Swindon
A Fourth Selection

IN OLD PHOTOGRAPHS

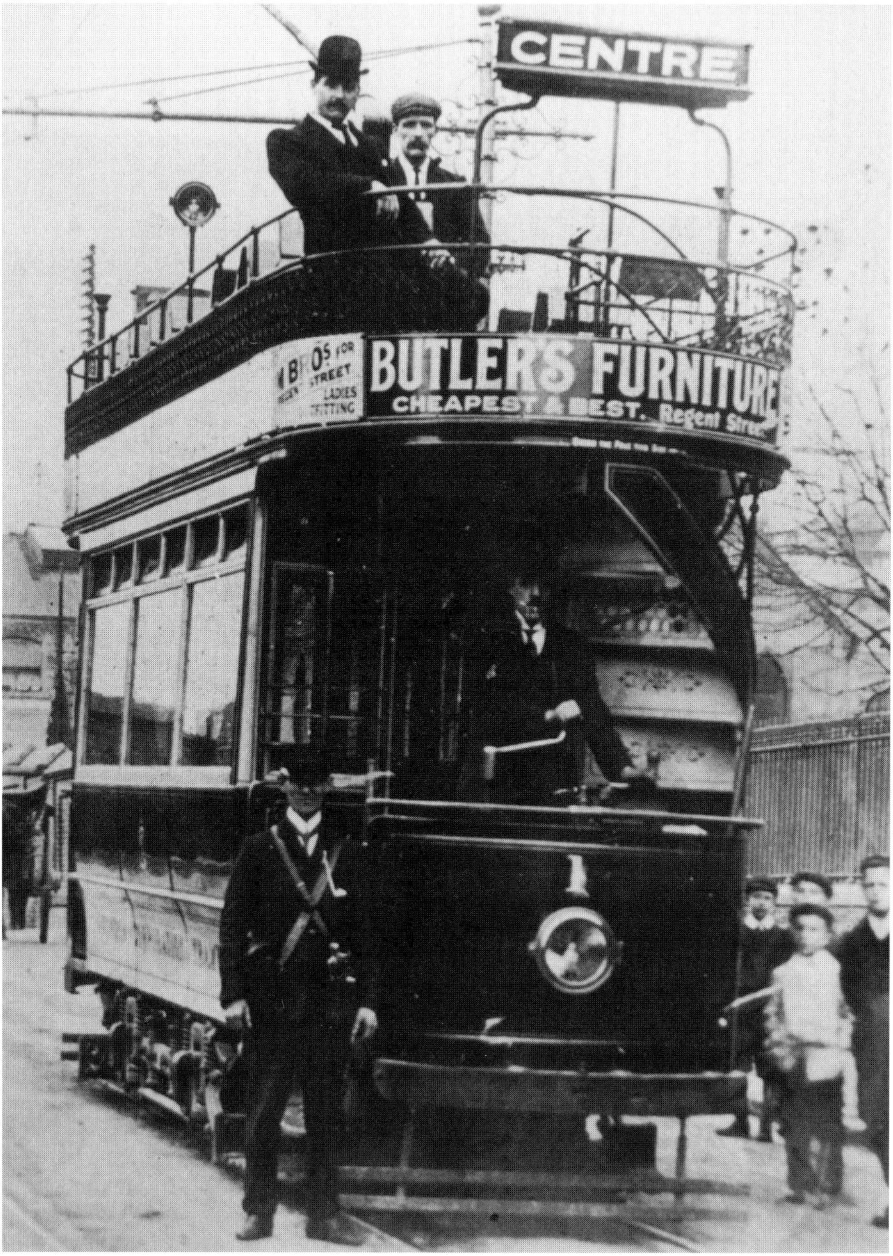

Tramcar No. 1, Park Lane, 1904. The tramway system opened in Swindon on 22 September 1904. Seven tramcars were purchased from Dick Kerr & Co., Preston, to commence the service. Livery was cream and crimson lake. They were fitted with a Tidswell lifeguard, a device which automatically dropped to road level on encountering an obstacle, thus preventing any person or object passing under the wheels.

Swindon

A Fourth Selection

IN OLD PHOTOGRAPHS

Collected by THE SWINDON SOCIETY

Alan Sutton Publishing Limited
Phoenix Mill · Far Thrupp
Stroud · Gloucestershire

First published 1993

British Library Cataloguing
in Publication Data.

Swindon Society
Swindon in Old Photographs:
Fourth Selection
I. Title
942.313

ISBN 0-7509-0366-X

Typeset in 9/10 Sabon.
Typesetting and origination by
Alan Sutton Publishing Limited.
Printed in Great Britain by
Redwood Books, Trowbridge.

Contents

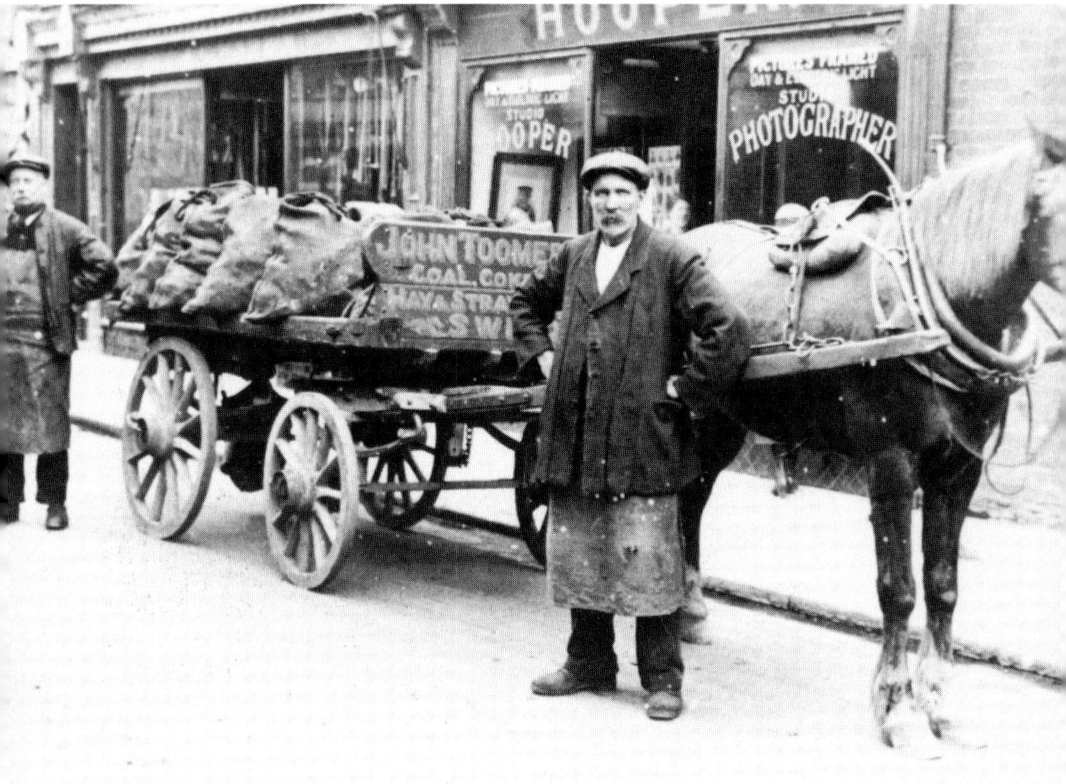

John Toomer, coal and coke merchant, Bath Road. A horse-drawn cart with delivery men stands outside the photographic studio of William Hooper, Cromwell Street (see p. 103).

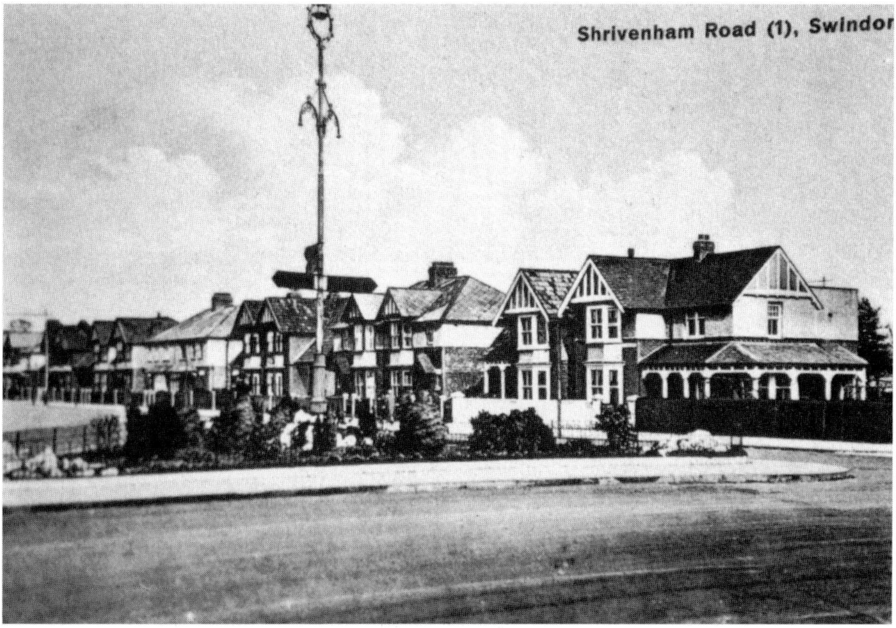

Shrivenham Road and traffic island, looking east, *c.* 1930. Today this is the site for the famous 'Magic Roundabout'. Lloyd's garage and filling station later occupied the space where the entry to Queen's Drive is now.

Introduction

For this fourth volume of old photographs of Swindon, the Swindon Society has continued with the formula that has proved so successful in the previous three volumes. Included in these pages are scenes of Swindonians at work and at play, photographs of buildings (many now gone) that have played their part in the story of the town, local personalities through the years, and street scenes and events, both local and national, that have touched upon the lives of the people of Swindon. Further views are included of the Great Western Railway and the great social events of 'Trip' and the Children's Fête.

The society has also included a section which shows aspects of the effect of the Co-operative Movement in the town. Co-operation began in Swindon as long ago as 1850, when a group of men in New Swindon held a meeting and resolved to follow the example of the Rochdale pioneers and to purchase goods from wholesalers and merchants to divide among themselves, thus saving the middleman's profits. A committee was set up and the Swindon Co-operative Provident Society was officially registered in 1853 with premises in High Street, New Swindon (on the corner of Oxford Street). The first secretary of the society was a Mr Alexander Jas. Braid, a teacher at the Bristol Street Boys'

School. It is recorded that his pupils used to sing the following ditty:

Mr Braid is a very good man,
He tries to teach us all he can,
In reading, writing and arithmetic,
But he never forgets to give us the stick.

A breakaway group formed the New Swindon Industrial Co-operative Society in 1861 when the parent society decided to discontinue the grocery trade and concentrate on the bakery. The new society soon outgrew its predecessor and expanded rapidly over the next seventy years or so with grocery, butchery, hardware, drapery, outfitting, boots and shoes, furnishing, and confectionery retail stores being opened throughout the town and in neighbouring parts of Wiltshire, Berkshire and Gloucestershire. Milk deliveries also commenced with a dairy in Colbourne Street. In 1880 a third society was formed in Swindon, called the Kingshill Co-operative Society, with offices in Radnor Street. After the Second World War increasing competition resulted in only the New Swindon Industrial Co-operative Society remaining in business by the end of 1953, and this was later renamed the Swindon & District Co-operative Society. In 1969 it amalgamated with the Oxford Society to form the Oxford & Swindon Co-operative Society Ltd.

Another section contains scenes of the town as it was during one year – 1968 – twenty-five years ago. These photographs, all taken by Swindon Society member Denis Bird, show Swindon and its inhabitants, young and old, during the change from old Victorian railway town to a more 'modern' community with high-rise office blocks and new industries. Perhaps when we look at these pictures we can regret the destruction of much of the old railway town, its sense of community and fellowship.

The Swindon Society hopes that this collection of photographs will, once again, bring back many memories to old Swindonians and stimulate younger readers to learn more about Swindon and its past.

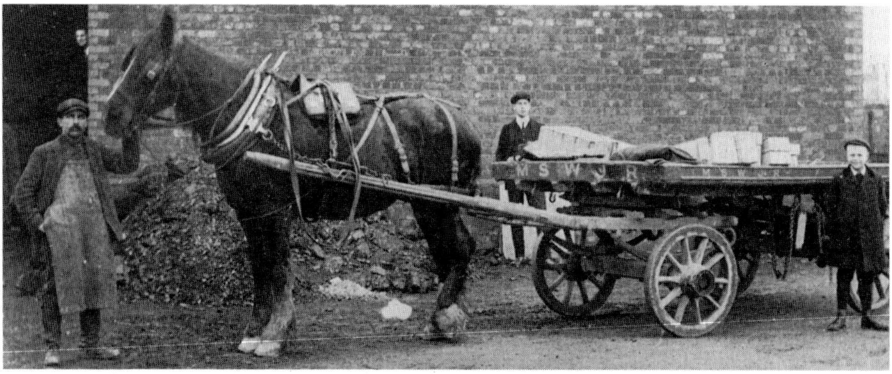

M&SWJR horse-drawn wagon, at the southern end of the goods transfer shed, Coate Road, *c.* 1905. The Midland & South Western Junction Railway was independent of the GWR until it was taken over by GWR in 1923.

SECTION ONE

Old Town through the Years

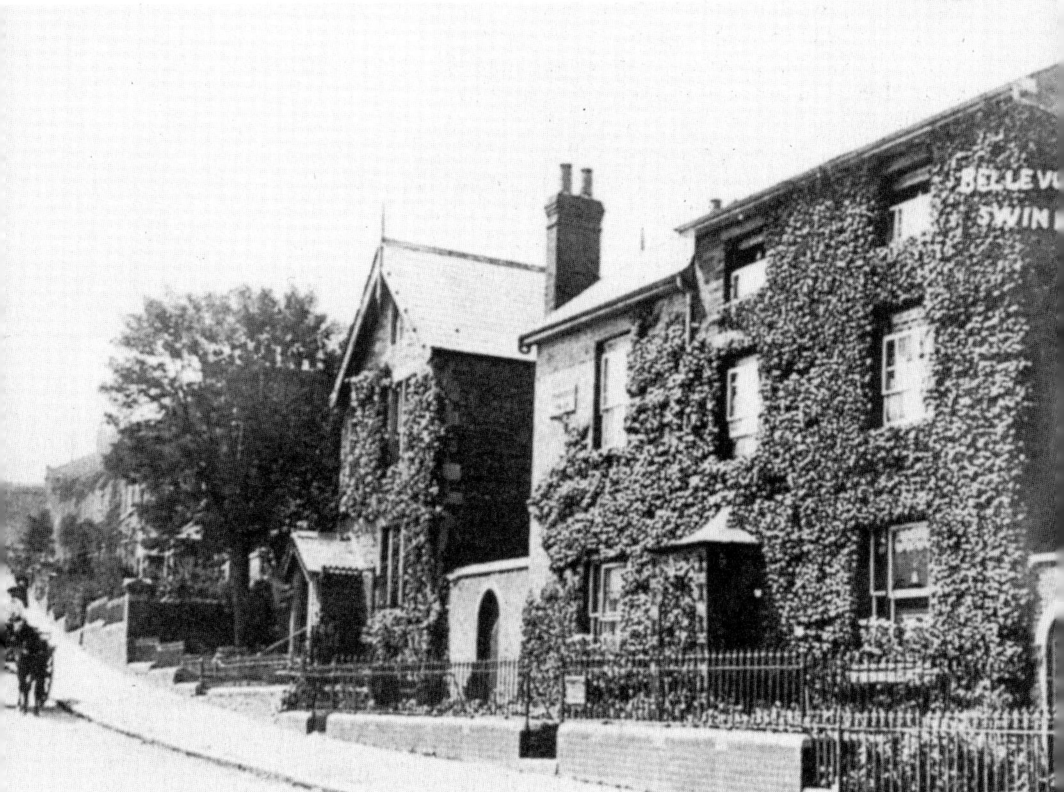

Belle Vue Road, *c.* 1910. In the foreground is the ivy-covered Standish Villa, today's Trenchard House, the headquarters of the Royal Air Forces' Association in Swindon.

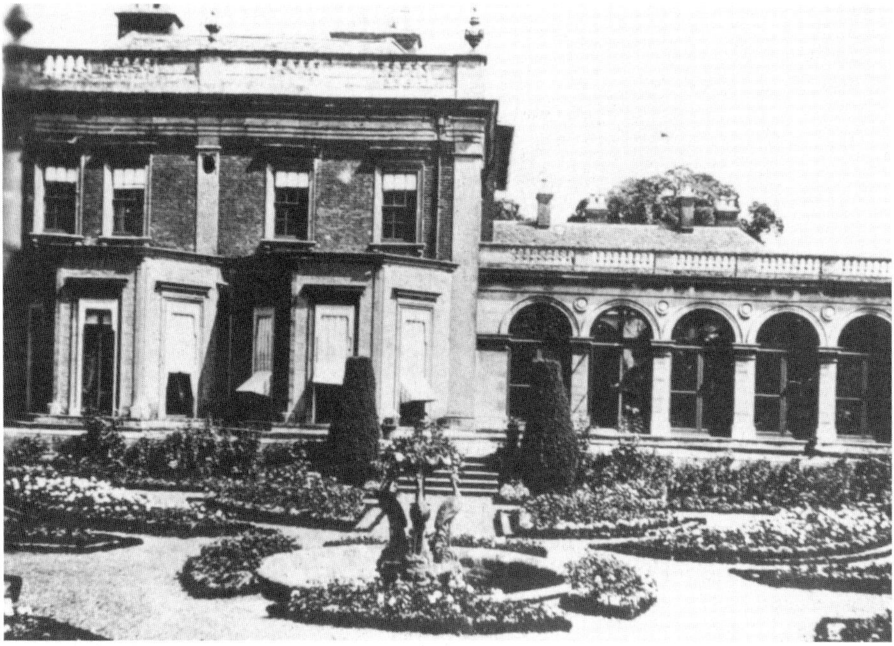

The Lawn (west front) and Italian garden, *c.* 1910. Home of the Goddard family, Lords of the Manor of Swindon, it was built in about 1770 and subsequently extended over the next eighty years. The last member of the family to live in the house, Major Fitzroy Pleydell Goddard, died in 1927, and his widow, Mrs E.K. Goddard, vacated The Lawn in 1931. It remained empty until the Second World War when American troops were billeted there. Demolished in June 1952, only the remains of the Italian garden are visible today in the grounds behind High Street.

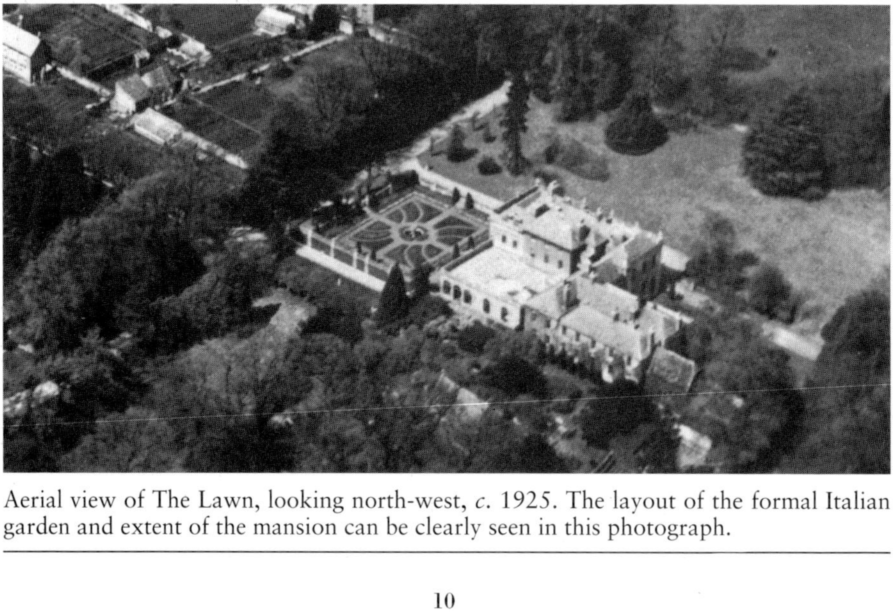

Aerial view of The Lawn, looking north-west, *c.* 1925. The layout of the formal Italian garden and extent of the mansion can be clearly seen in this photograph.

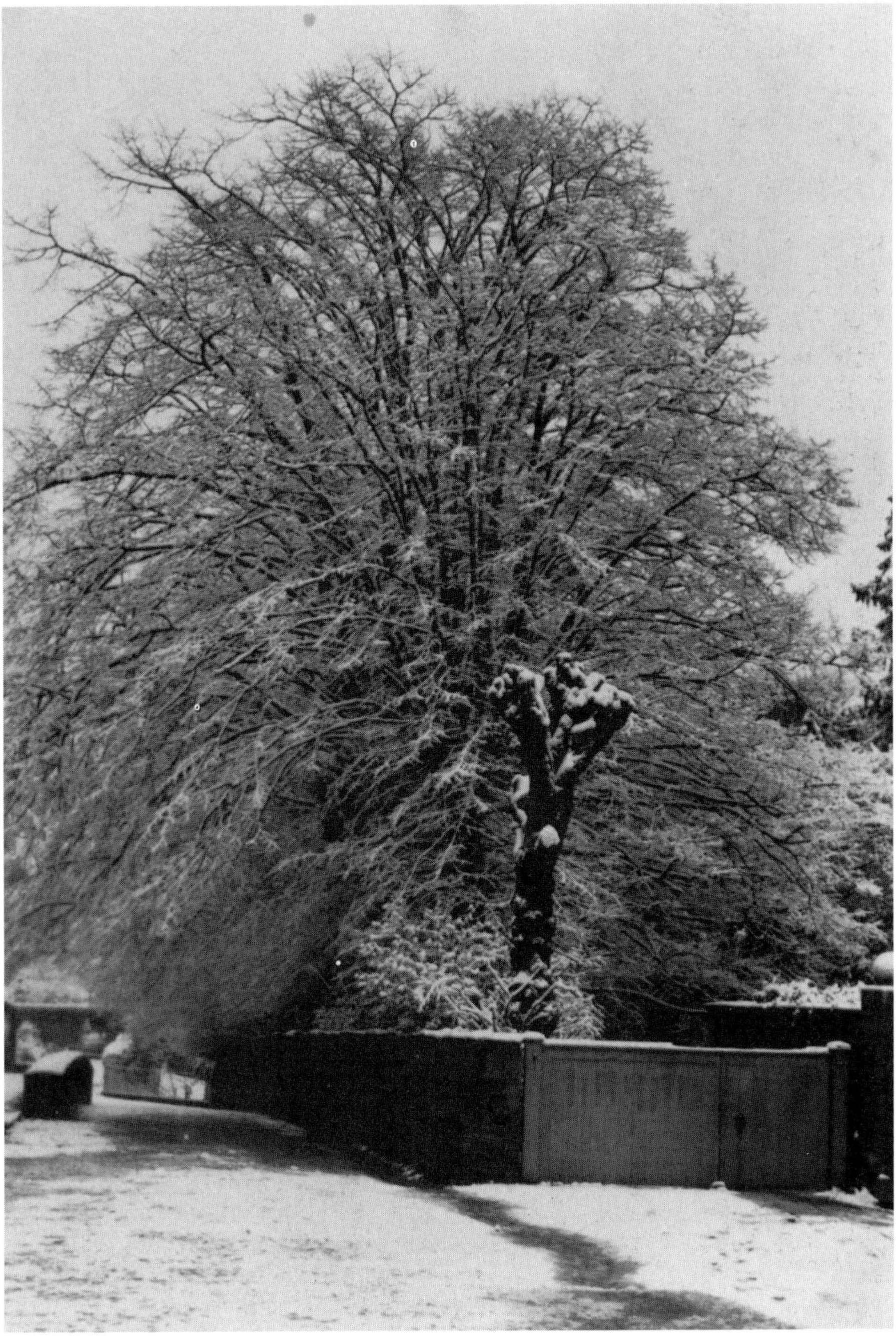

The Planks, looking east, 24 April 1908. A view of the freak snowfall. (William Hooper photograph)

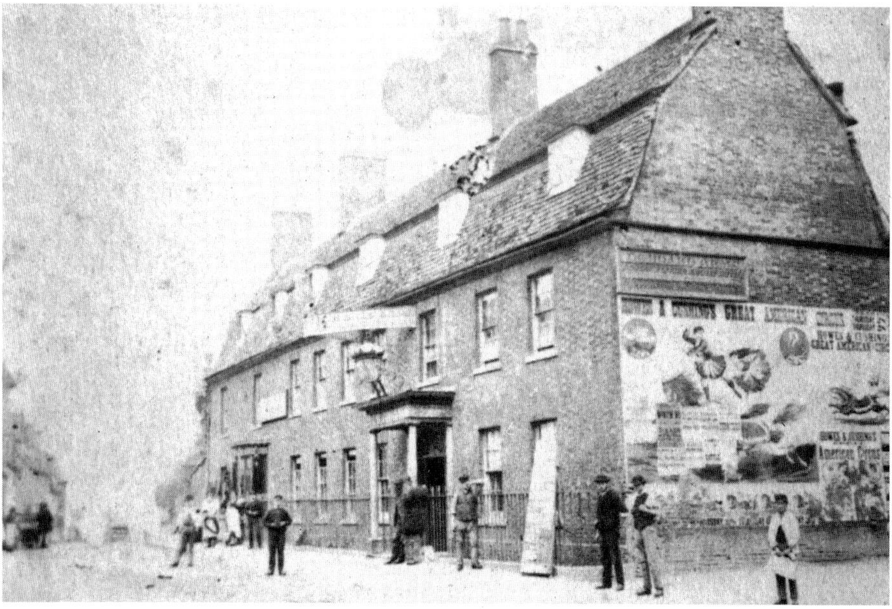

Goddard Arms, High Street, *c.* 1885, photographed by Zephaniah Dodson, an early photographer, who had premises in Victoria Street. Note the extensive advertising for Howes & Cushings Great American Circus.

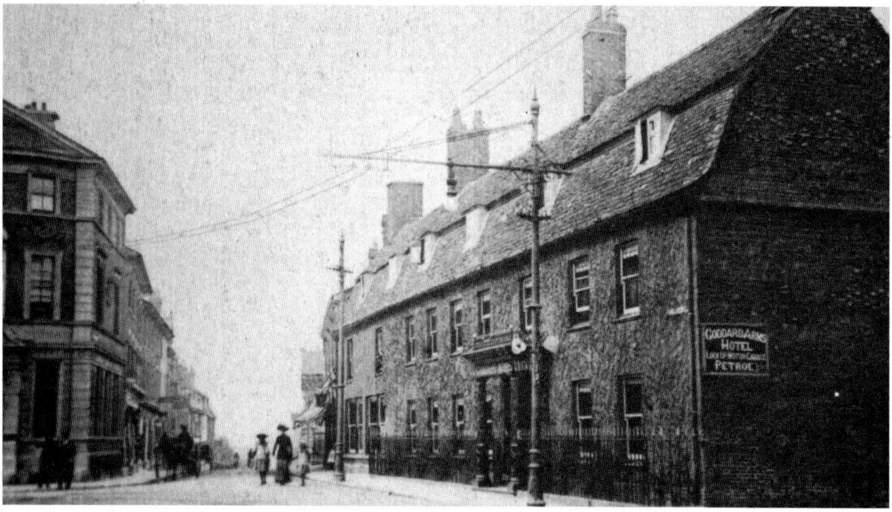

Goddard Arms, High Street, *c.* 1910. An inn has stood on this site since the seventeenth century. Known as The Crown until about 1810, the building was used as the Magistrates Court in the early nineteenth century before the building of the (Old) Town Hall in the Market Square in 1852. In April 1914 Frances Priscilla Hunter, aged 23, a between-maid at the Goddard Arms, was shot dead by her jealous lover, Walter James White. He was executed for the murder at Winchester in June 1914.

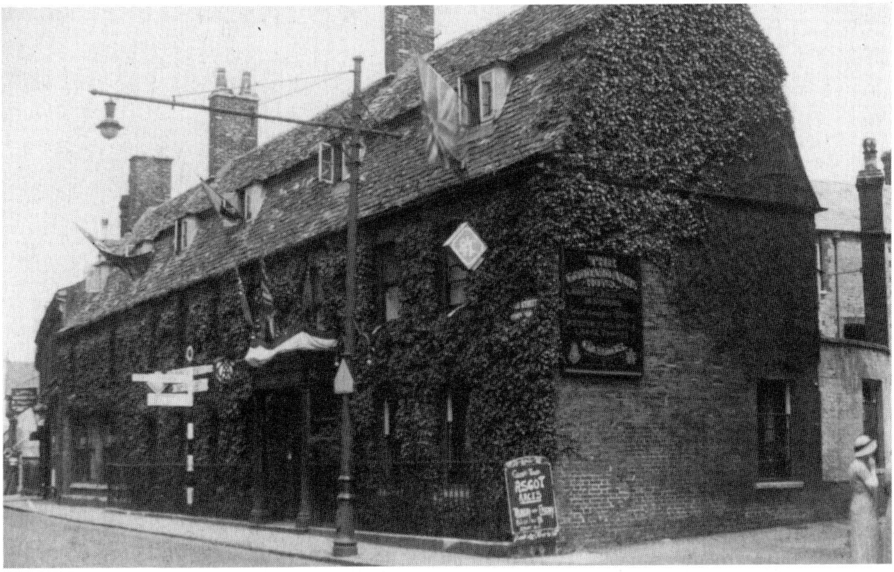

Goddard Arms, High Street, 1920s. Note the advertisement for races at Ascot, and the lady on the right in her fashionable hat.

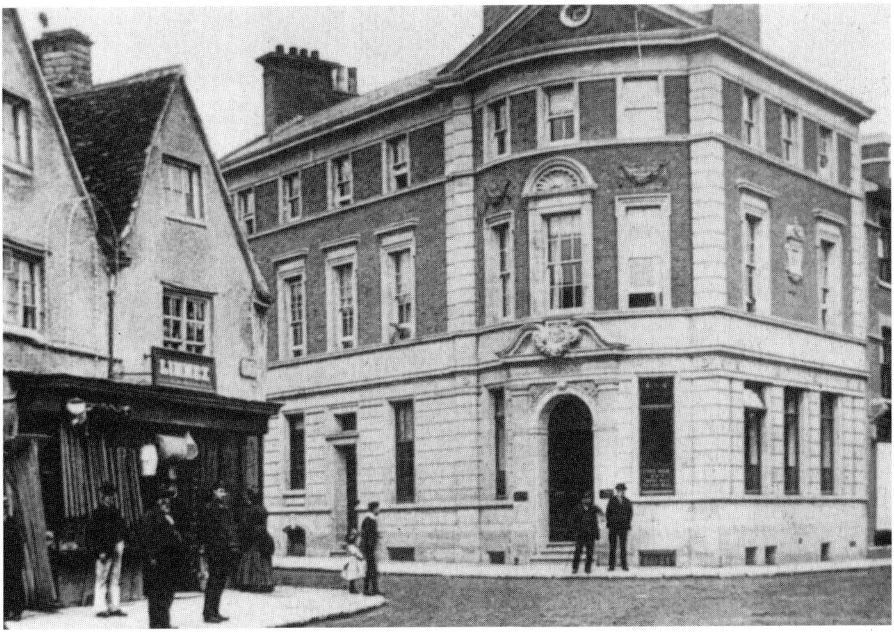

The corner of Wood Street and High Street, 1885. The newly opened Wiltshire & Dorset Bank is at the junction of Wood Street and Cricklade Street. On the left is the Limmex hardware store, which was established in the 1870s and is still trading today. The large man to the left is William Morris, founder of the *Swindon Advertiser* in 1854.

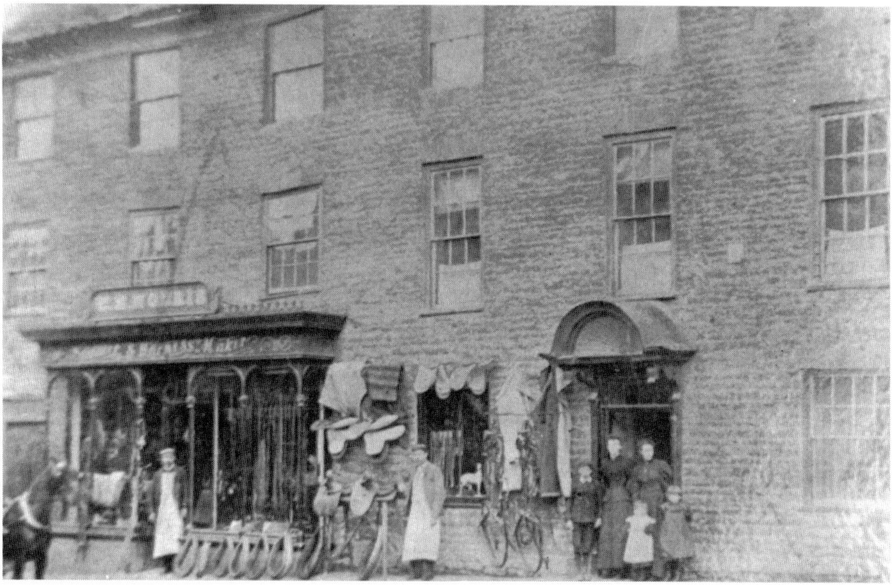

W.H. Norris, saddler and harness maker, 34 High Street, *c.* 1899. To the right is the ornate doorway of Manchester House, which was an early eighteenth-century merchant's house. For a view of the same property in the 1960s see *Swindon in Old Photographs (3)*, p. 33. The Co-operative supermarket now occupies this site.

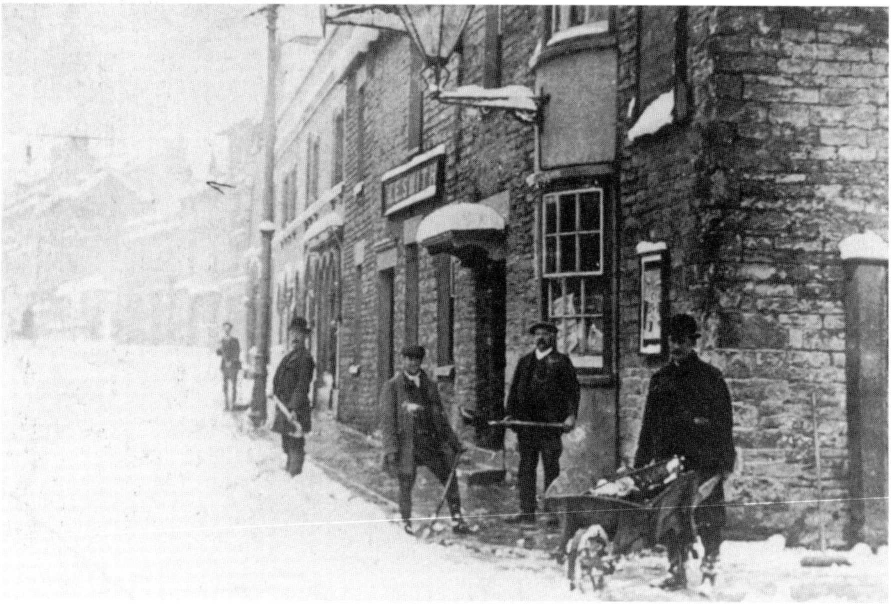

Masons Arms, High Street, *c.* 1905. To the right is the entrance to the yard and stables. Today the Midland Bank occupies this site opposite Newport Street.

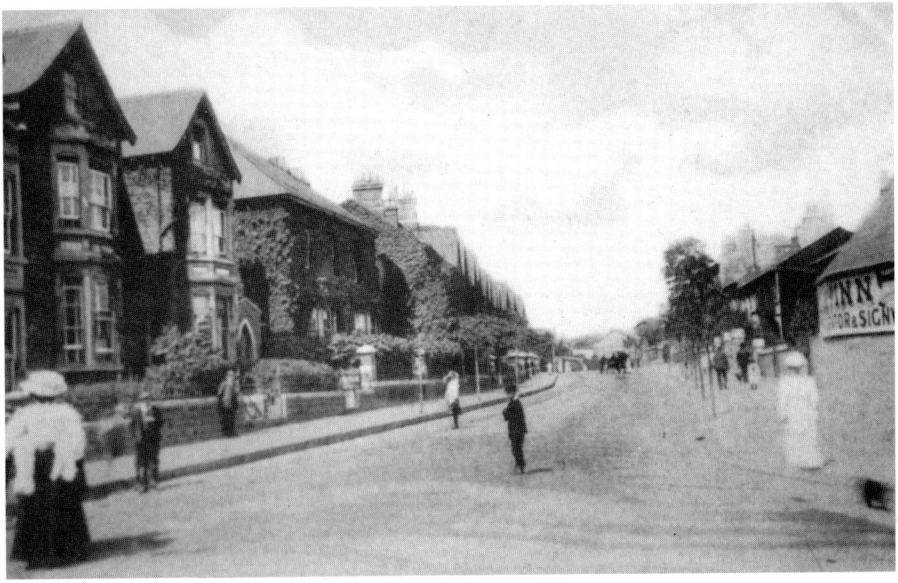

Devizes Road, looking north, *c*. 1905. To the right are the premises of Tom Finn, decorator and signwriter, his sign claiming 'only skilled men employed'.

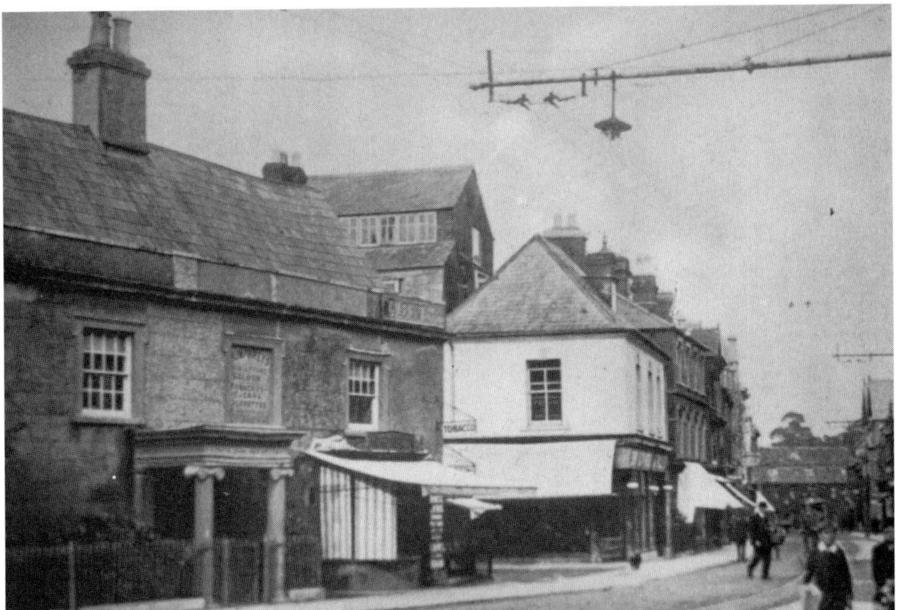

A view east to Wood Street, *c*. 1918. On the left is an old building known as 'The Manor House', about which little is known. Demolished in the 1960s, the site is now occupied by Queen Victoria House, with shops and offices.

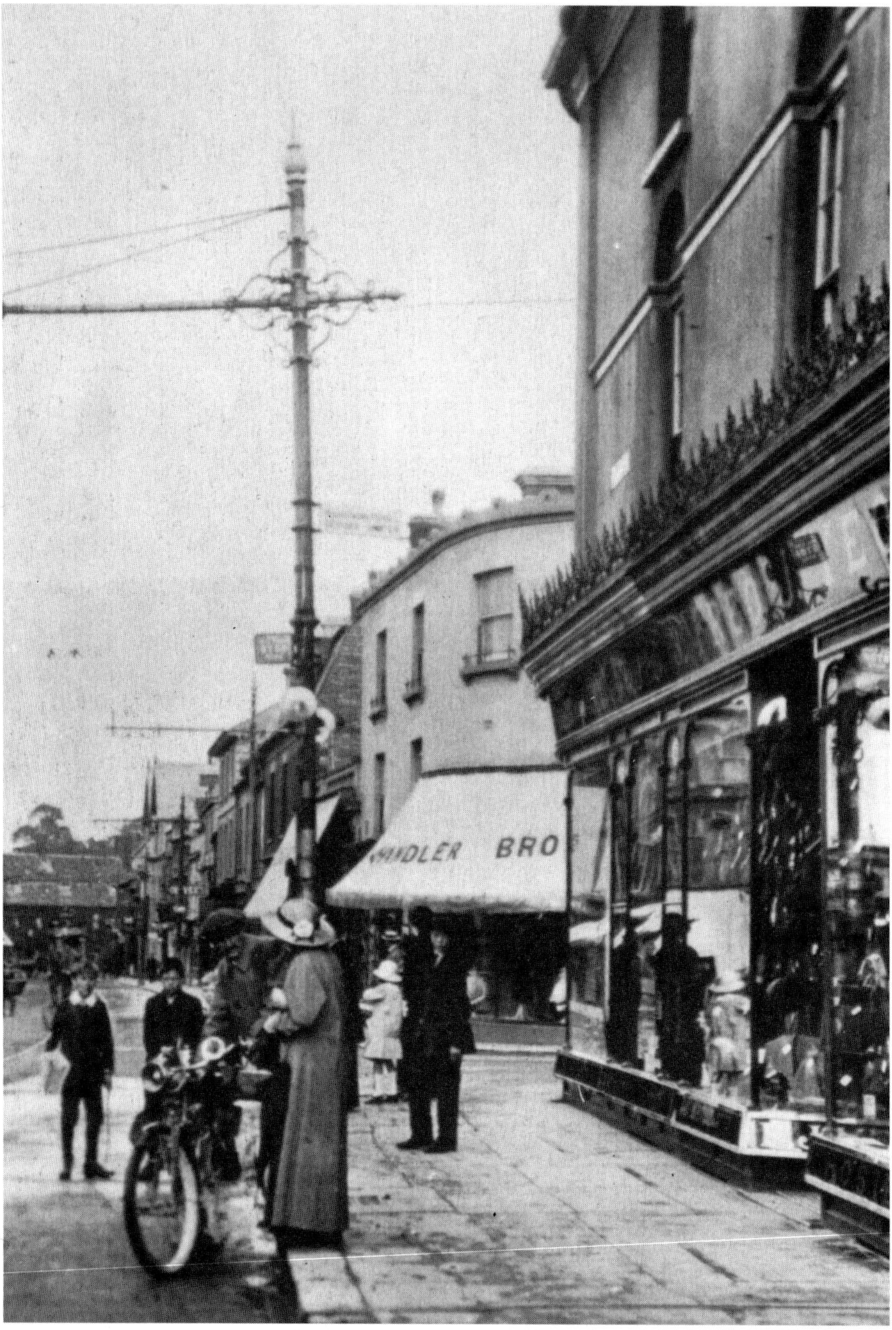

Bath Road and Devizes Road junction, 1918, known for many years as Chandler's Corner, after the drapers shop on the corner of Wood Street and Devizes Road (now Dentry's).

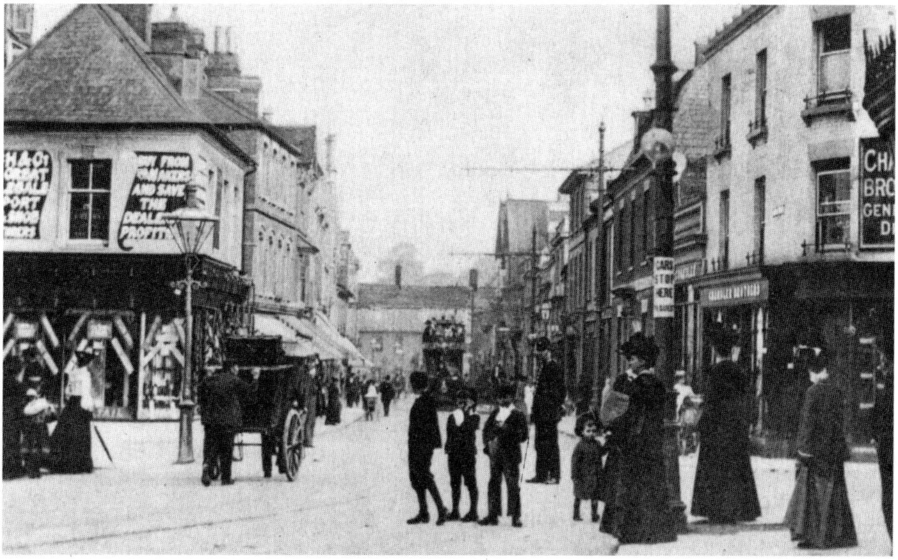

Wood Street, looking east, 1904. This photograph was taken shortly after the introduction of the tramway system. Note the temporary tramcar stop sign on the lamp-post on the right.

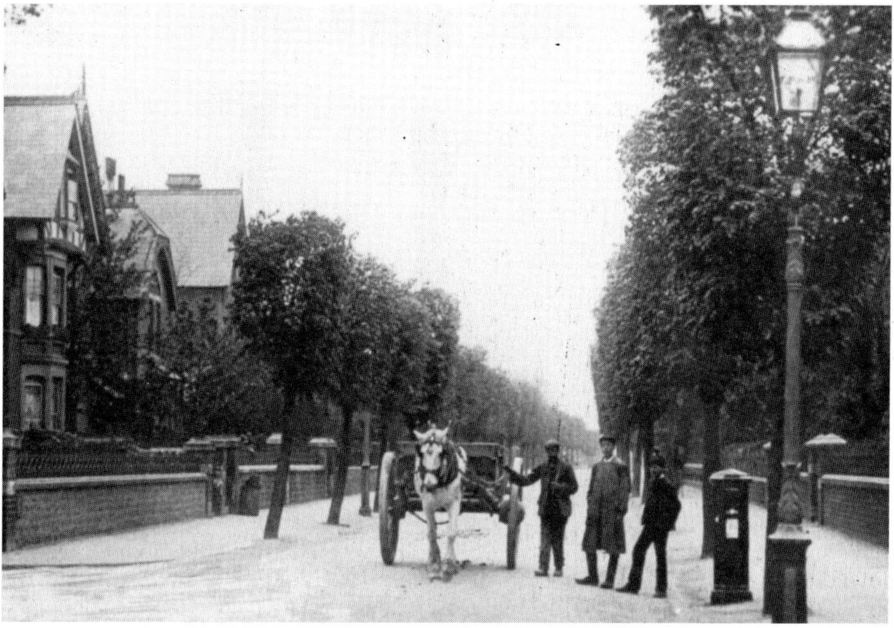

A view down tree-lined Bath Road, *c.* 1910. This elegant thoroughfare was also known as The Sands, after the sandy nature of the soil hereabouts, until the name was officially changed in 1904.

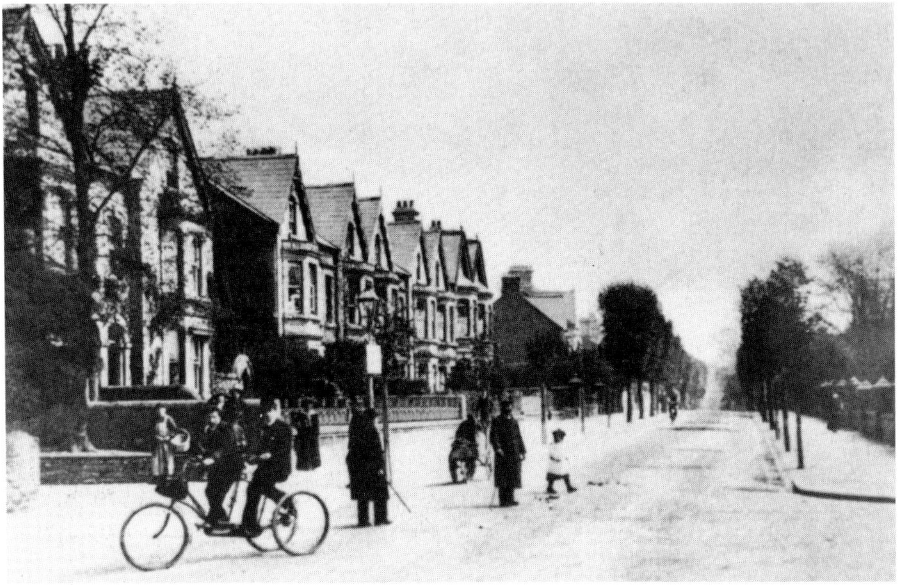

Bath Road, looking east from the junction of Goddard Avenue and Kent Road, *c.* 1905. Note the two men on a strange, tandem tricycle.

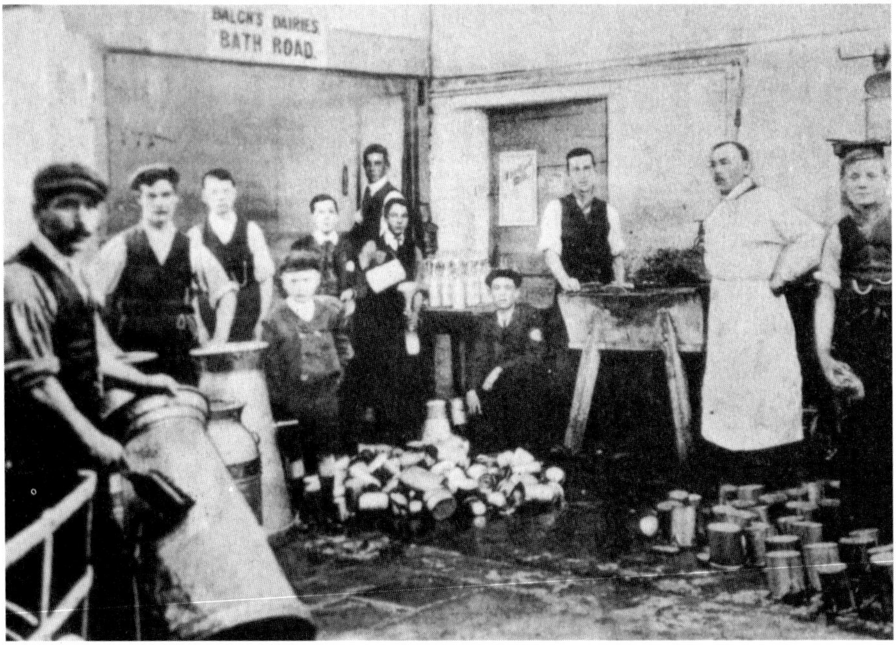

Balch's Dairies can-cleaning and sterilizing section, 8 Bath Road, *c.* 1905. Not a bottle in sight, the milk was ladled into jugs in the street, but one dairy in Old Town advertised three deliveries a day.

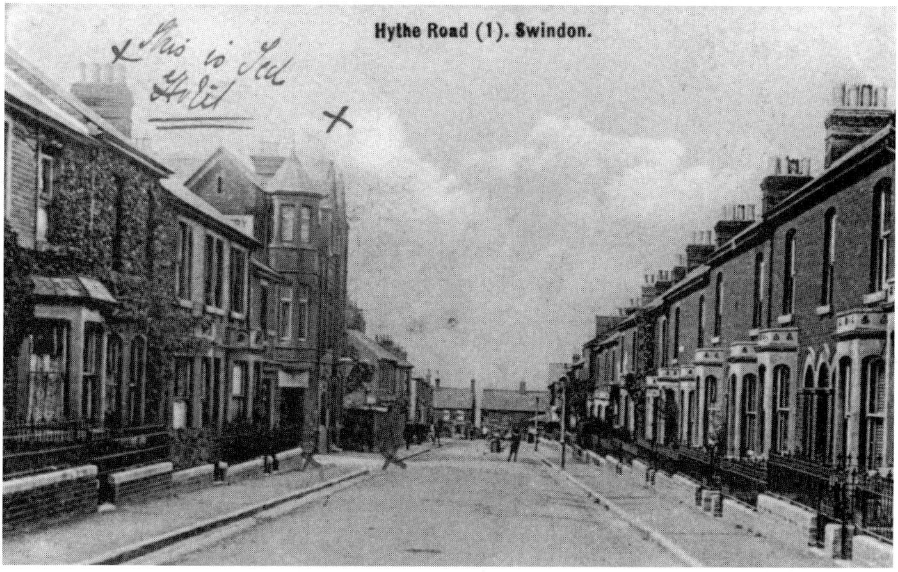

Hythe Road, looking north towards Stafford Street, *c.* 1910. The large building on the left was the Frome Hotel, commonly known as 'Ted's Hotel' at this time. It closed in 1978 and is now private apartments.

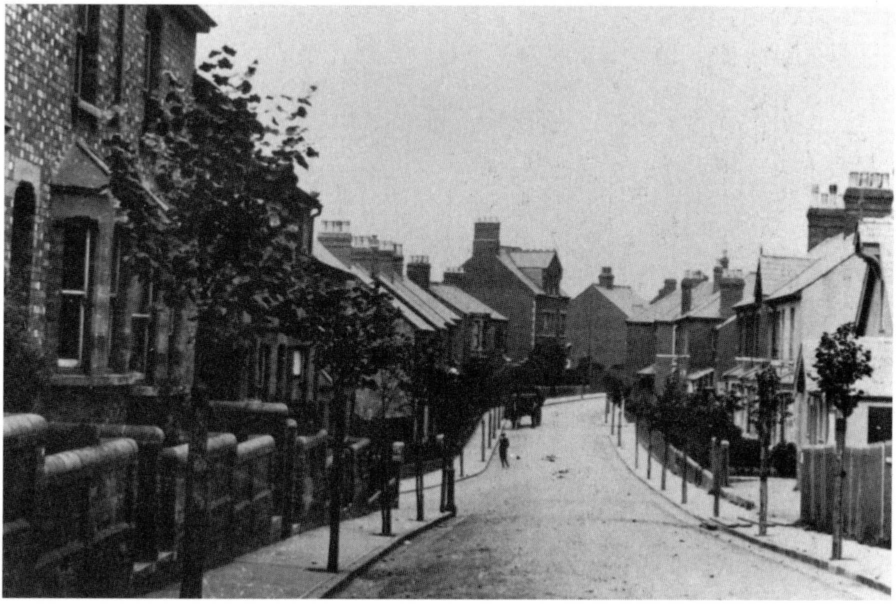

Ashford Road, looking north, *c.* 1910. To the right is St Saviour's church, built in wood in 1889 by voluntary labour and by GWR factory workers in their spare time, and enlarged, again by voluntary labour, in 1904.

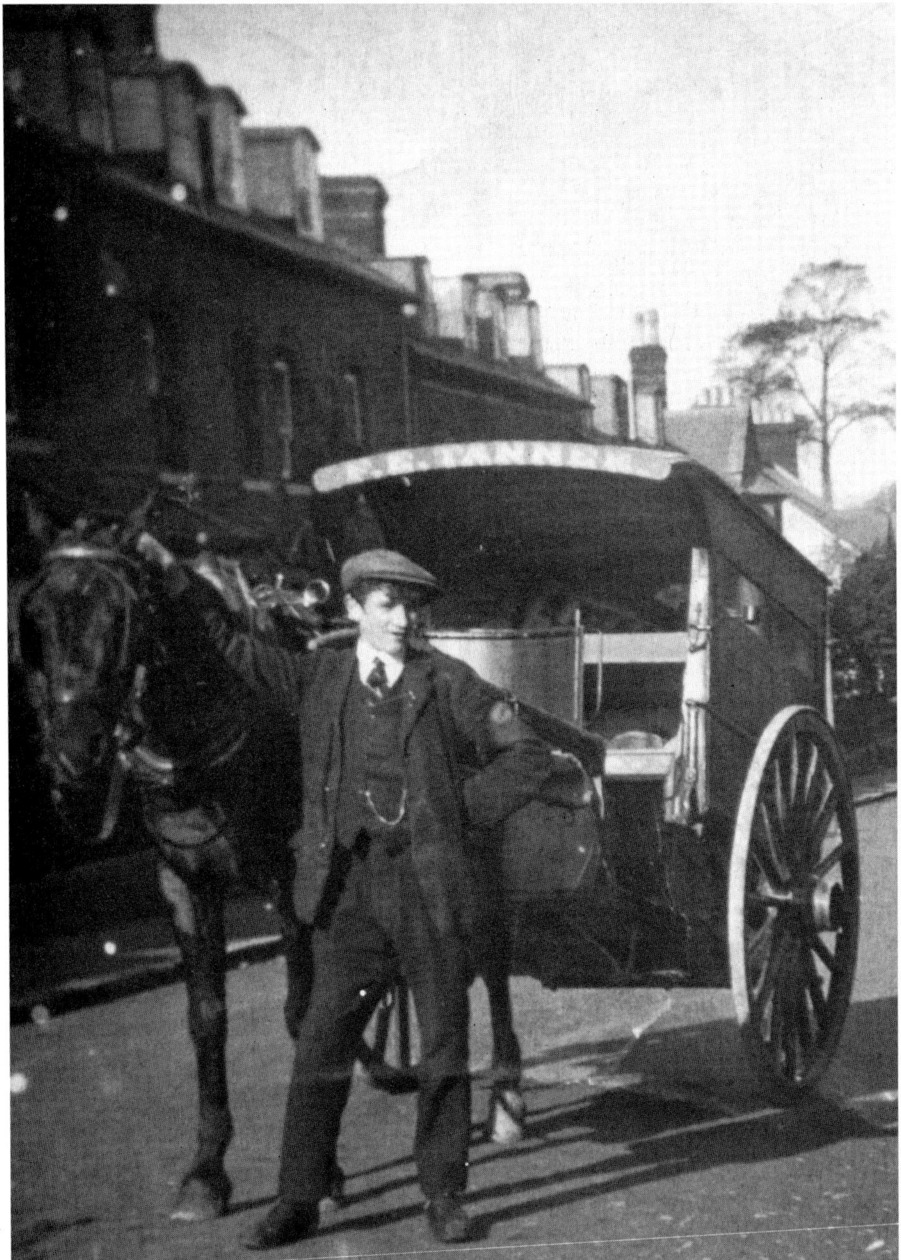

Horse-drawn baker's delivery van, Clifton Street, *c.* 1908. F.E. Tanner had his 'Machine Bakery' at 1 Manchester Road. It was said to be 'a high class shop with its own bakehouse at the back . . . with a display of silver cups and shields won in various bread-making competitions'.

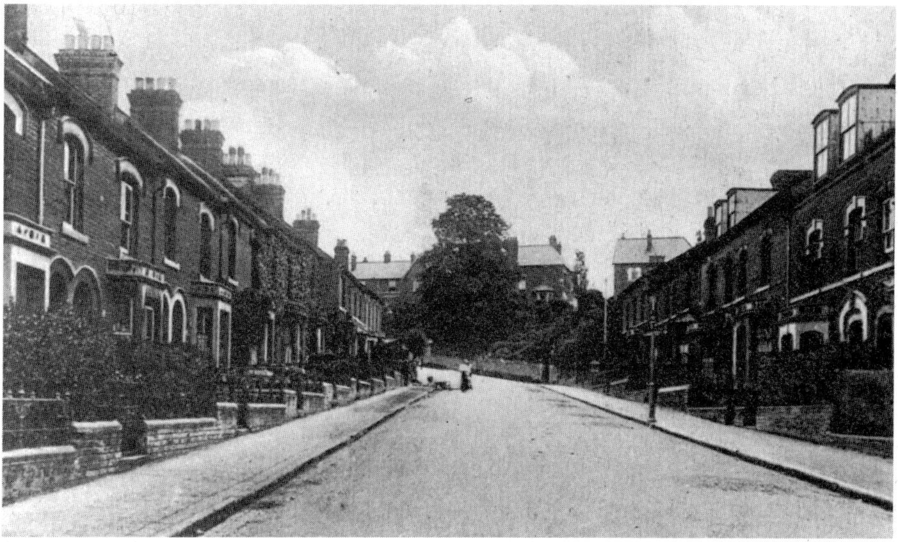

Clifton Street, looking south towards Kingshill, *c*. 1910.

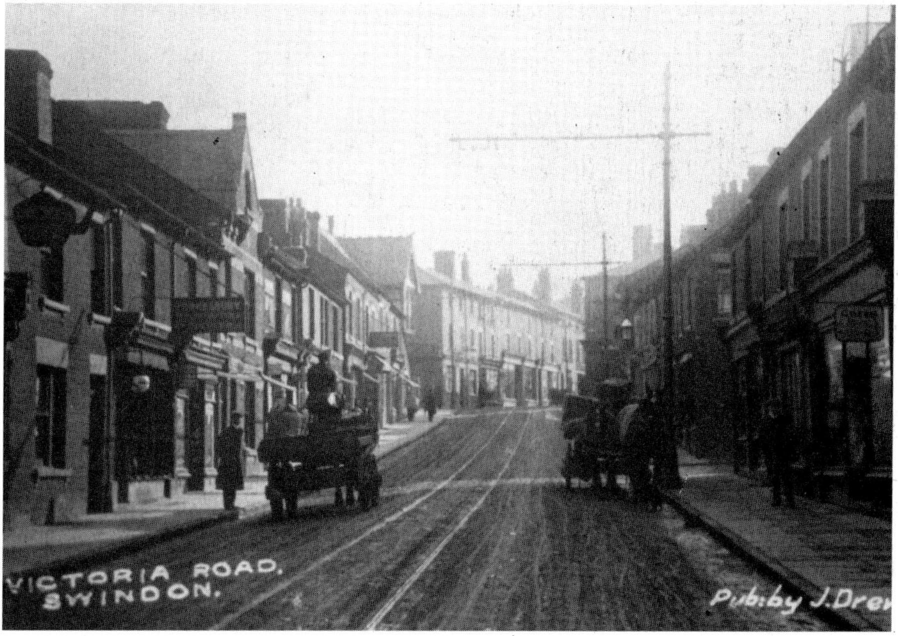

Victoria Road, looking south towards the Belle Vue and Victoria public houses, *c*. 1910. The horse and cart on the left is outside Tewkesbury's, the tailor, hatter and outfitters.

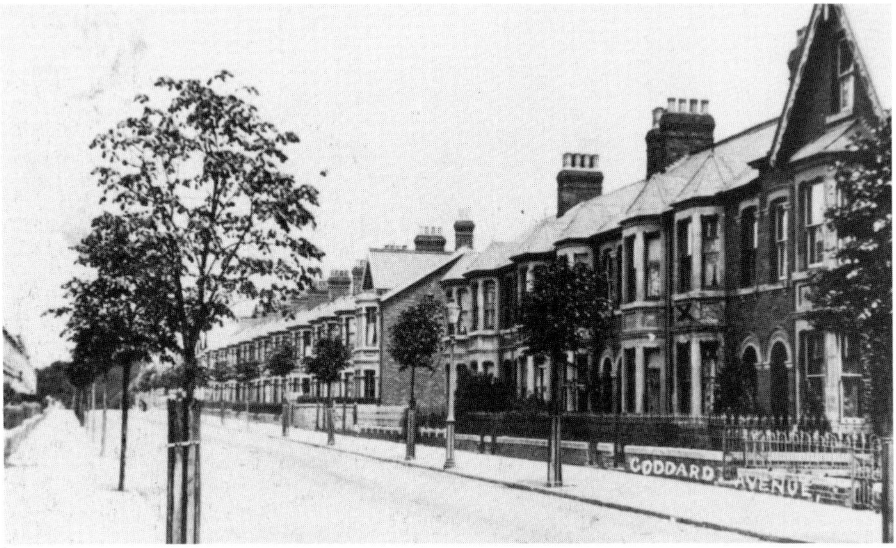

Goddard Avenue, *c.* 1910. Named after the Goddard family, Lords of the Manor of Swindon, this street of stylish Victorian villas is at the highest point of Swindon Hill (485 ft).

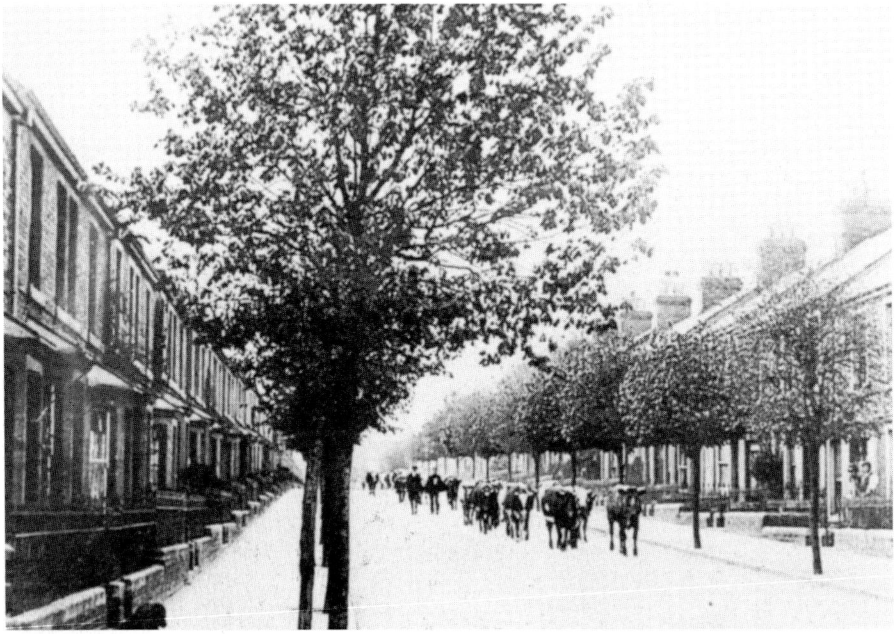

Avenue Road, *c.* 1910. This photograph was probably taken on a Monday, market day in Old Town, as a herd of cows is being driven along the road. The livestock market was founded in 1254 and was held in High Street until 1887 when it moved to a site off Marlborough Road behind Newport Street. It remained there until the mid-1980s.

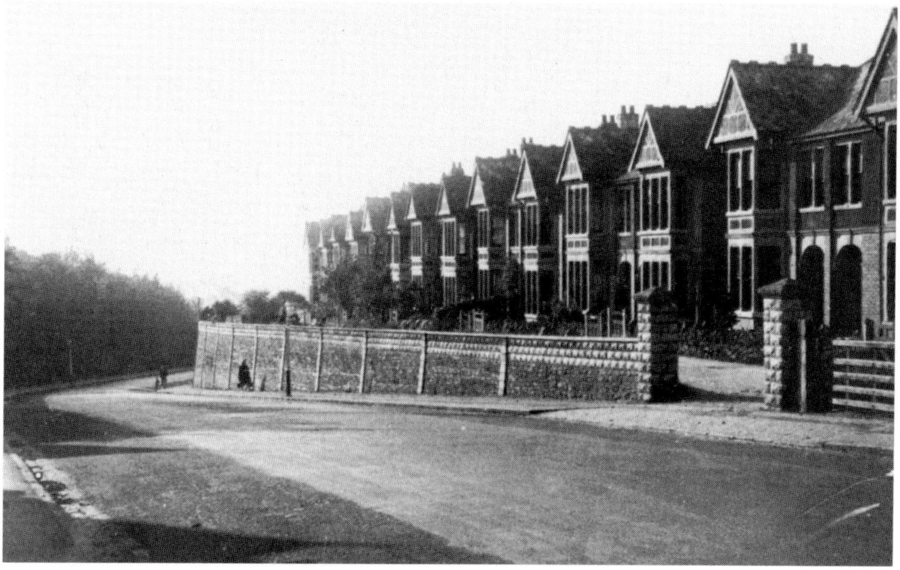

Croft Road and The Knoll, looking south towards Wroughton, *c.* 1928. A plaque in the wall on the right marks the site of Wroughton Road springs, an early water supply.

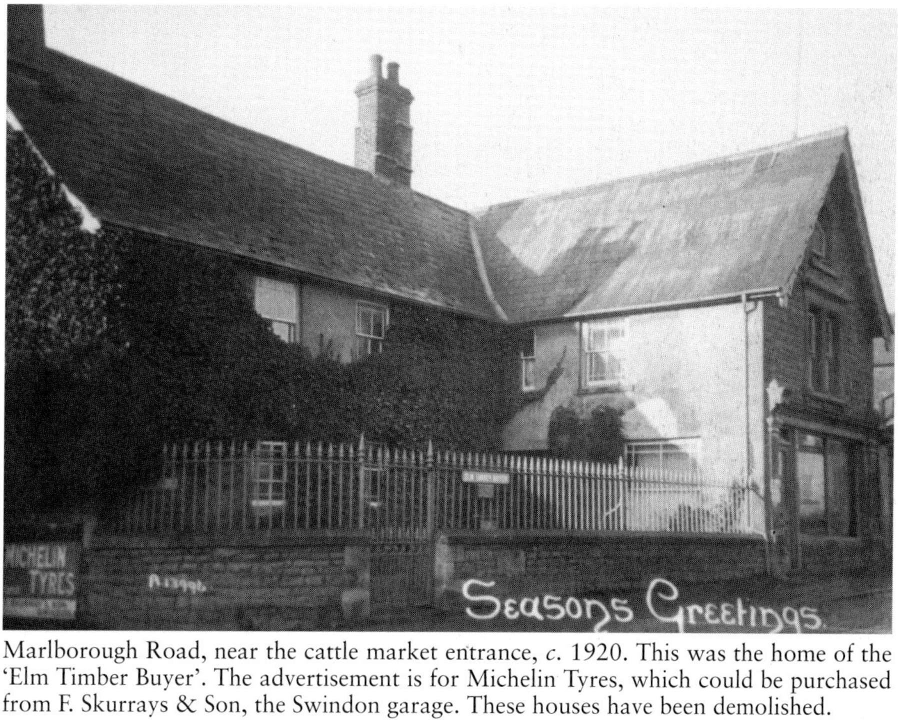

Marlborough Road, near the cattle market entrance, *c.* 1920. This was the home of the 'Elm Timber Buyer'. The advertisement is for Michelin Tyres, which could be purchased from F. Skurrays & Son, the Swindon garage. These houses have been demolished.

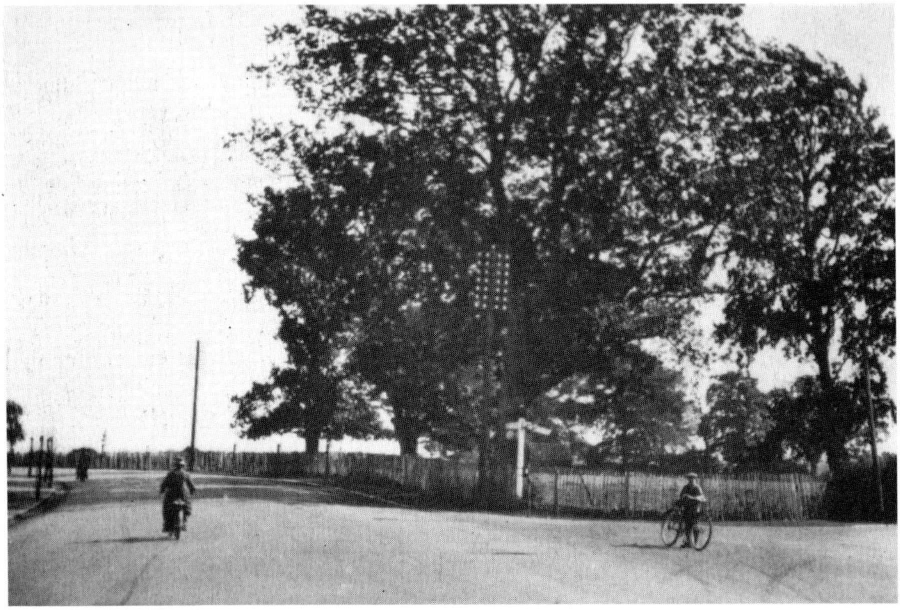

Coate Road, looking south, *c.* 1925. The Hodson road (Broome Manor Lane) is to the right.

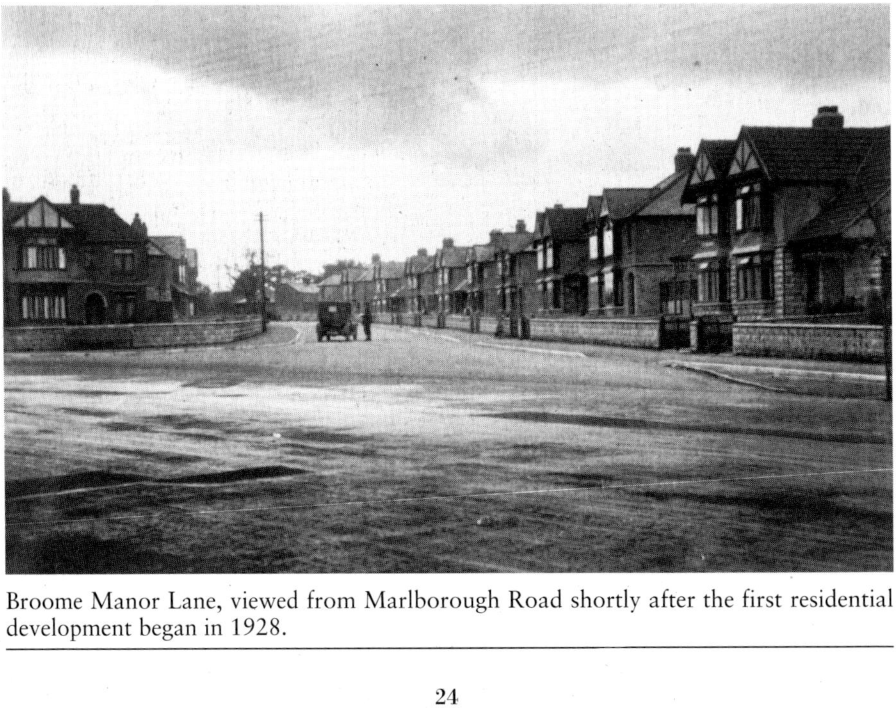

Broome Manor Lane, viewed from Marlborough Road shortly after the first residential development began in 1928.

The Railway Village & Works

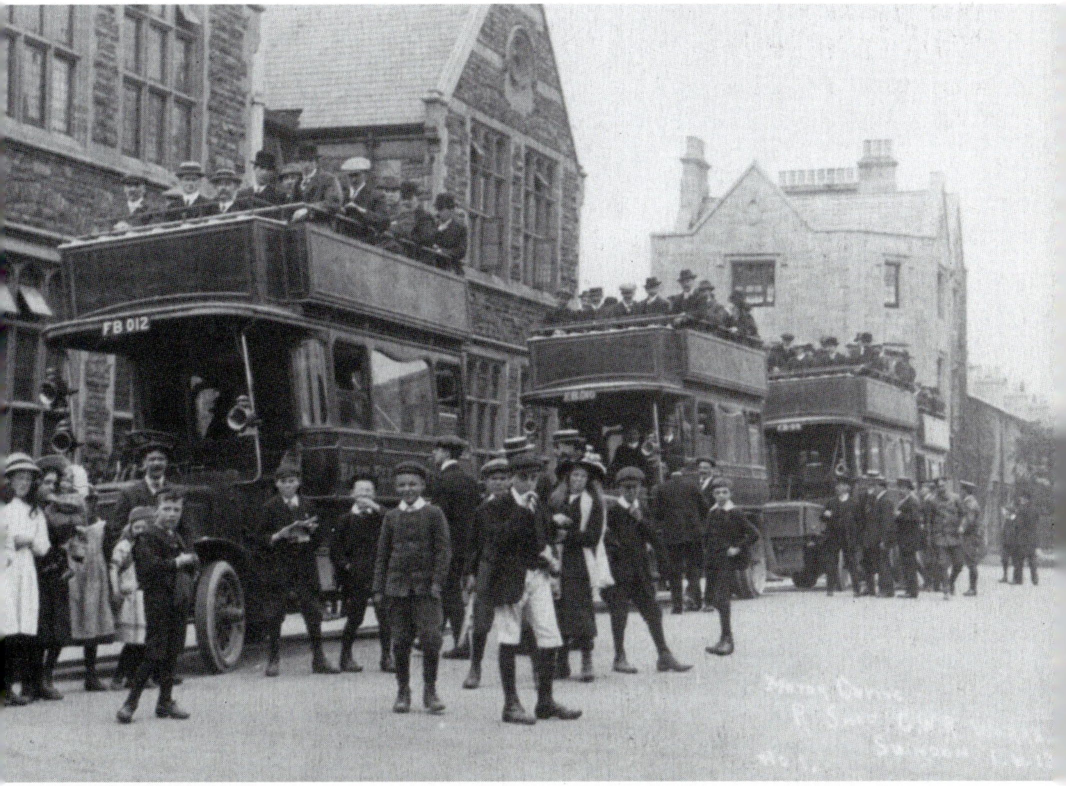

Family outing for 'R' (machine) shop, GWR Works, from Mechanics Institute, 1 June 1912. Transport was provided by motor buses supplied by Bath Tramways.

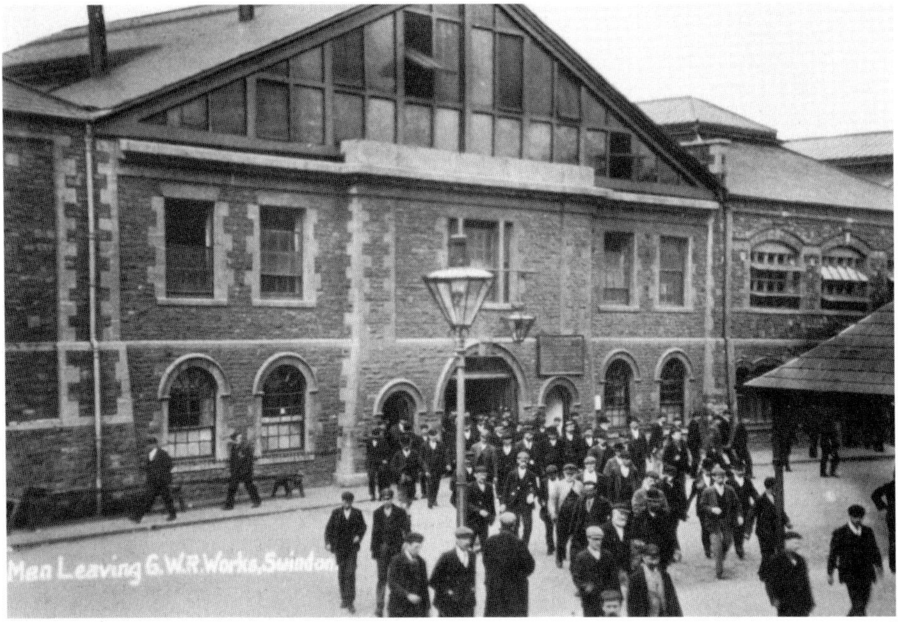

Men leaving the GWR Works from the London Street entrance, *c.* 1910. At this time men worked a 54-hour, six-day week.

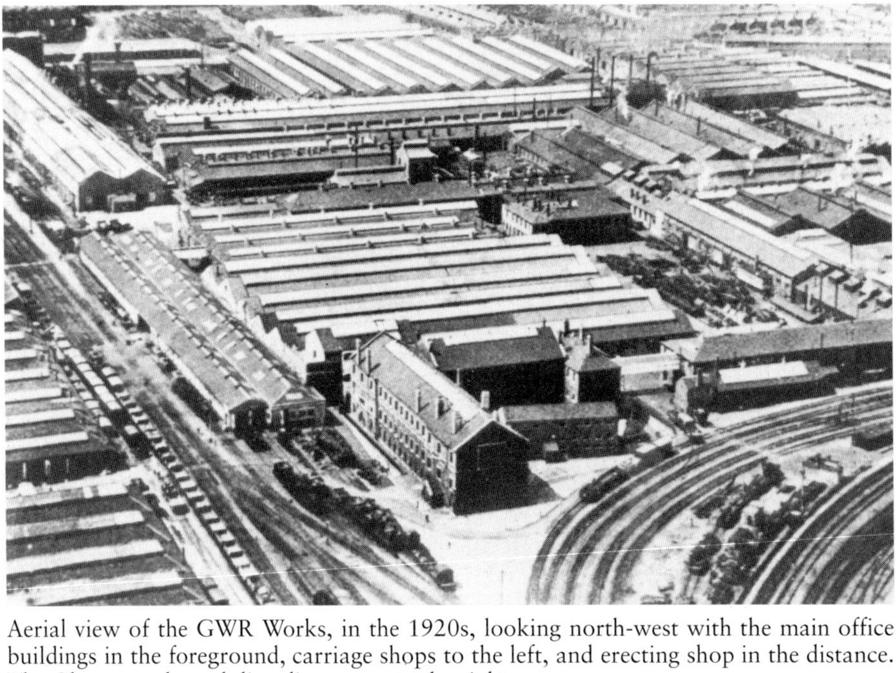

Aerial view of the GWR Works, in the 1920s, looking north-west with the main office buildings in the foreground, carriage shops to the left, and erecting shop in the distance. The Gloucester branch line disappears to the right.

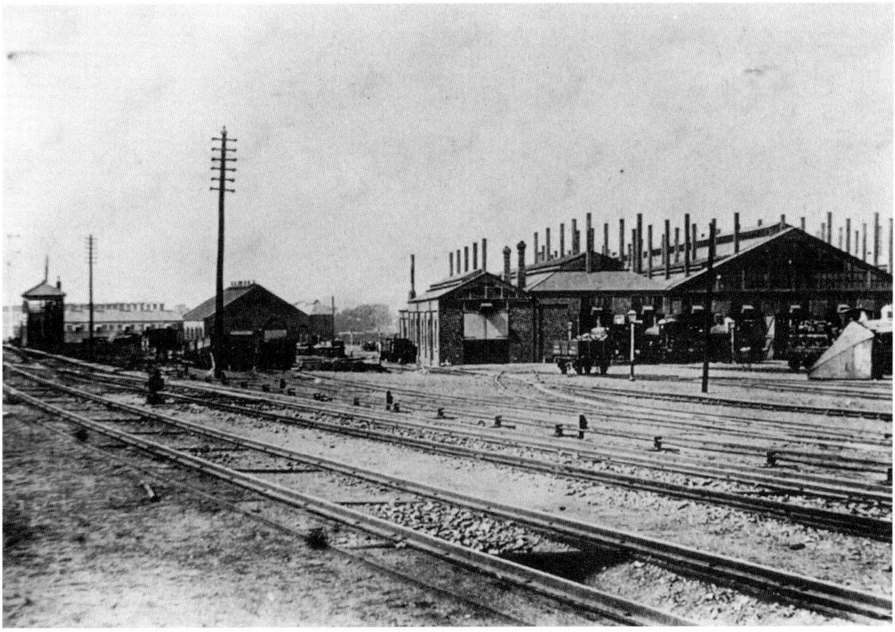

Swindon running shed, *c.* 1890. Some broad gauge track is still in evidence at this time. The photograph looks north with running sheds to the right and stock sheds to the left.

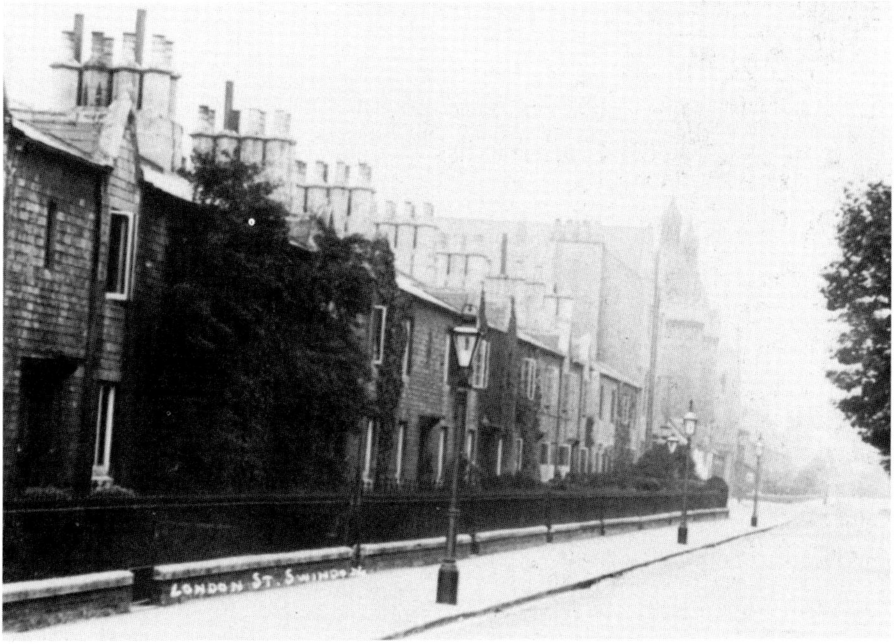

London Street, looking south-west towards Mechanics Institute, *c.* 1910.

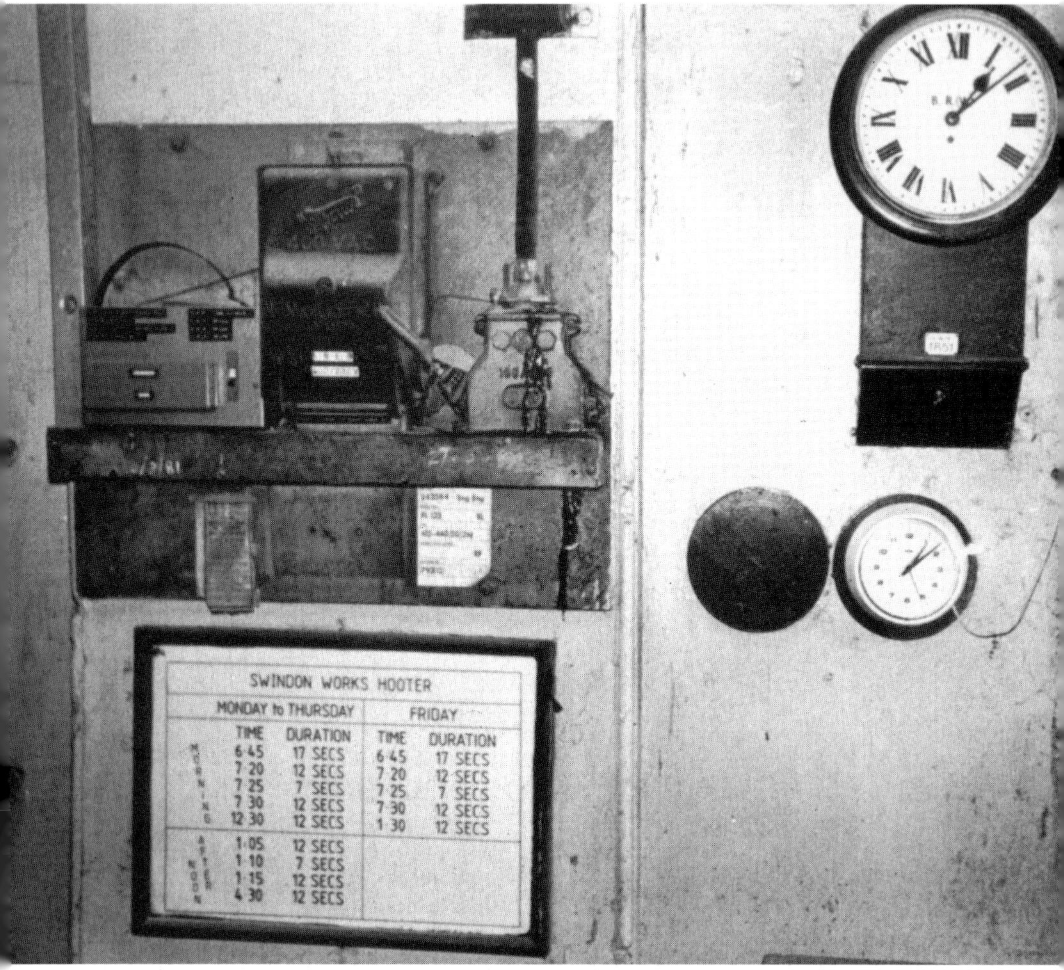

Swindon Works' hooter. Originally, to summon and dismiss its workforce, the GWR fixed a large bell on the roof of 'C' shed. This was adequate while the town was small in size, but by 1867 more noise was needed and a steam hooter was installed. The hooter at this period was first blown for ten long minutes at 5.20 a.m., for three minutes at 5.50 a.m. and then, to make sure, another minute at 6.00 a.m. Soon objections were received from outlying villages (the hooter could be heard for up to twenty miles) and the Local Government Board decided, after five years' deliberation, that the hooter should not blow. The company fixed another hooter on the roof within a few yards of the disused one and, as the local MP for the Cricklade Division (which included Swindon), the Hon. F.W. Cadogan, pointed out, no injunction had been granted against the second one – incidentally louder than the first! The authorities soon realized they could not win and the matter was allowed to drop. This second hooter remained in use until the works closed in the mid-1980s, and blew its final blast at 4.30 p.m. on 26 March 1986. During the Second World War it was also used to warn of approaching enemy aircraft on nearly 1,000 occasions between 1940 and 1944. The final timetable, operative until closure, can be seen on the photograph.

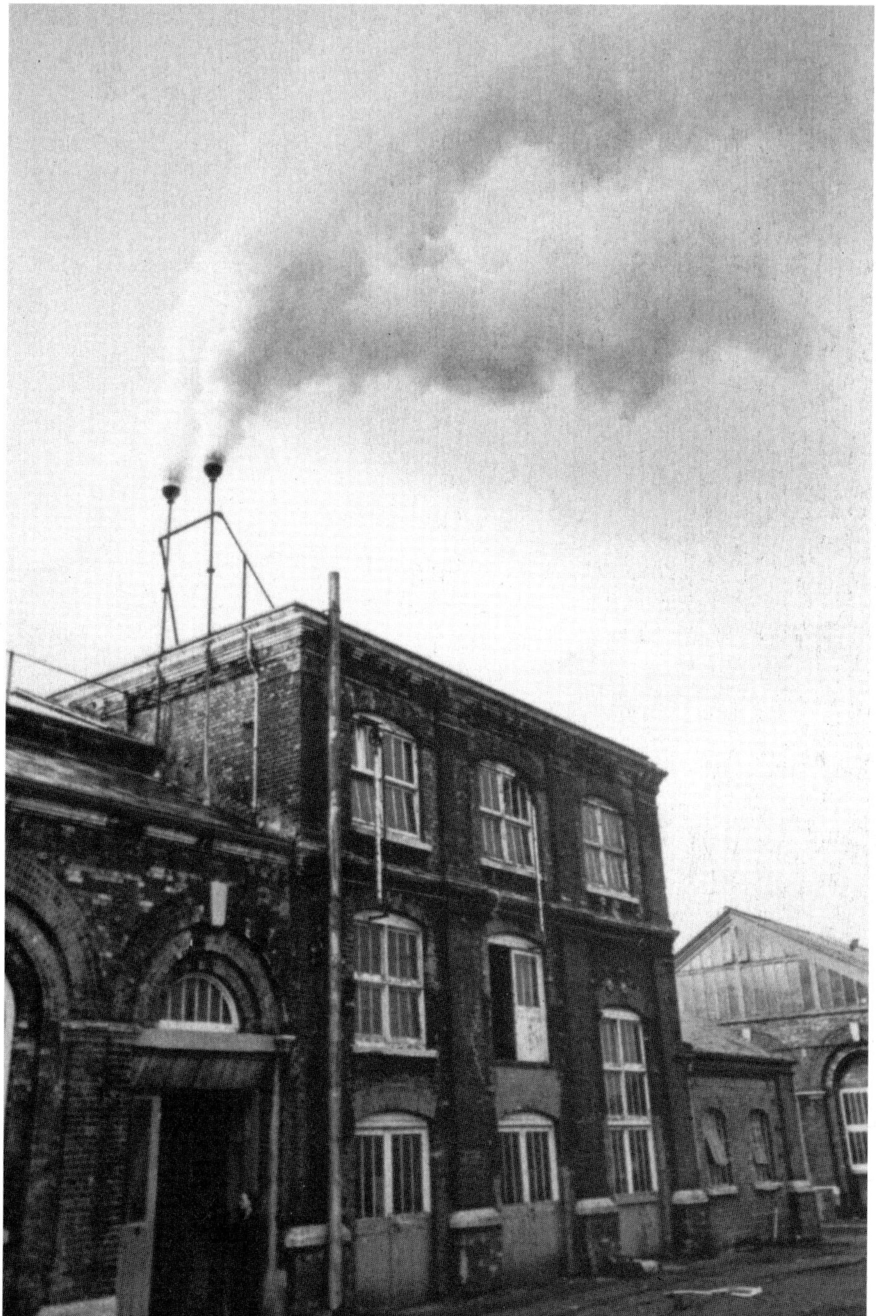

Swindon GWR Works' hooter. The twin domes of the works' hooter were adapted by the company from their original design of ships' sirens.

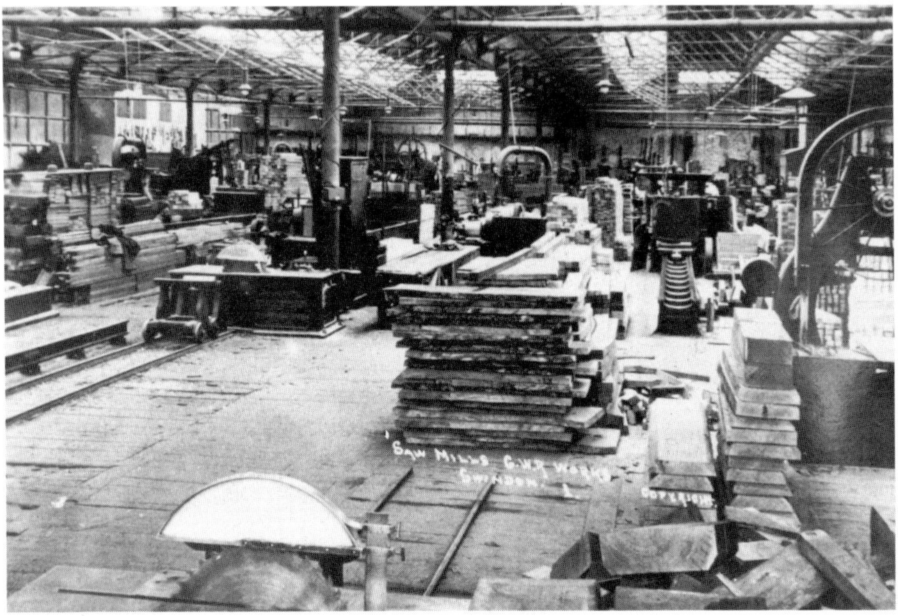

Saw mills, GWR Works, 1907. (William Hooper photograph)

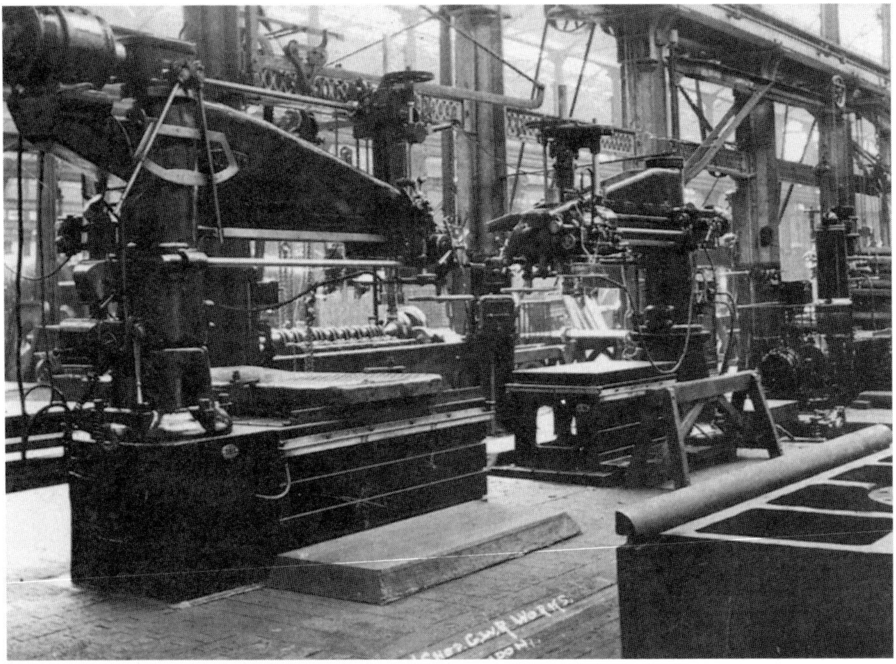

'V' (boiler) shop, GWR Works, 1907. (William Hooper photograph)

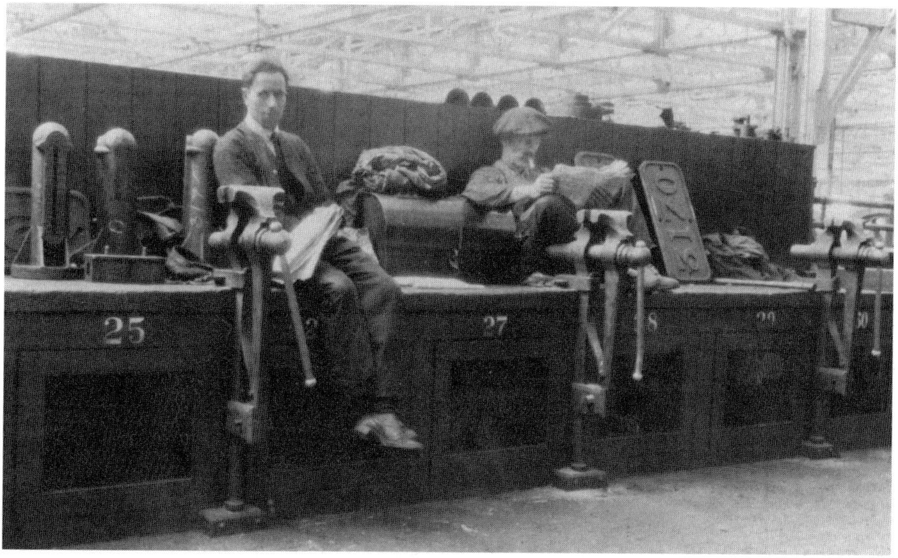

'Tea break', GWR Works, *c.* 1939. Note the plate for locomotive No. 3170. This was one of the 3150 class of 2–6–2 tank engines built in 1907. It was intended that they be rebuilt just before the Second World War but only five were completed. No. 3170 was sent out unaltered as all this type of work was stopped on account of the war.

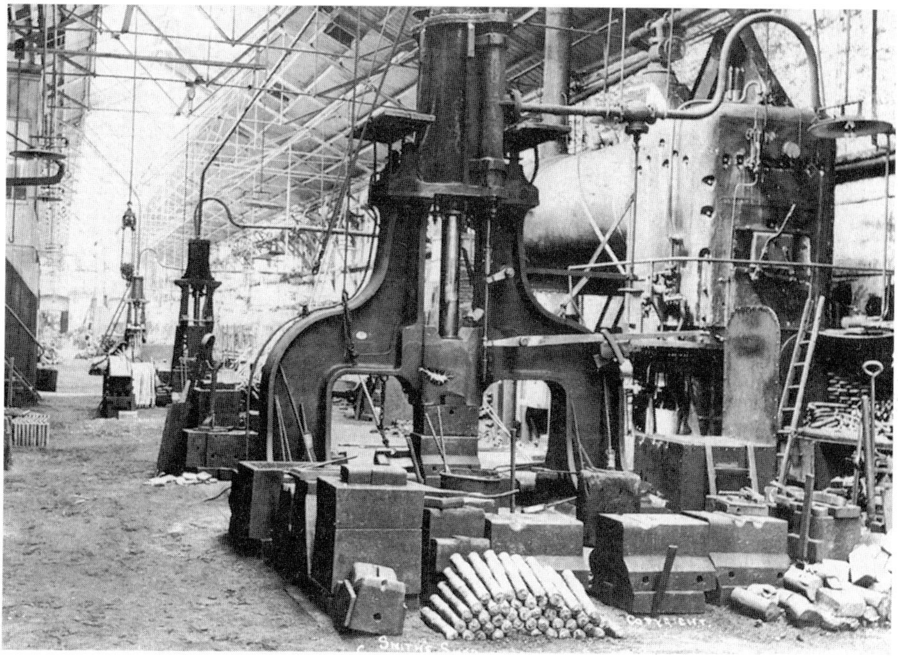

Smith's shop, GWR Works, 1907. The blow of the 5 cwt steam-hammer is equivalent to about a 30-ton load. (William Hooper photograph)

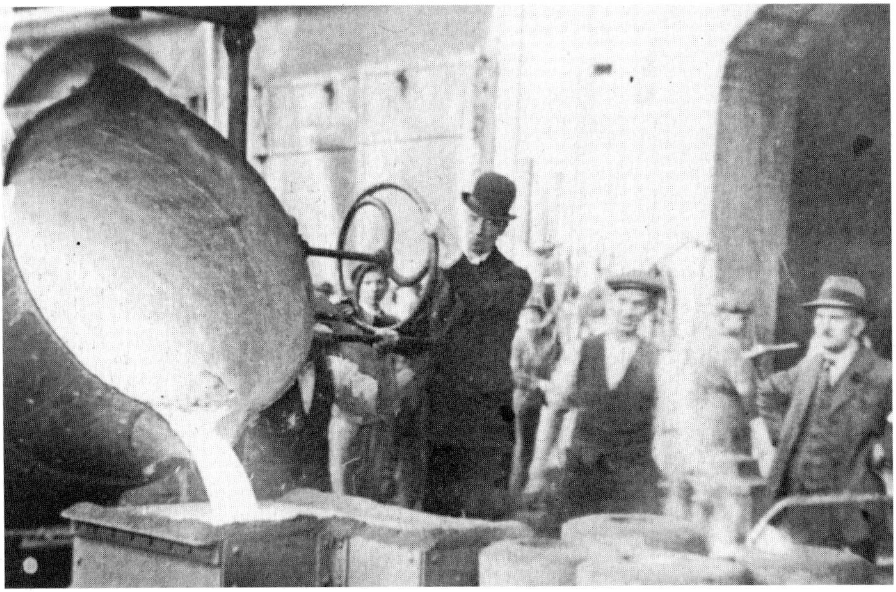

Iron foundry, GWR Works, *c*. 1931. The man on the right in the trilby hat is believed to be Vic Gregory, the pattern shop foreman for many years.

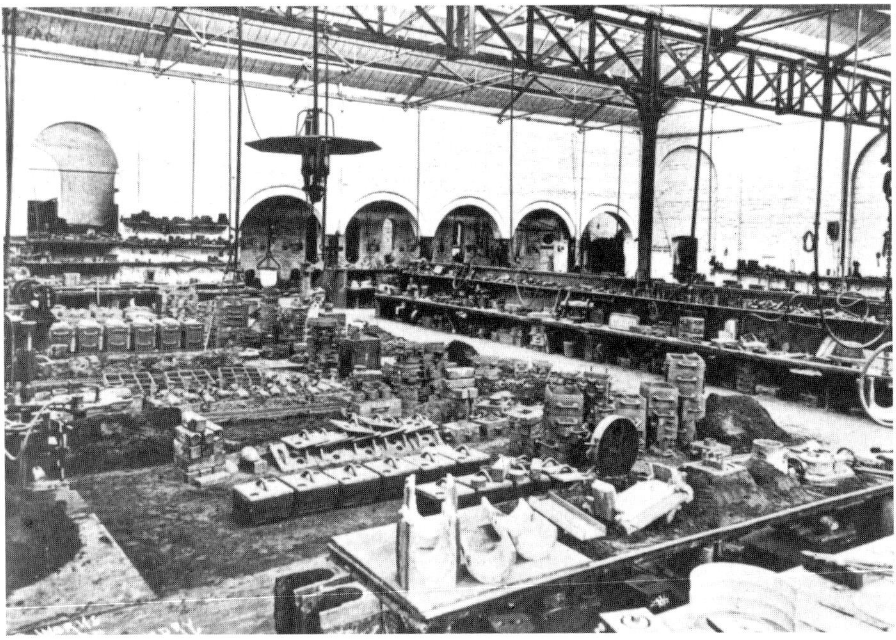

Brass foundry, GWR Works, 1907. The foundry housed thirty-three crucibles, three air furnaces and four moulding machines. Annual output at this time was about 1,700 tons. (William Hooper photograph)

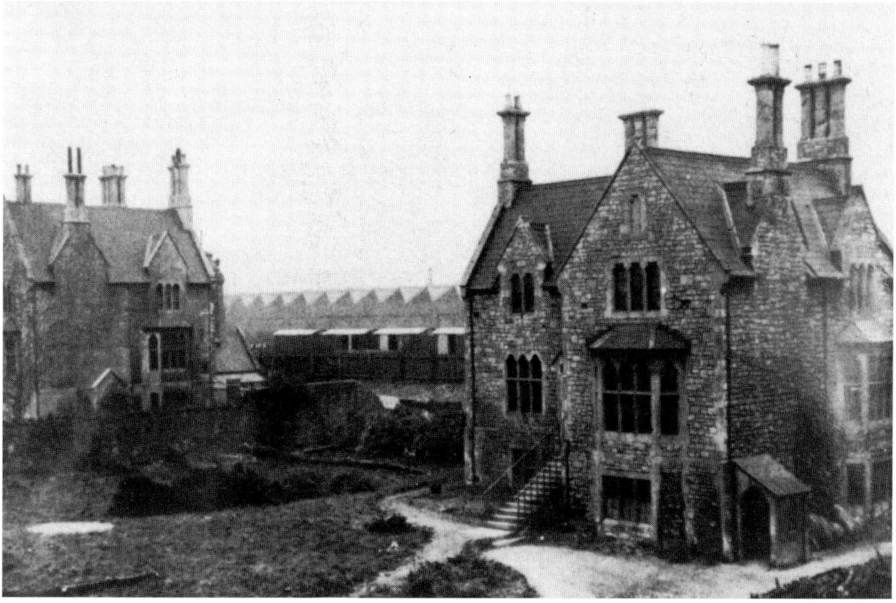

GWR managers' houses, awaiting demolition for extension to the wagon works, *c.* 1914. In the foreground is Station House with Marlow House to the left.

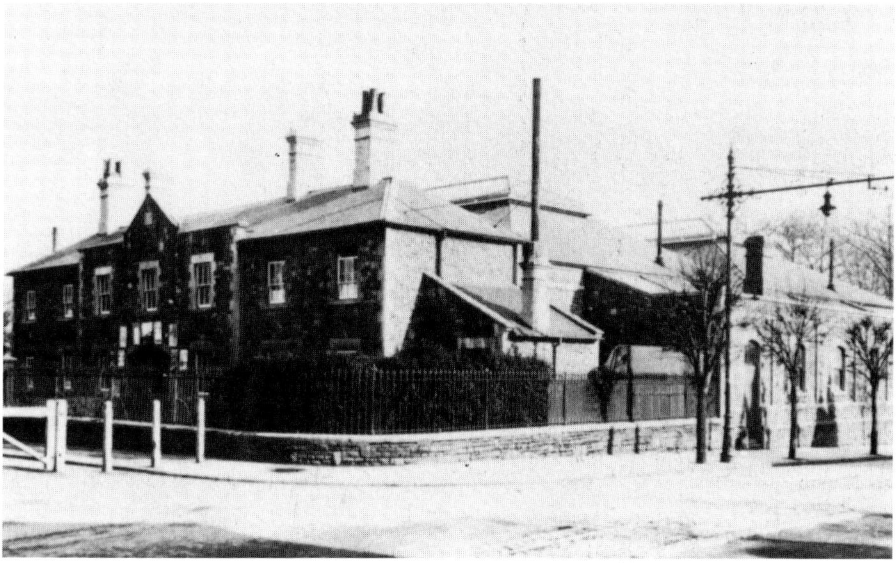

Drill Hall, Church Place, 1927. The hall was built in 1871 at a cost of £1,500 for the GWR Volunteer Rifle Corps. The building was also used as an overflow girls' school while awaiting the opening of College Street School in 1874. Gates at the end of Church Place marked the boundary between railway property and common ground.

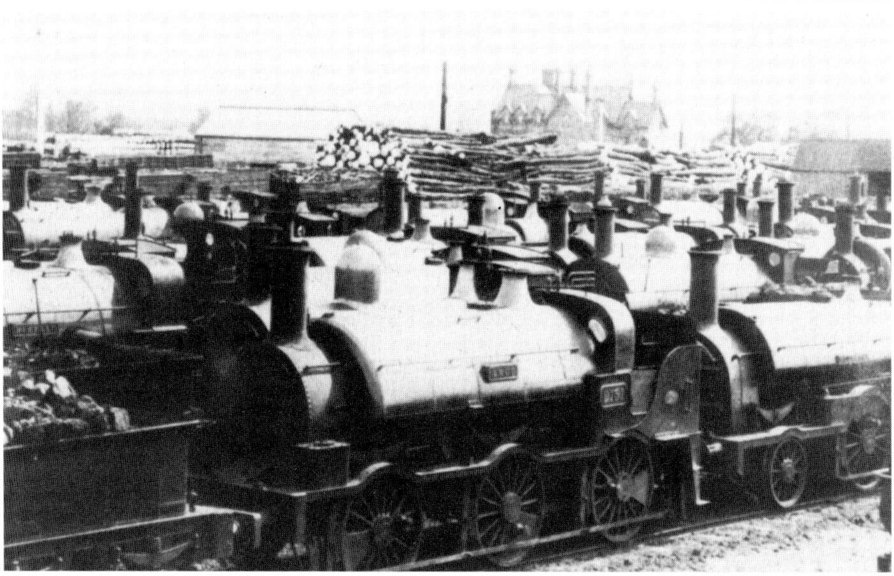

Broad gauge 'graveyard', GWR Works, 1892. Locomotives await scrapping or conversion to standard gauge. In the background can be seen 'Newburn', then home of William Dean, the Locomotive, Carriage and Wagon Superintendent at Swindon. Built in 1873 for his predecessor, Joseph Armstrong, Newburn House was demolished in the late 1930s and a carriage stock shed built in its place.

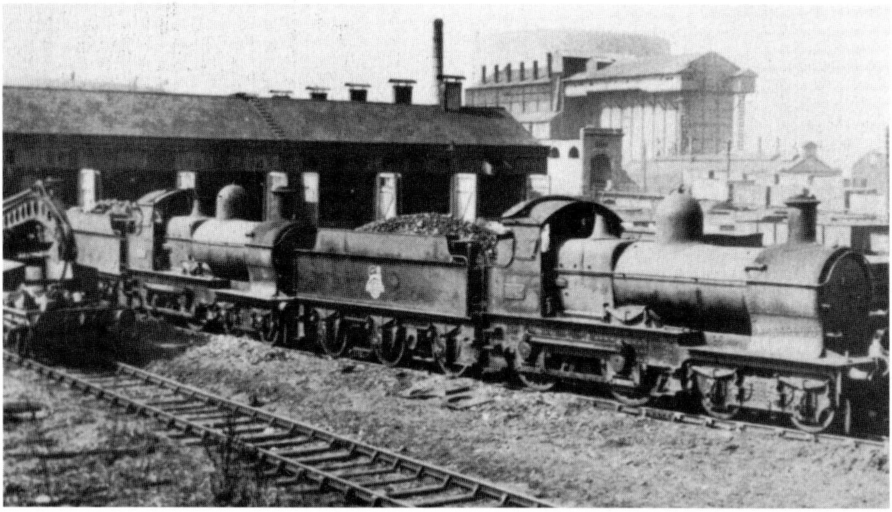

Swindon stock sheds and gasworks, *c.* 1950. The locomotive on the right is a so-called 'Dukedog' No. 9012, originally *Earl of Ducie*. These engines were rebuilt in the 1930s and used Bulldog frames and motion with Duke boilers and cabs. In 1946 the whole class was renumbered in the 90XX series. In the background can be seen the railway gasworks and vertical retort. The gasworks finally closed in 1959, and the stock sheds in 1964. This area is now all under Hawkesworth Trading Estate.

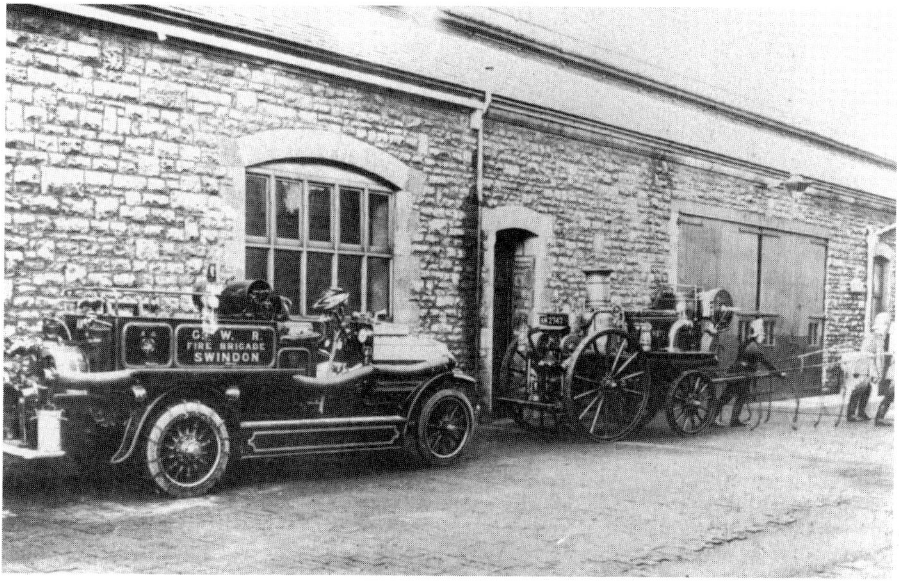

GWR Works' Fire Brigade. On the left is a Dennis fire-engine No. 3 (delivered in 1912), and on the right a stationary Merryweather engine (both now preserved at the GWR Museum).

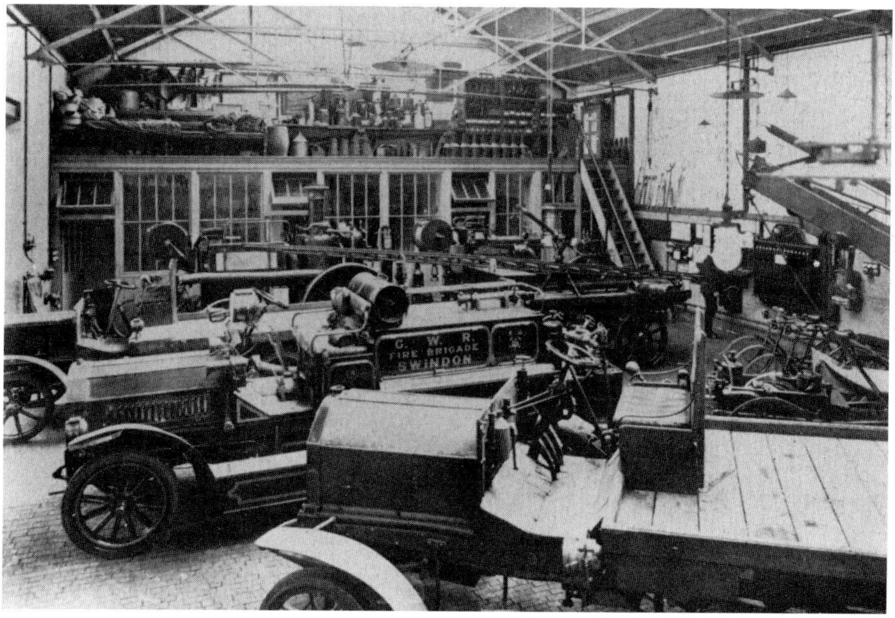

Bristol Street fire station, *c.* 1913, with the Dennis engine at the centre of the photograph.

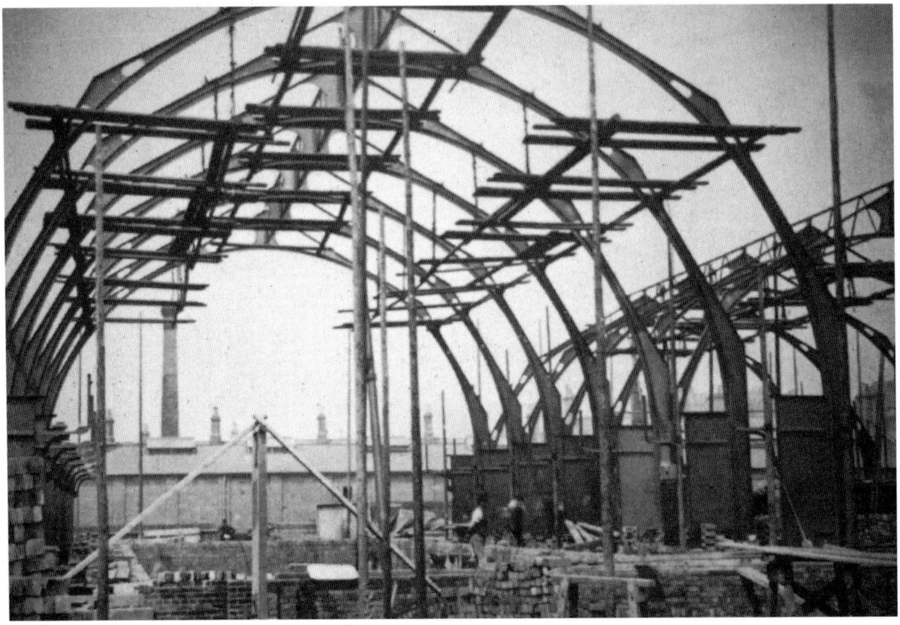

GWR Medical Fund Society swimming baths under construction in 1891/2. Two swimming baths were built, one 30 ft by 111 ft, the other 24 ft 6 in by 60 ft, with diving facilities and gallery accommodation. The large building could hold up to 750 people.

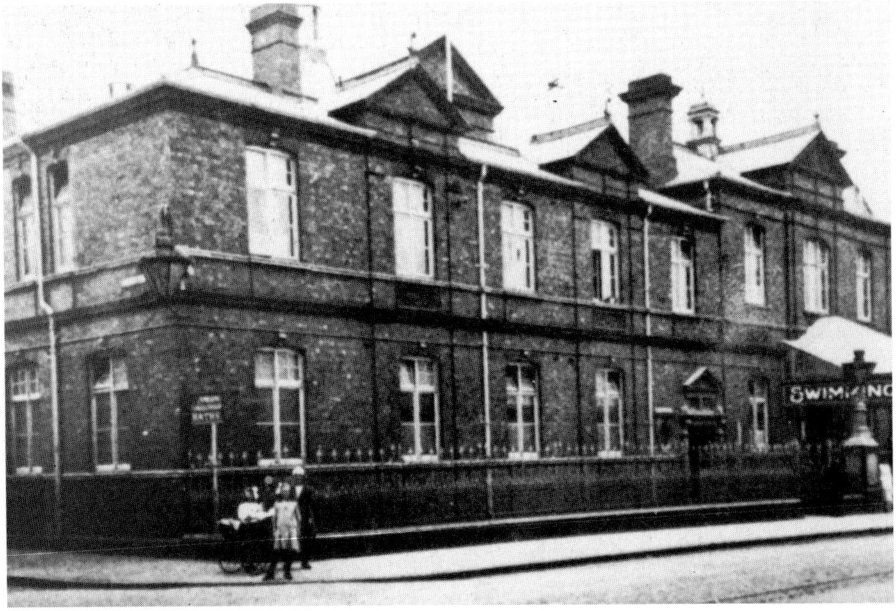

GWR Medical Fund Society swimming baths, Faringdon Road, *c.* 1905. The baths were opened in 1892 with Turkish and Russian baths added later in 1899.

SECTION THREE

Streets, Shops & Industries

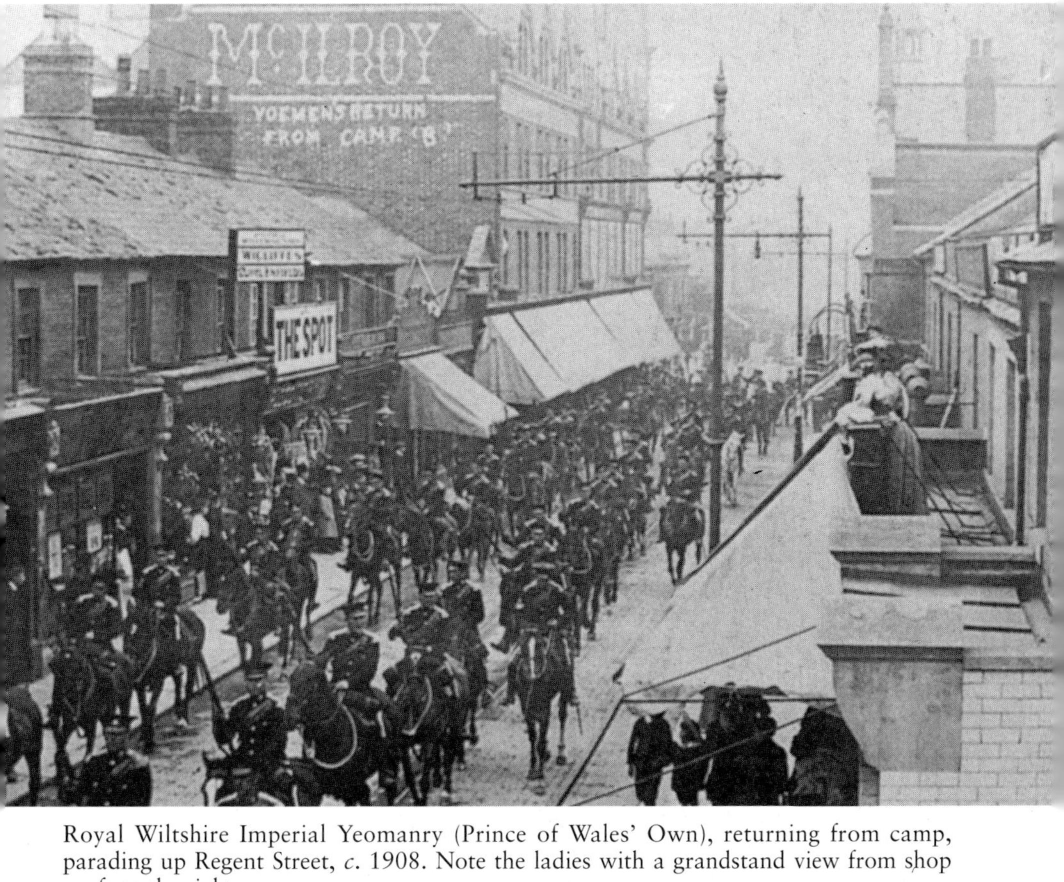

Royal Wiltshire Imperial Yeomanry (Prince of Wales' Own), returning from camp, parading up Regent Street, *c*. 1908. Note the ladies with a grandstand view from shop roofs to the right.

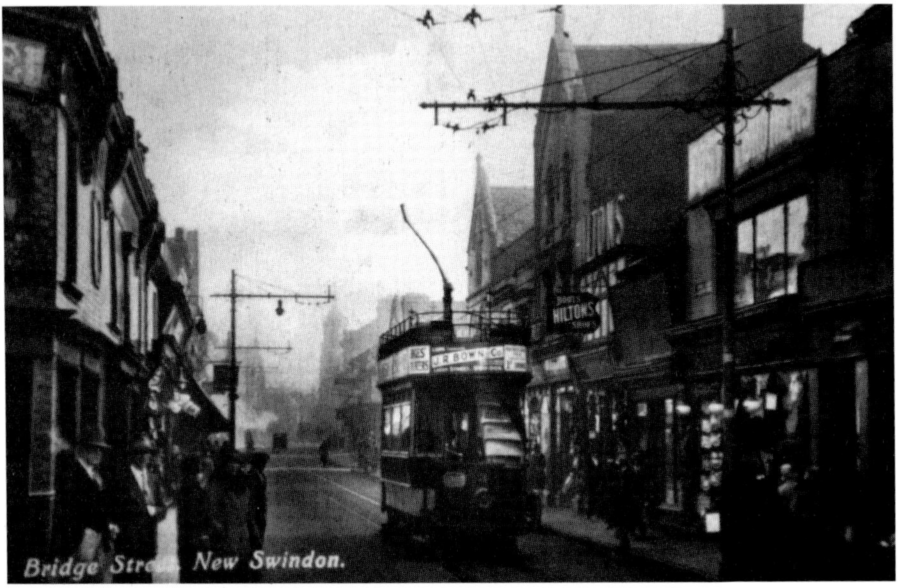

Tramcar No. 3, Bridge Street (looking south), *c.* 1925. On the left is the Oxford Hotel on the corner with Fleet Street.

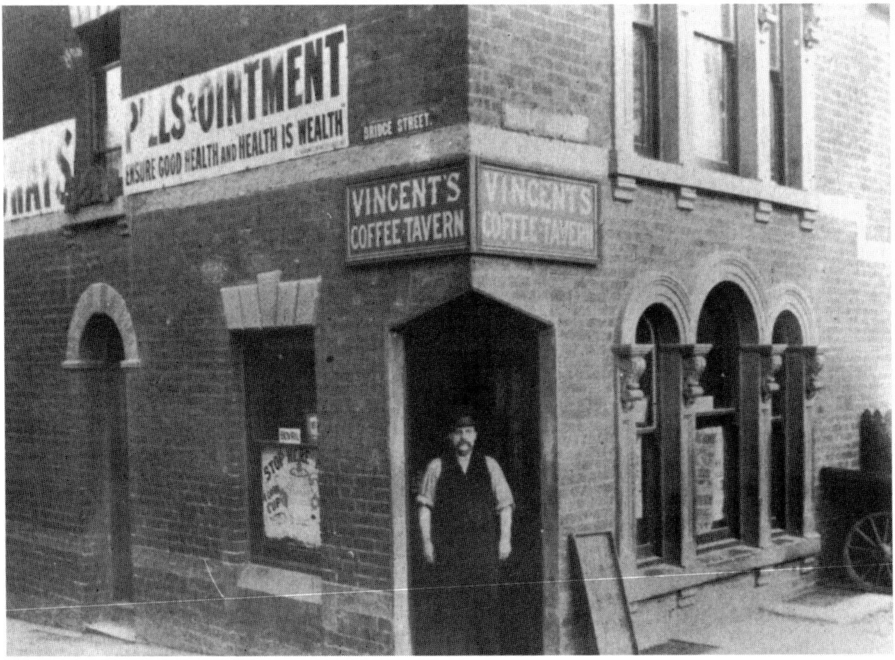

F.W. Vincent's Coffee Tavern, 78 Bridge Street, at the corner with Sheppard Street, *c.* 1910. These premises are now offices for Workout.

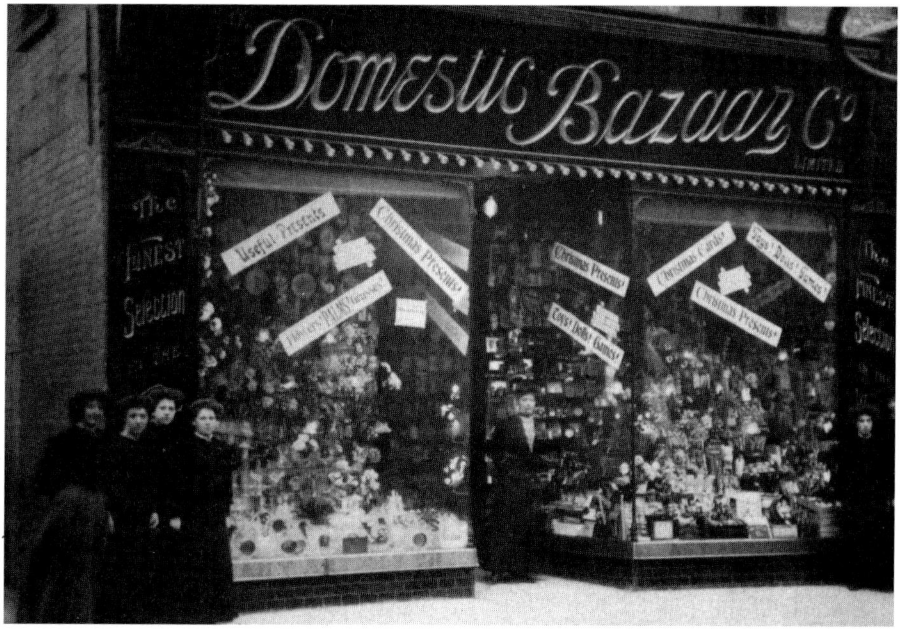

Domestic Bazaar Co. Ltd, 47 Bridge Street, *c.* 1910. Photographed at Christmas time with stickers on the windows advertising 'useful presents', 'toys, dolls, games', 'Christmas cards' and 'Christmas presents'. This shop, on the corner with Queen Street, is now The Pine Shop.

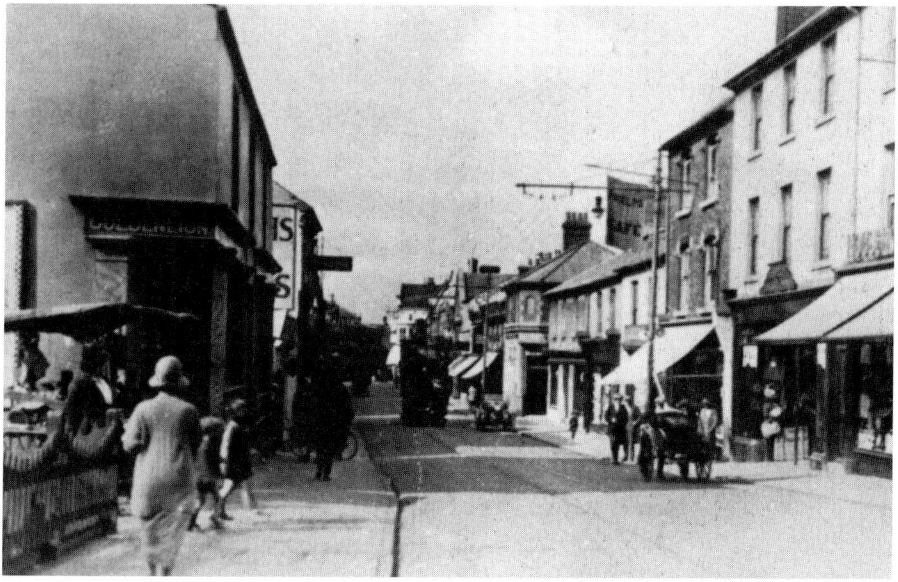

Bridge Street, looking north from the site of the Golden Lion bridge (demolished in 1918), *c.* 1925. The Golden Lion public house is on the left.

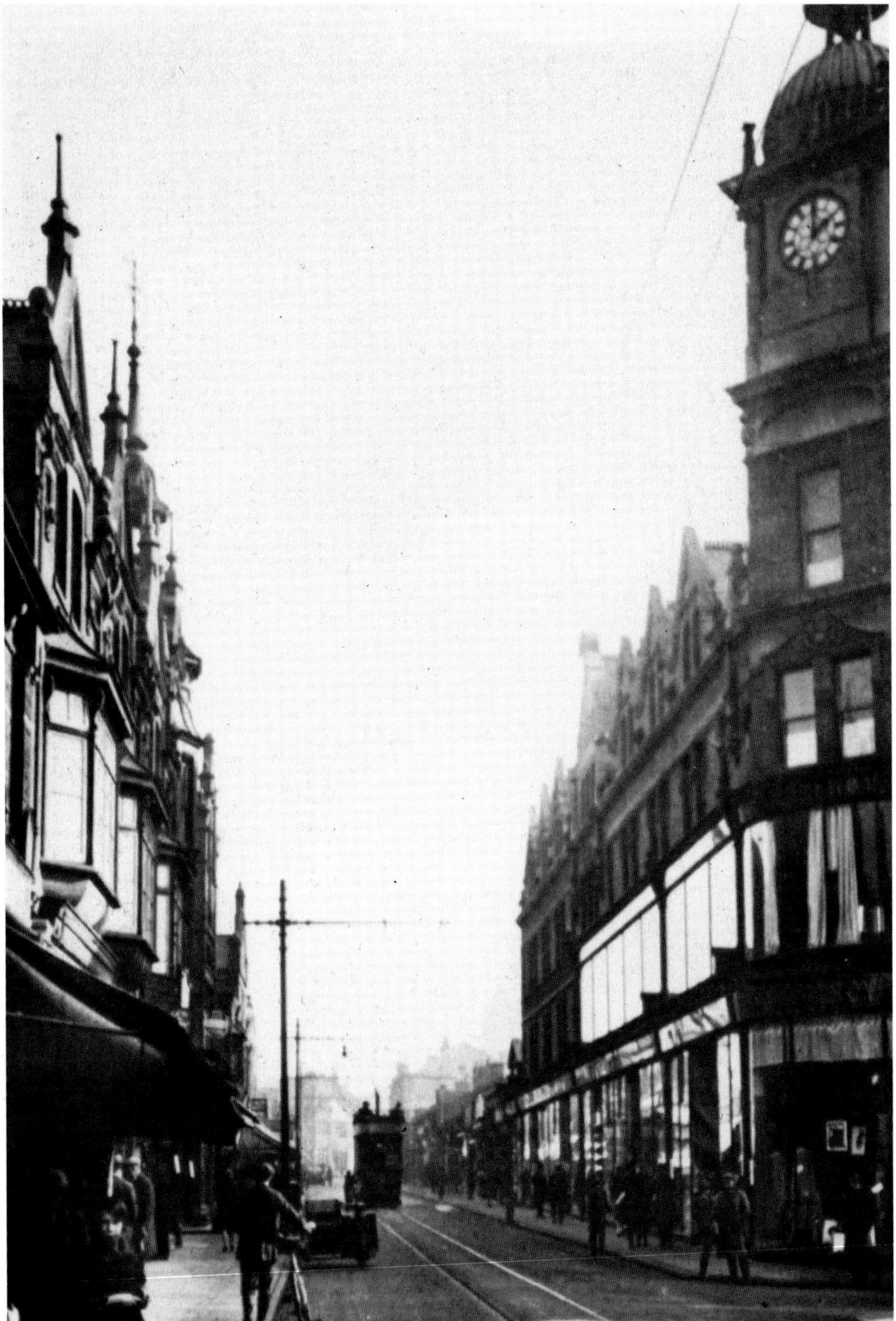

Regent Street, looking south, *c.* 1925. McIlroy's clocktower was built in 1904. It was demolished in the mid-1960s when the store was modernized.

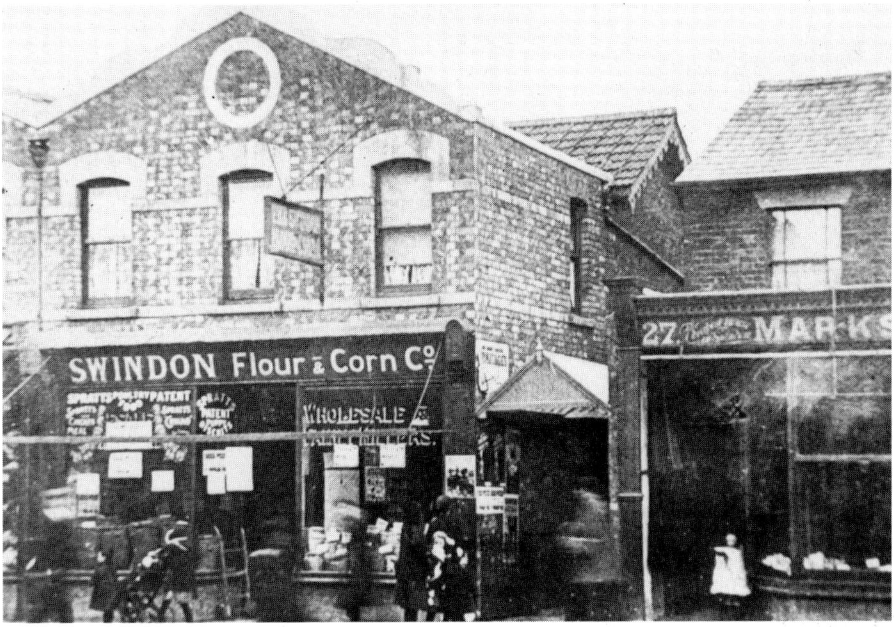

Swindon Flour & Corn Co., 26 Cromwell Street, and S. Marks, clothiers, *c.* 1910.

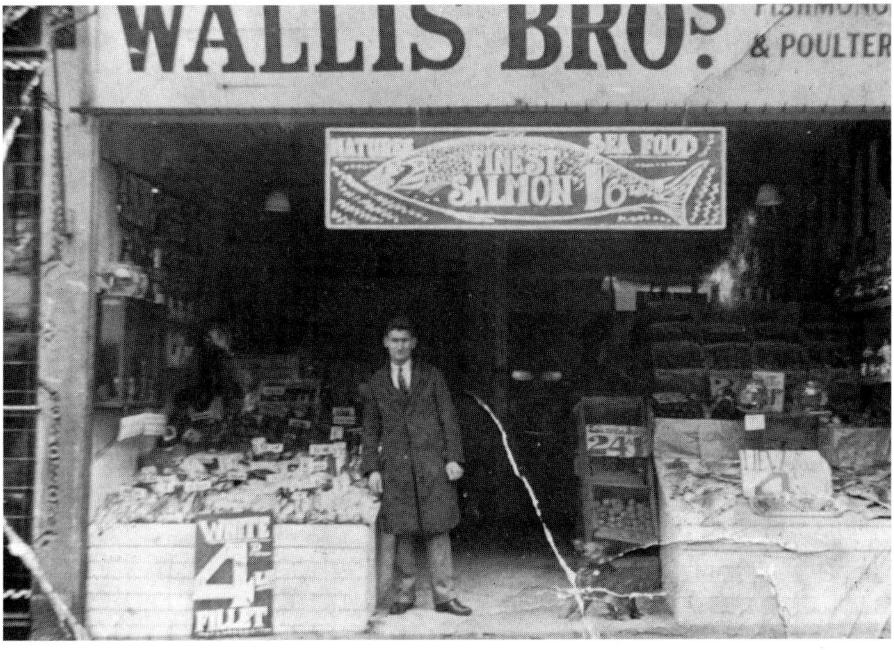

Wallis Bros., fishmongers and poulterers, 22 Cromwell Street, *c.* 1932.

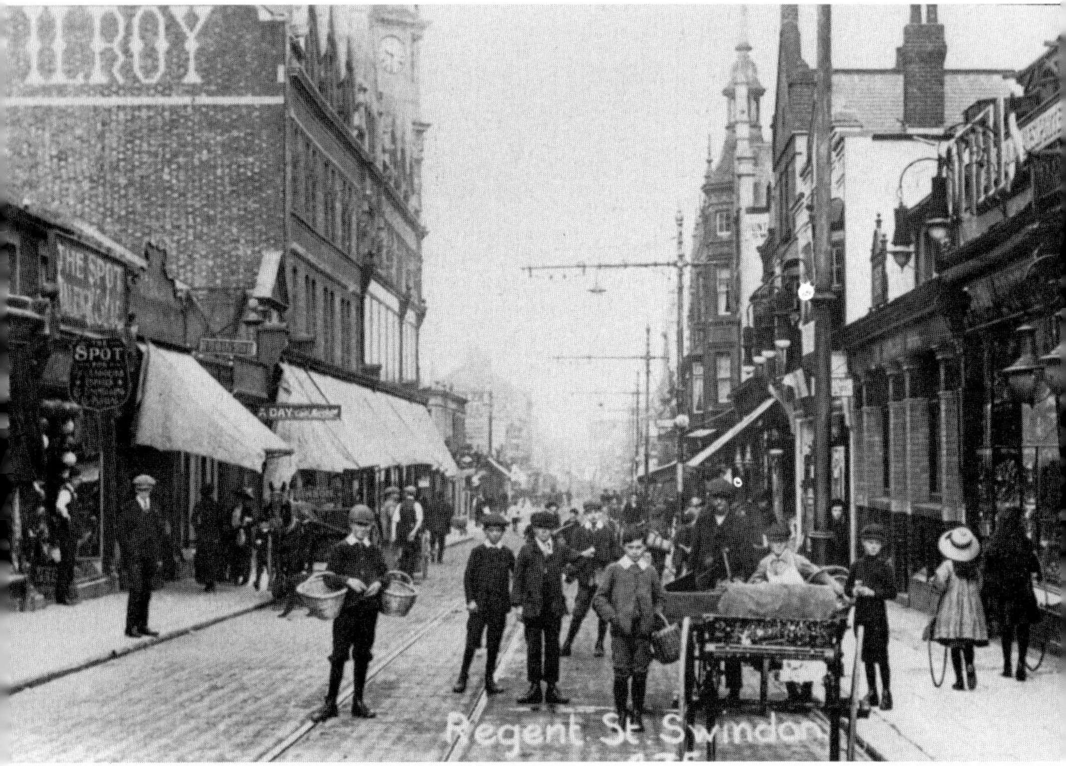

Regent Street, looking north, 1913. Several young tradesmen's delivery boys ensure they are recorded on camera, but two young girls, on the right with their hoops, ignore the photographer. To the left is the imposing façade of McIlroy's departmental store, built by John Norman, a Swindon builder who had offices in Victoria Road. Regent Street was originally the southern part of Bridge Street and was lined with terraced houses (see *Swindon in Old Photographs (2)*, p. 34). Its present name, derived from the famous London Street, was bestowed in the 1860s when the original workmen's cottages were being converted into shops.

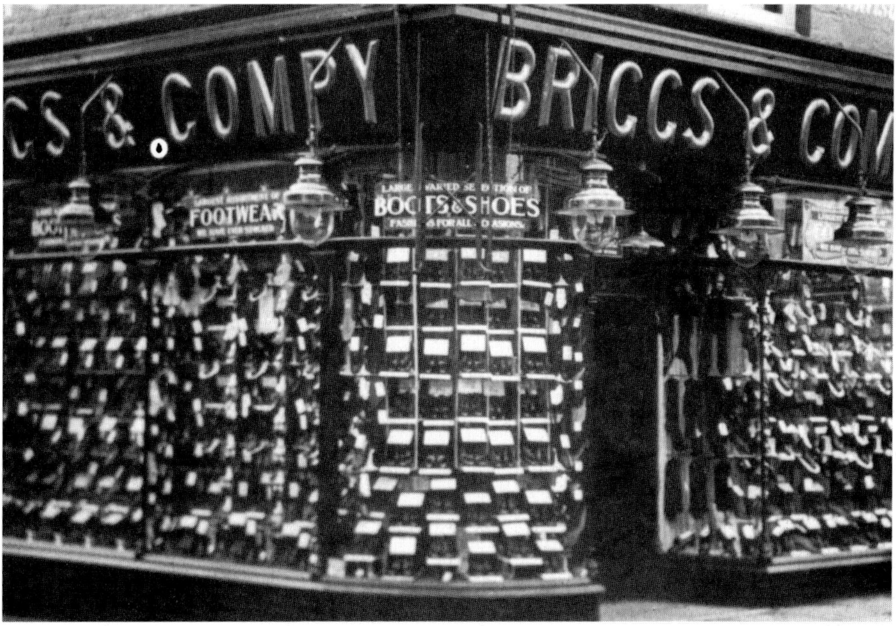

Briggs & Co., which sold boots and shoes, at 89 Regent Street, *c.* 1910. This company remained trading in Regent Street until very recently, but from a different shop.

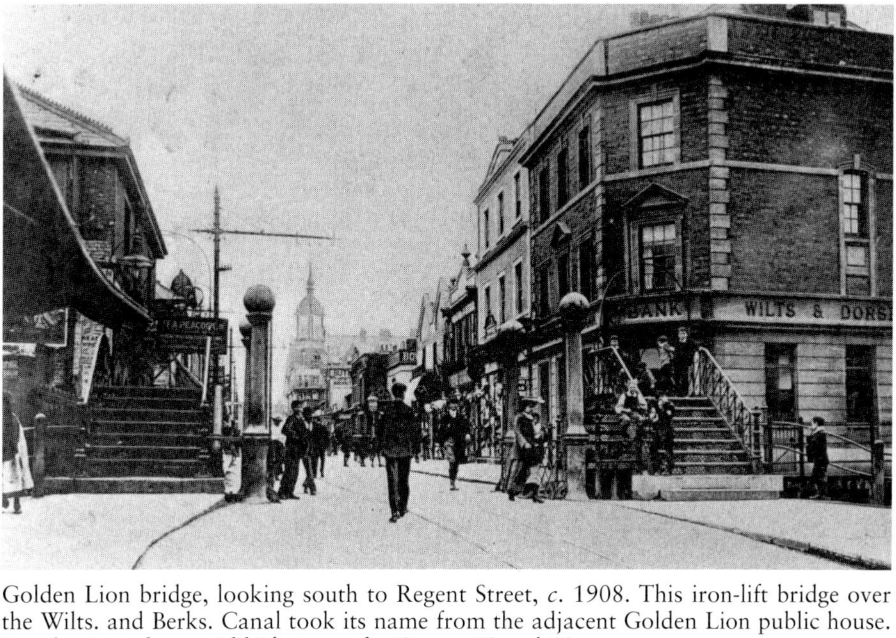

Golden Lion bridge, looking south to Regent Street, *c.* 1908. This iron-lift bridge over the Wilts. and Berks. Canal took its name from the adjacent Golden Lion public house. See also *Swindon in Old Photographs (3)*, pp. 78 and 79.

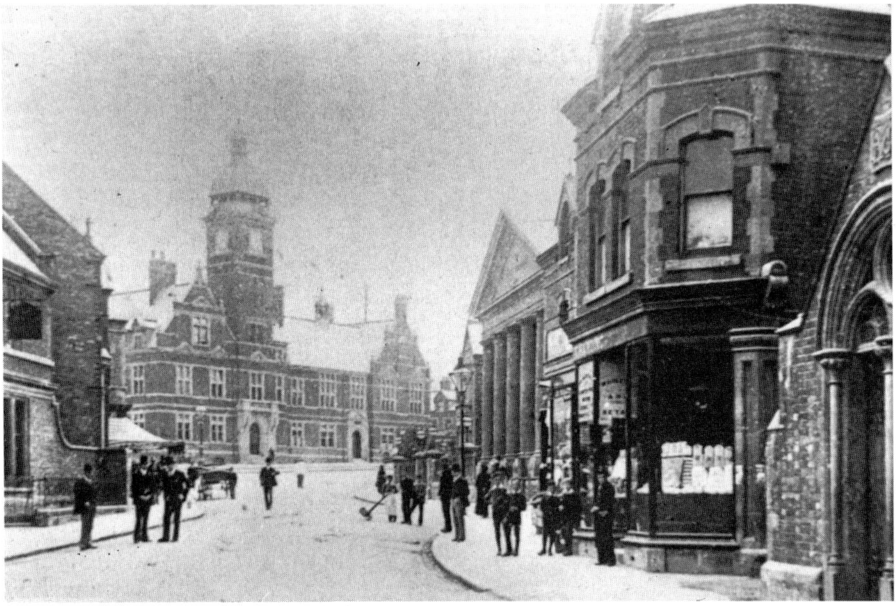

The Town Hall, viewed from Regent Street, *c.* 1900. Opened on 2 October 1891 by the Marquis of Bath as the 'new public offices building', it has remained a landmark of New Swindon ever since. The imposing façade of the Baptist Tabernacle can be seen to the right.

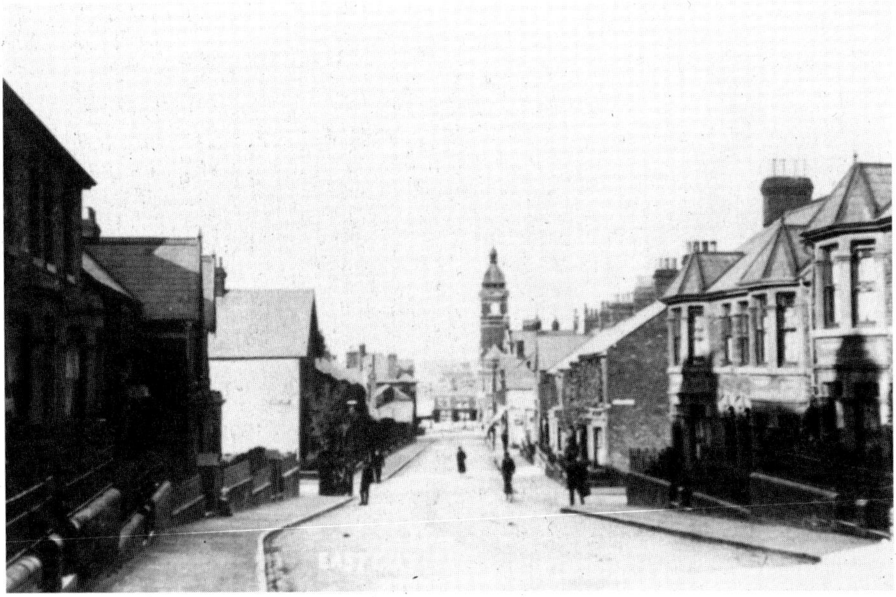

Eastcott Hill, looking east towards the Town Hall, *c.* 1910. This was one of the original routes to reach Old Town when the two were separate.

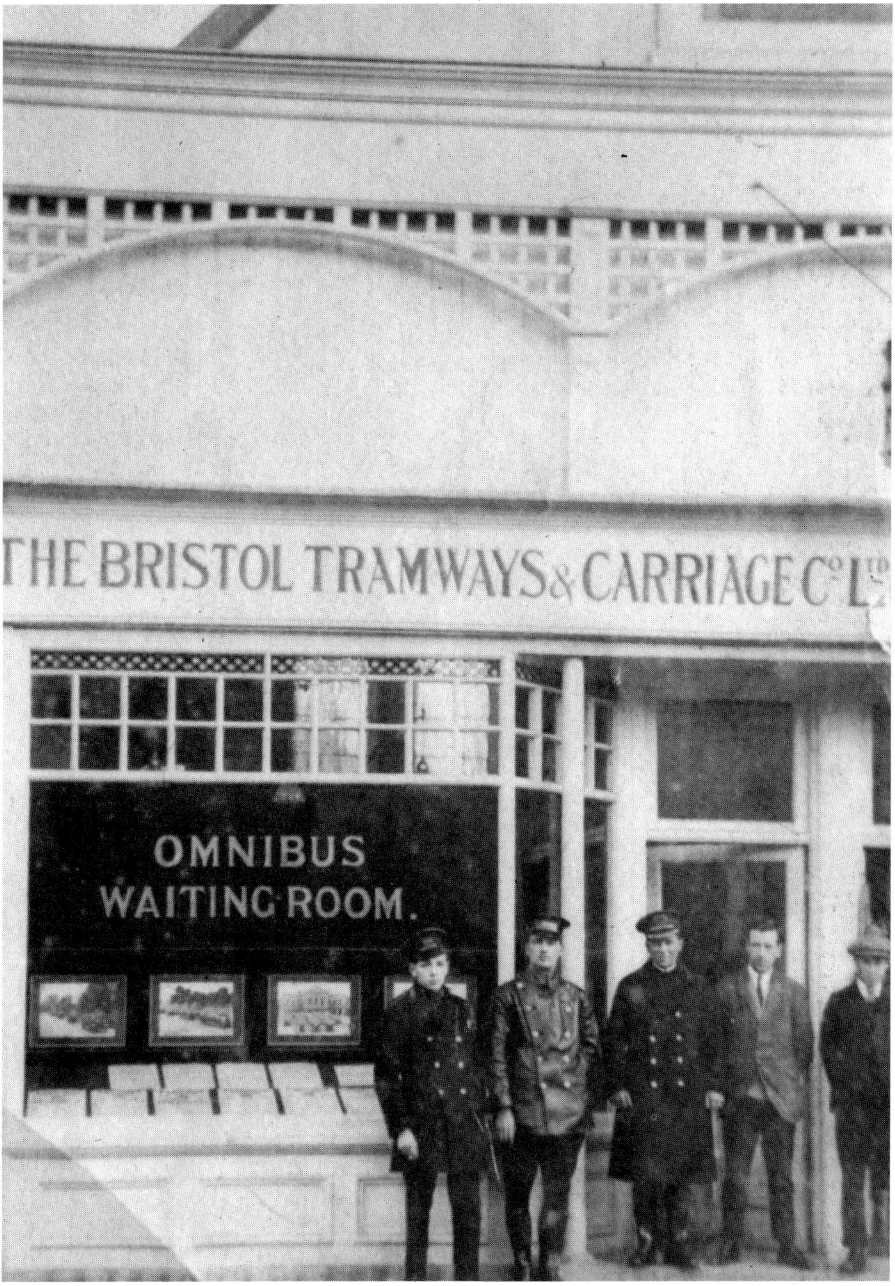

The omnibus waiting room and office of The Bristol Tramways & Carriage Co. Ltd, Regent Circus, *c.* 1931. These premises had formerly been The Picture House, one of Swindon's first cinemas (see p. 133). Left to right: S. Curtis (conductor), R.J. Moore (driver), W. Winter (inspector), W. Frewin (clerk), W. Beasley (clerk).

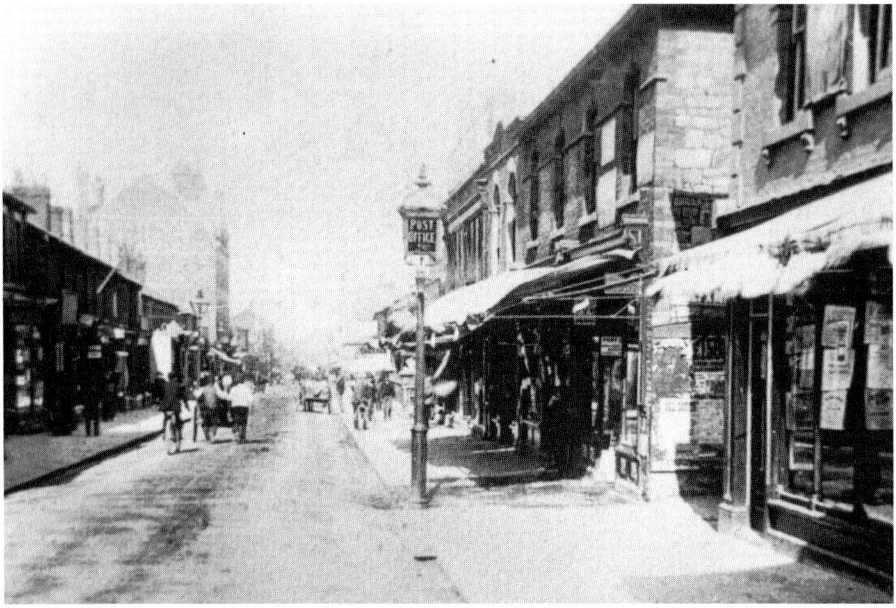

Regent Street, looking north towards McIlroy's, *c.* 1904. Note the post office sign on the pavement to the right.

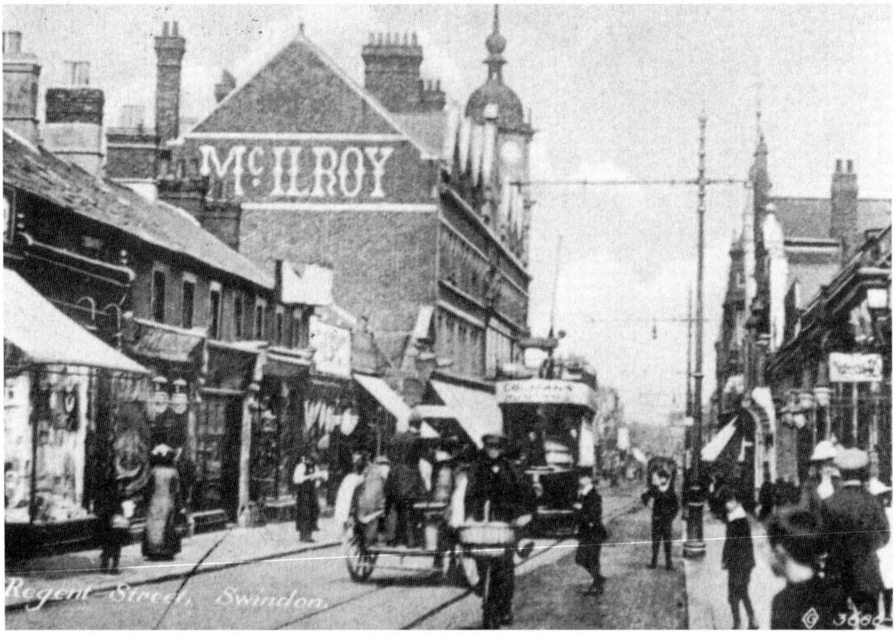

Regent Street, looking north, *c.* 1908. Many of the first-floor windows of the old cottages on the left can still be seen behind modern shop fronts.

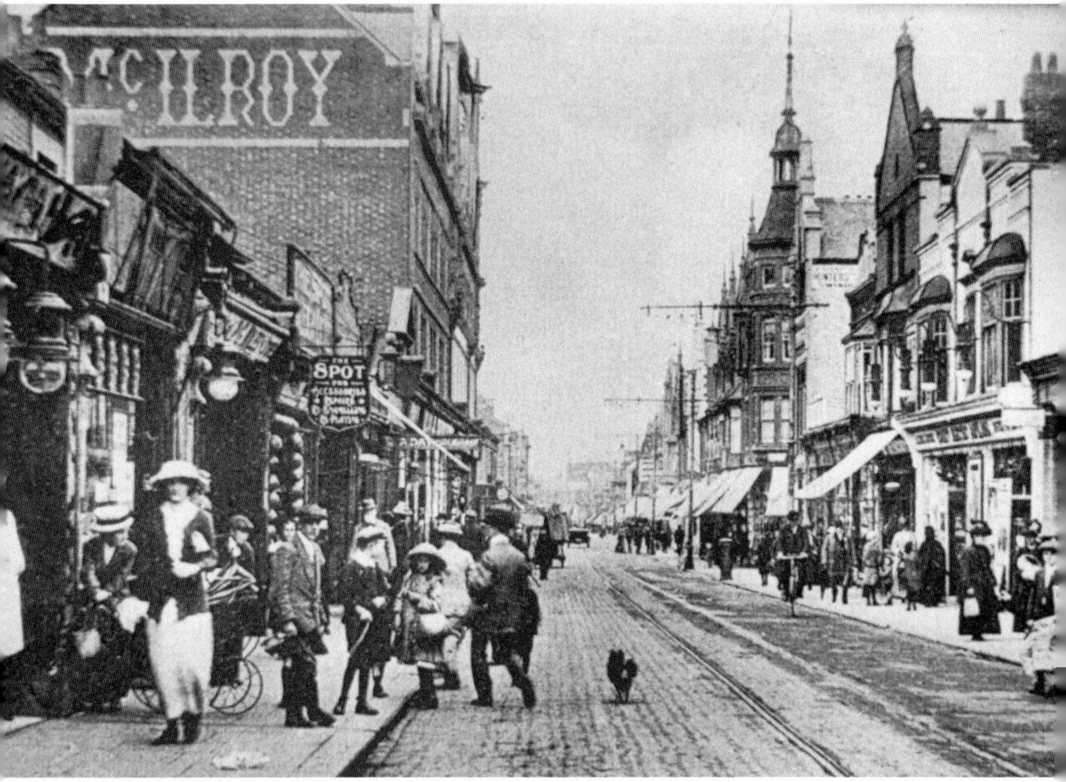

Regent Street, looking north, *c.* 1912. On the right is the Artillery Arms public house, which opened here around 1858, and the County Electric Pavilion, Swindon's first cinema. The Artillery Arms was closed and demolished in 1936 for extensions to Woolworth's store. On the left can be seen 'The Spot', where many generations of Swindon's youth purchased their models, cycles and sports equipment until closure in 1979.

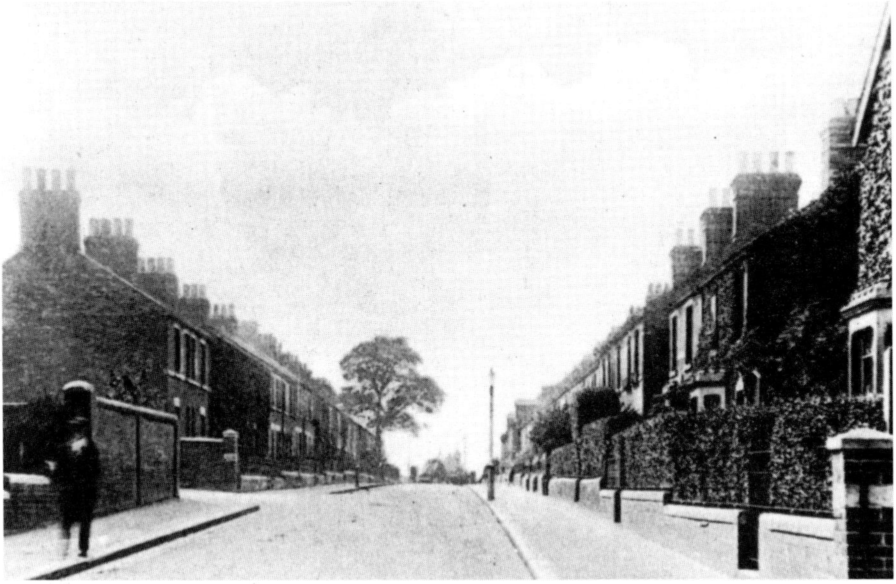

Stafford Street, looking west, *c.* 1910. The Gorse Hill Brick & Tile Co. built the first houses here, and in adjacent Dixon Street, on a large field called Gilberts Hill.

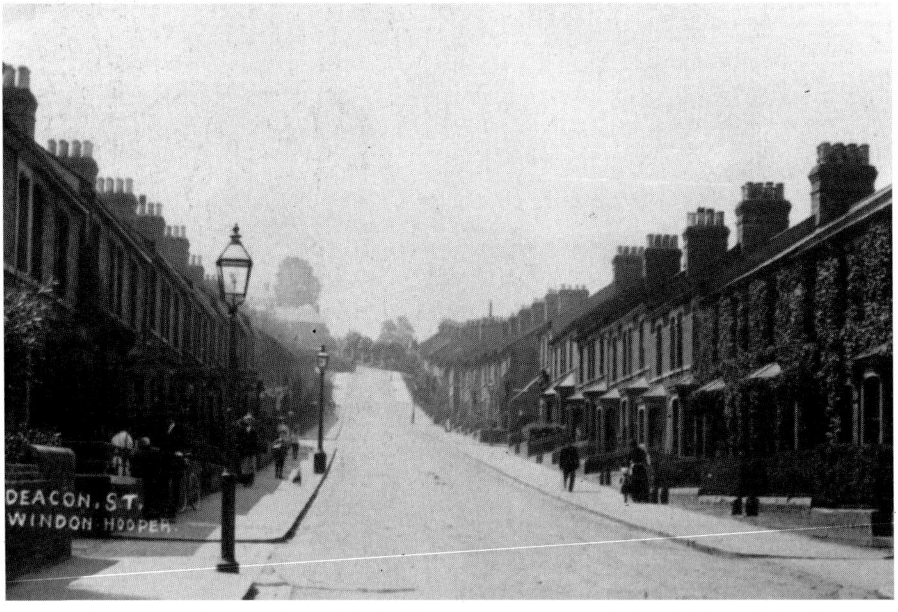

Deacon Street, looking south, *c.* 1910. The road was named after Hubert John Deacon, an Old Town jeweller, who bought the land and built on this part of the Rolleston estate in the 1890s.

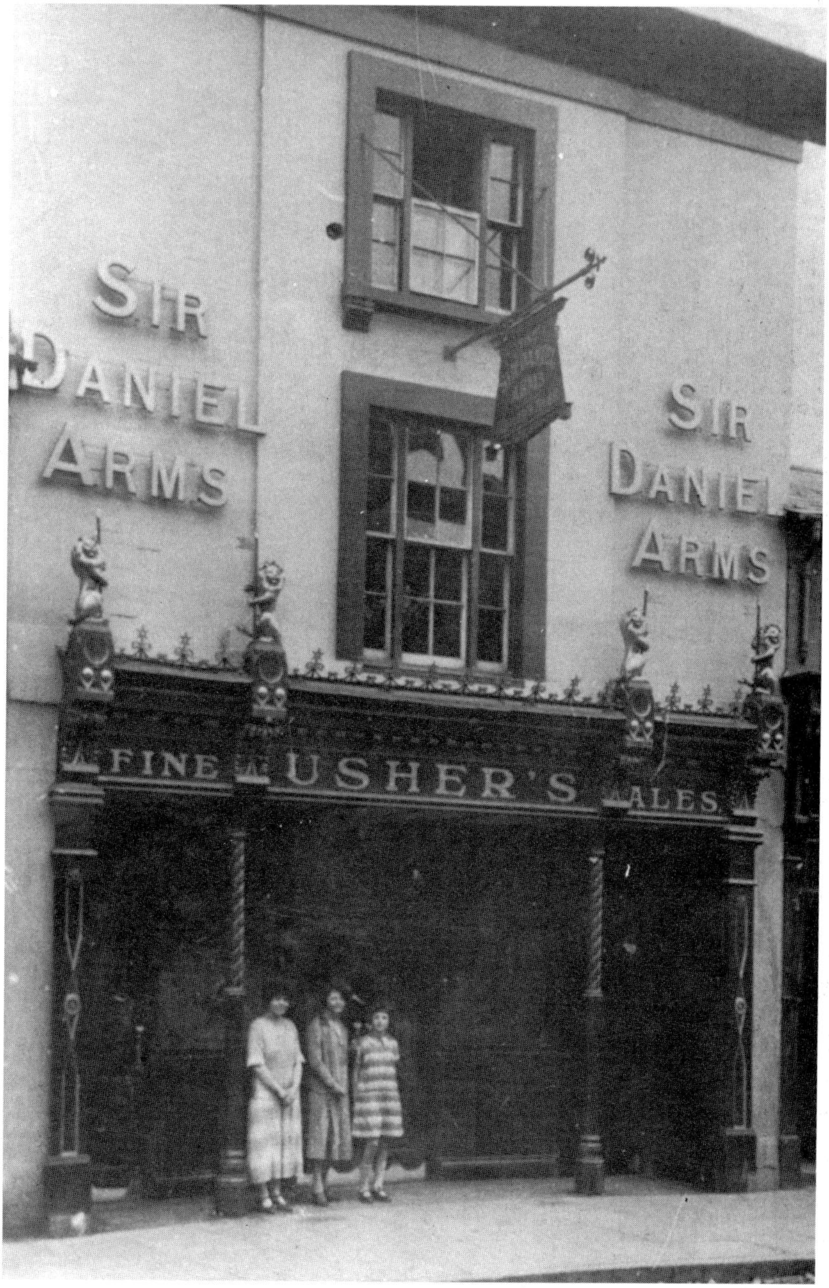

Sir Daniel Arms, 4 Fleet Street, in the 1930s. Named after Sir Daniel Gooch (1816–79), the first Locomotive, Carriage and Wagon Superintendent of the GWR Works at Swindon, it was built in the mid-1800s as a beerhouse. Although renovated in 1984 it is now closed, but may be re-opened as a night-club in the future.

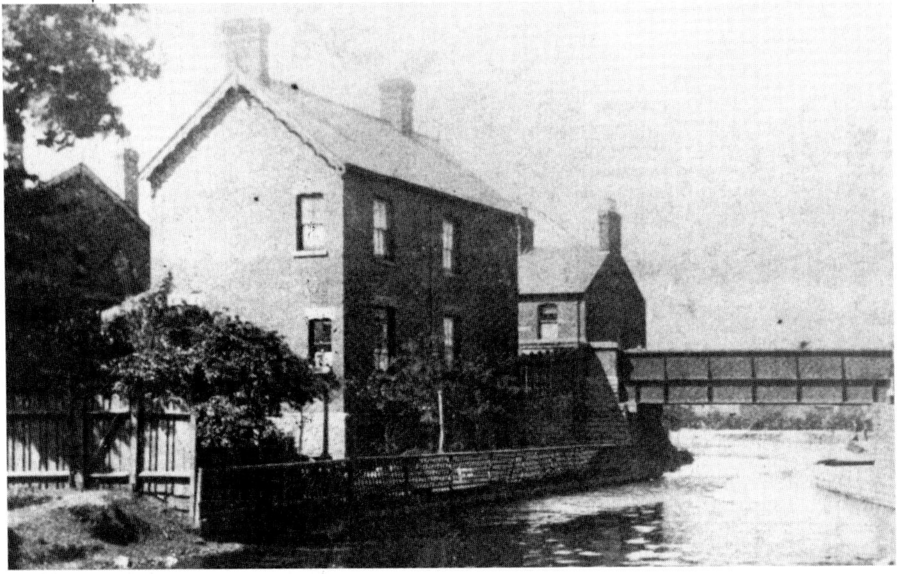

Wellington Street (Queenstown) Bridge, over the Wilts. and Berks. Canal, *c.* 1890. Fleming Way now runs along the canal route and the site of the bridge is near the entrance to Falcon House (Allied Dunbar).

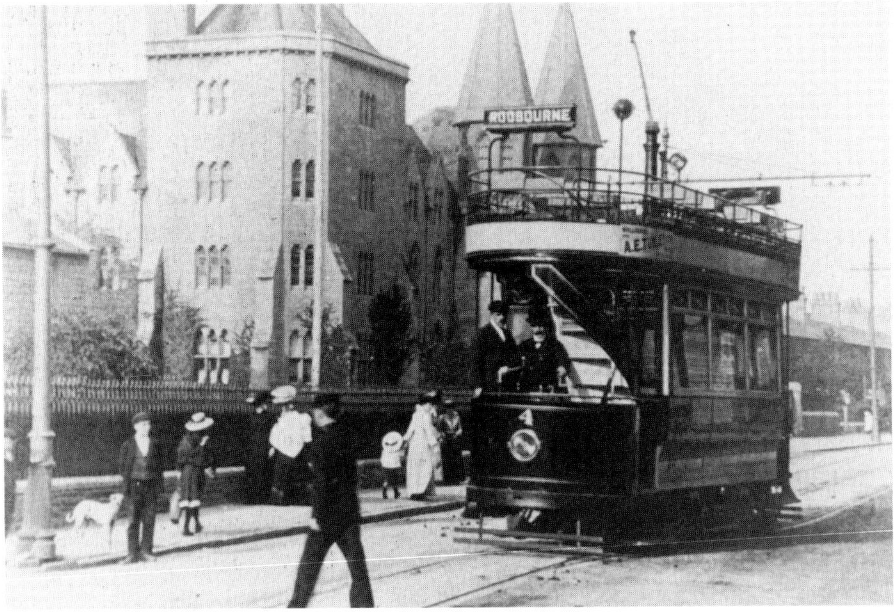

Tramcar No. 4, *en route* to Rodbourne, in Faringdon Road, *c.* 1905. In the background is the Wesleyan Methodist church (now the Railway Museum), which was built originally as a 'barracks' for single men working at the GWR factory.

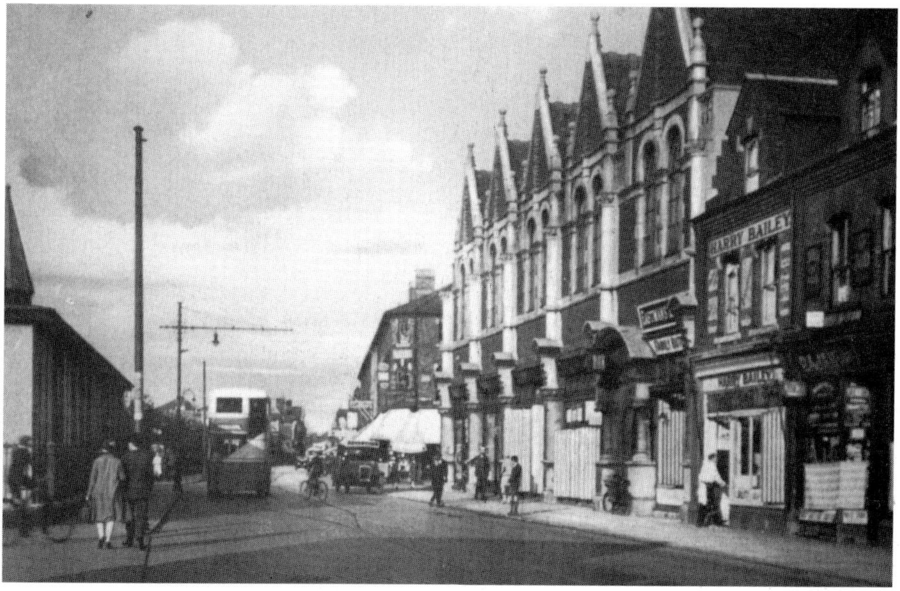

Faringdon Road, looking east from near the junction with Milton Road, *c.* 1930. To the left is the extension to the GWR Medical Fund Hospital added in 1927, and to the right the Wesleyan Methodist Schools.

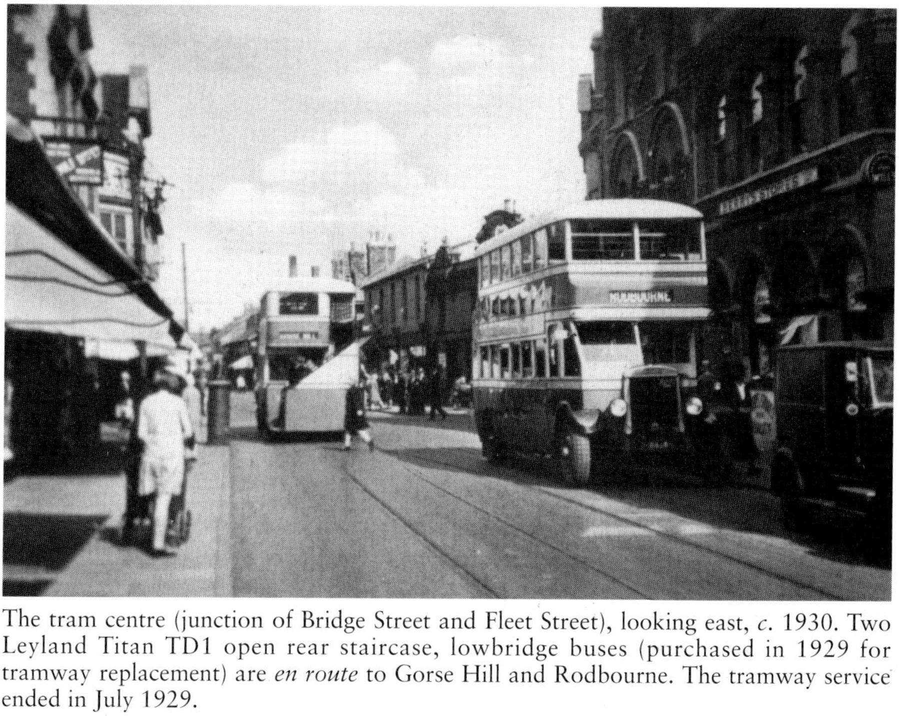

The tram centre (junction of Bridge Street and Fleet Street), looking east, *c.* 1930. Two Leyland Titan TD1 open rear staircase, lowbridge buses (purchased in 1929 for tramway replacement) are *en route* to Gorse Hill and Rodbourne. The tramway service ended in July 1929.

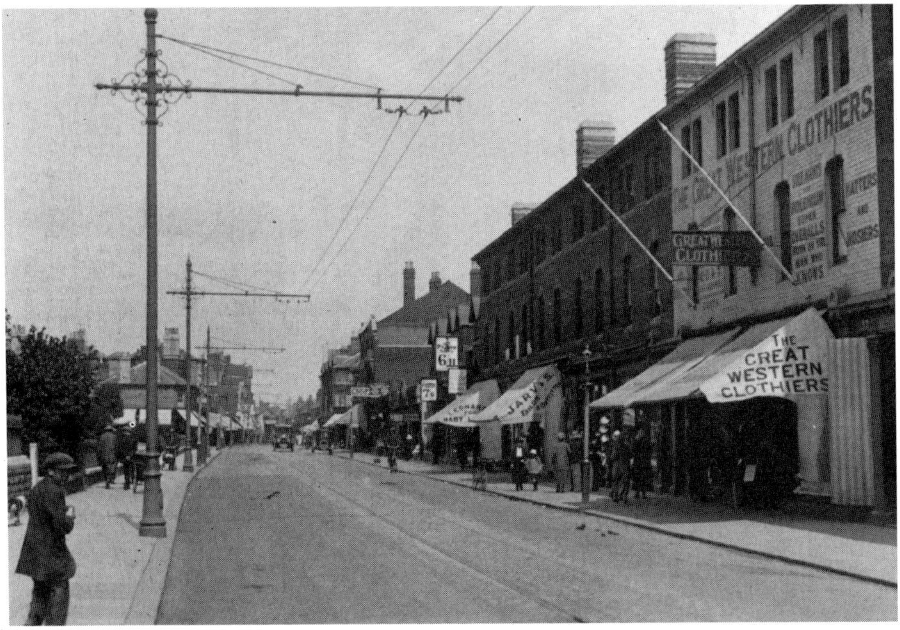

Faringdon Road, looking east towards Fleet Street, *c.* 1925. The Great Western Clothiers, established in 1899, traded here for many years. The upper storeys of the buildings remain very similar today.

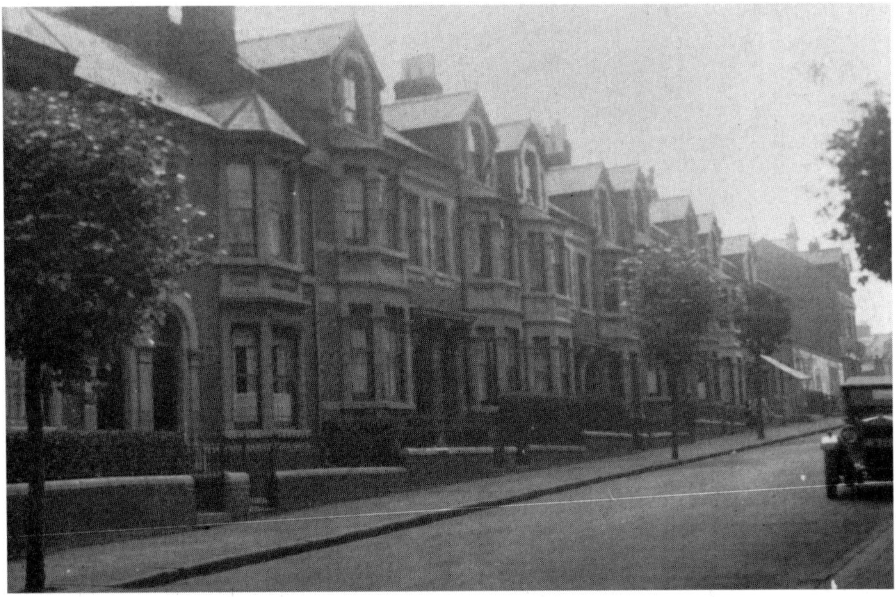

Milton Road, looking south-east, *c.* 1925. The houses in this road boasted attics and basements. Today many have been completely rebuilt.

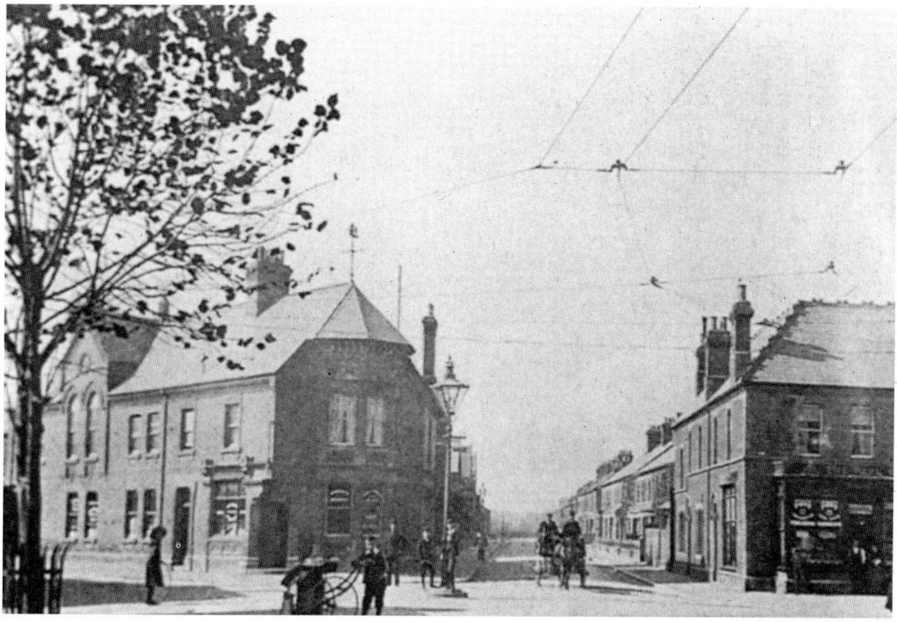

Birch Street and Westcott Place, at the junction with Park Lane and Faringdon Road, *c.* 1905. The Ship Hotel, on the corner of Birch Street and Westcott Place, was the scene of a murder in 1903 (see *Swindon in Old Photographs (1)*, p. 106).

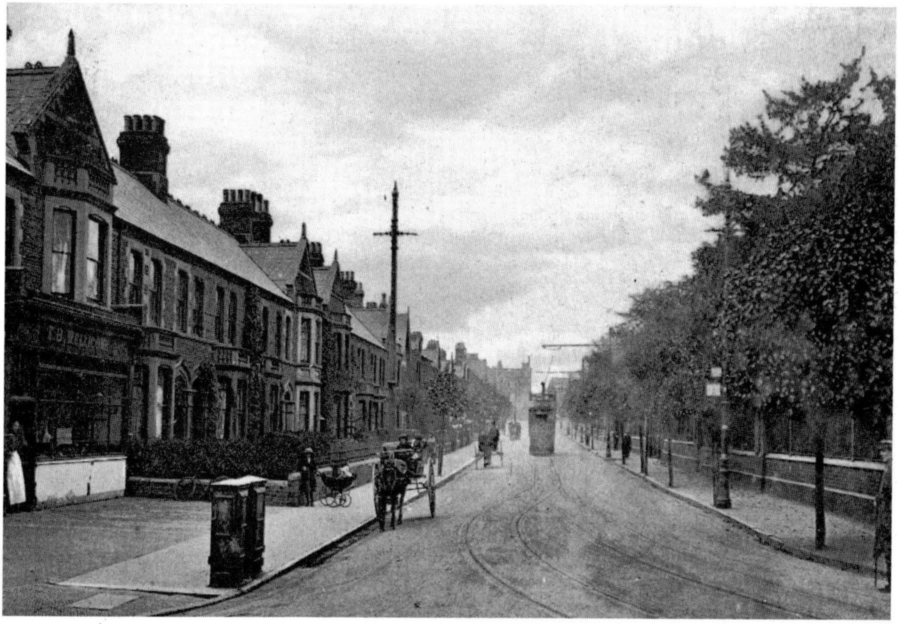

Park Lane, looking north towards Rodbourne, *c.* 1908.

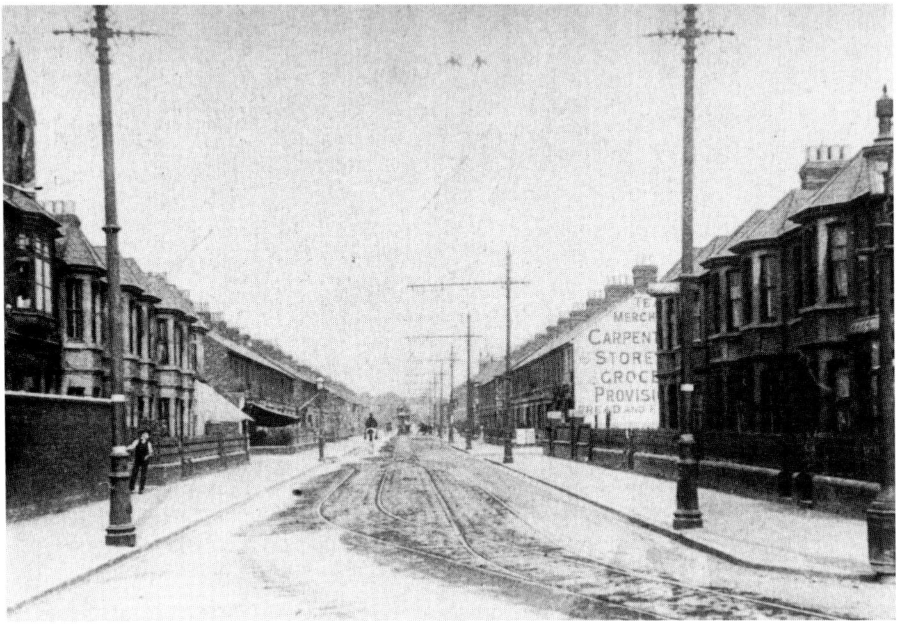

Manchester Road, looking east towards County Road, with a tram in the distance, *c.* 1910.

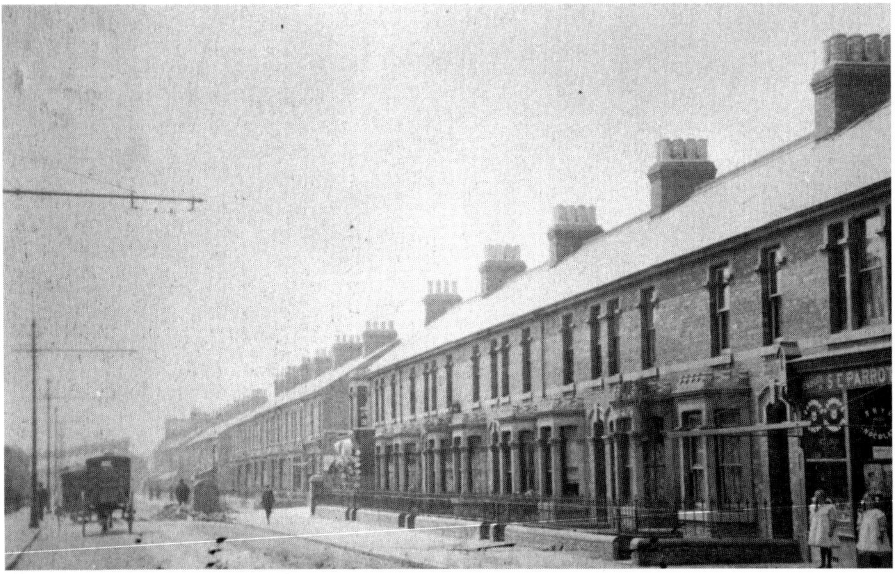

Manchester Road, looking west towards Corporation Street, *c.* 1903. S.E. Parrott's shop on the right, at the junction with Salisbury Street, is now the premises of B. & S. Supplies Ltd.

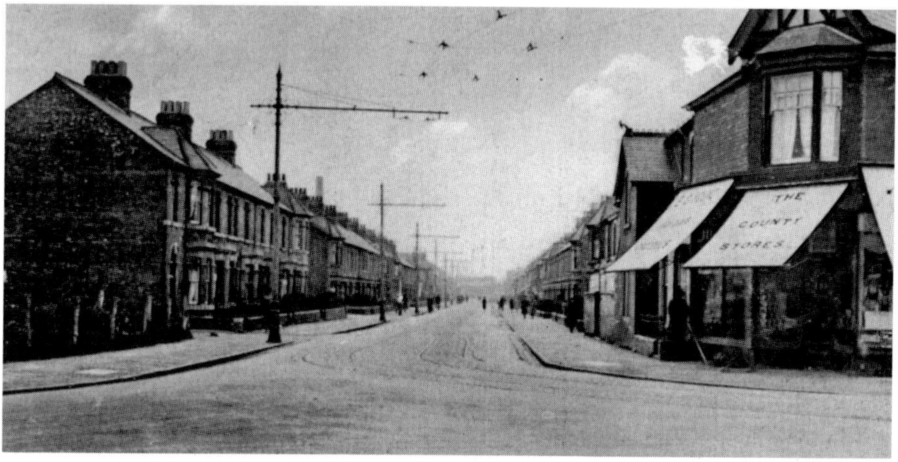

Manchester Road, looking west from the junction with County Road, *c.* 1905. The shop on the corner – the County Stores – is the present day café.

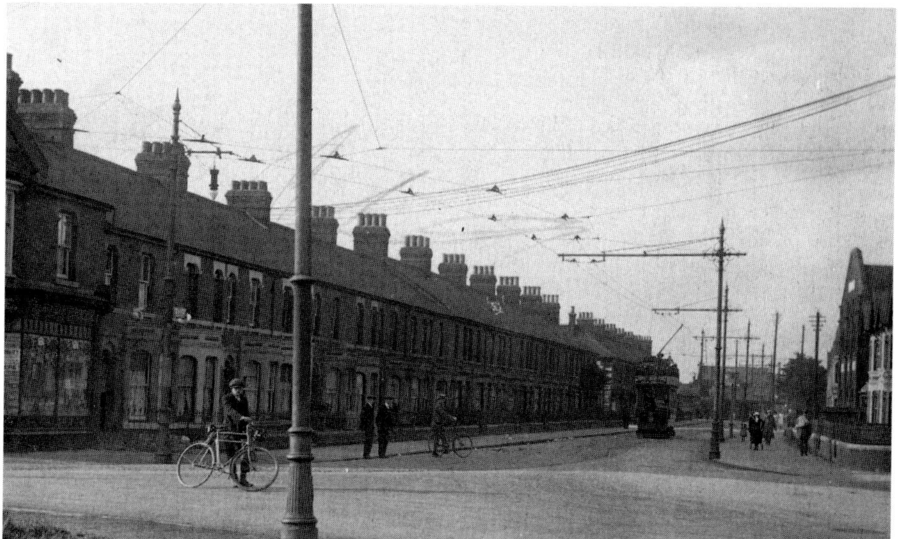

County Road, looking north from the junction with Manchester Road towards Gorse Hill, 1913. To the right, on the corner of Colbourne Street, stands a building which was originally a sweet factory, then used by Compton & Sons of Sheppard Street, before being taken over by Nicholson & Co. in 1919 for the manufacture of raincoats. The factory building remained here until recent years when it was demolished and residential properties were built on the site.

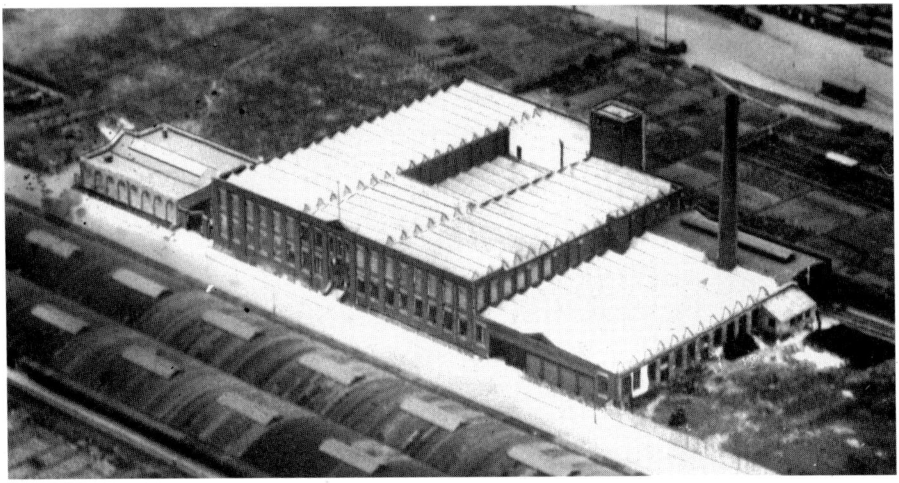

Aerial view of W.D. & H.O. Wills tobacco factory in Colbourne Street, *c*. 1920. Building work commenced on the No. 5 Wills factory in September 1913, but the factory was not opened until 1915 due to the start of the First World War. In May 1916, however, the building was taken over by Ministry of Munitions and additional sheds and storage provided. The whole complex was used for storage of live ammunition and other military equipment (including army boots). At one time 3,000,000 live shells were held here. In July 1919 the military vacated the premises and the factory was restored to the manufacture of tobacco products. By the end of the 1920s the factory employed around 900 workers, 600 being women and girls. The factory was demolished in the late 1980s and the new Tesco superstore was built on the site.

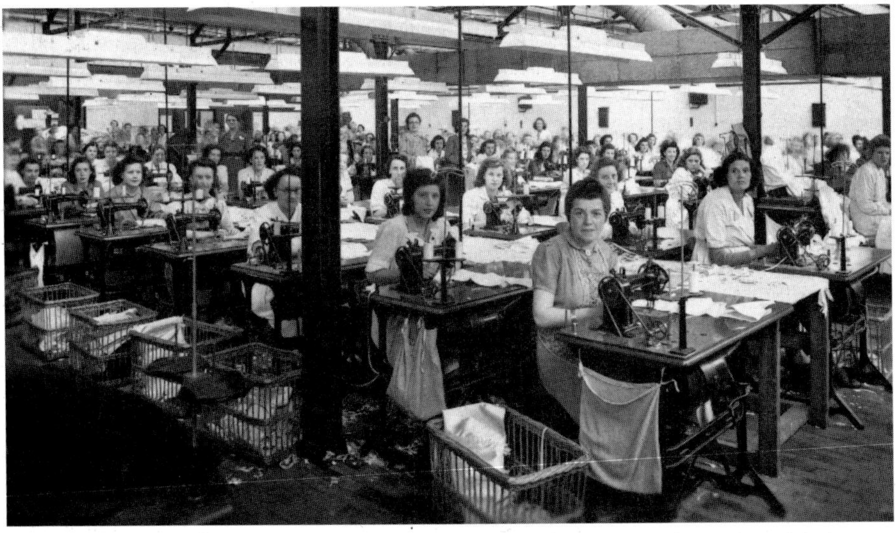

Cellular Clothing Co. (shirt factory), Morris Street, 1947. Opened in 1902, this factory provided employment for female workers for many years. It was demolished in the 1980s and residential housing was built on the site.

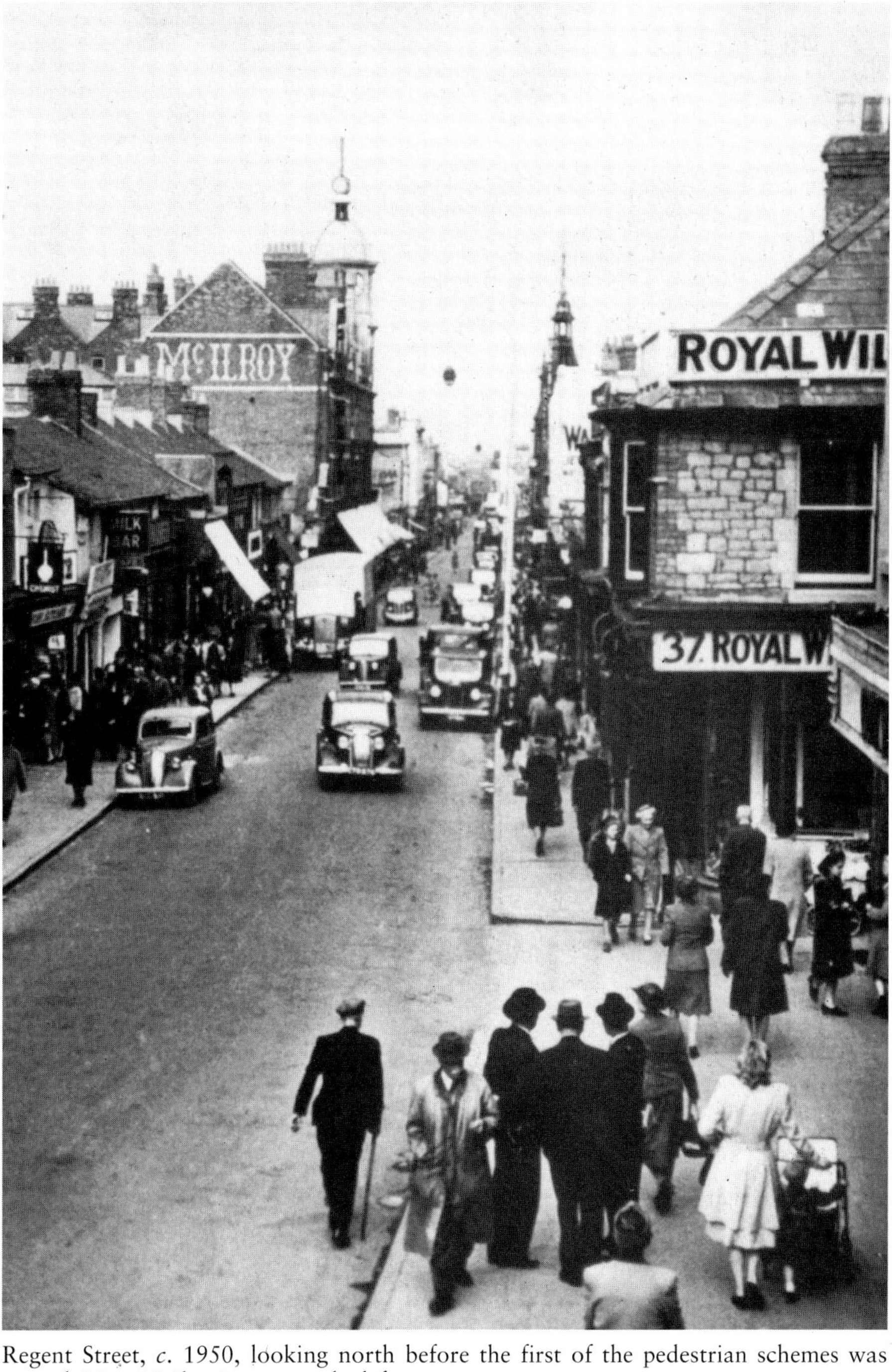

Regent Street, *c.* 1950, looking north before the first of the pedestrian schemes was started. Note McIlroy's store to the left.

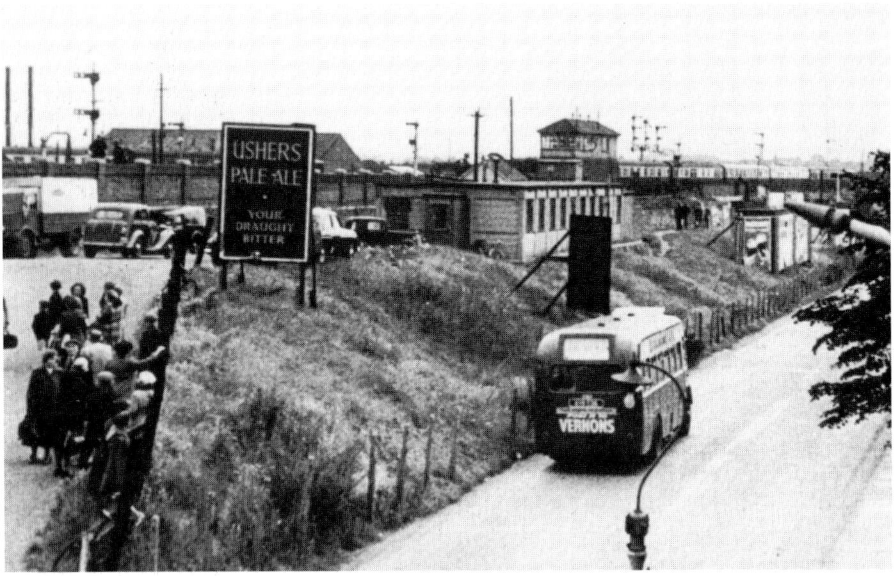

'The Milk Bank', Station Road, *c.* 1950. This was a favourite vantage point for generations of Swindon's youthful train-spotters, where they would sit on the wall or climb on the hoardings to gain a better view. In later years this became a car park and is used as such today.

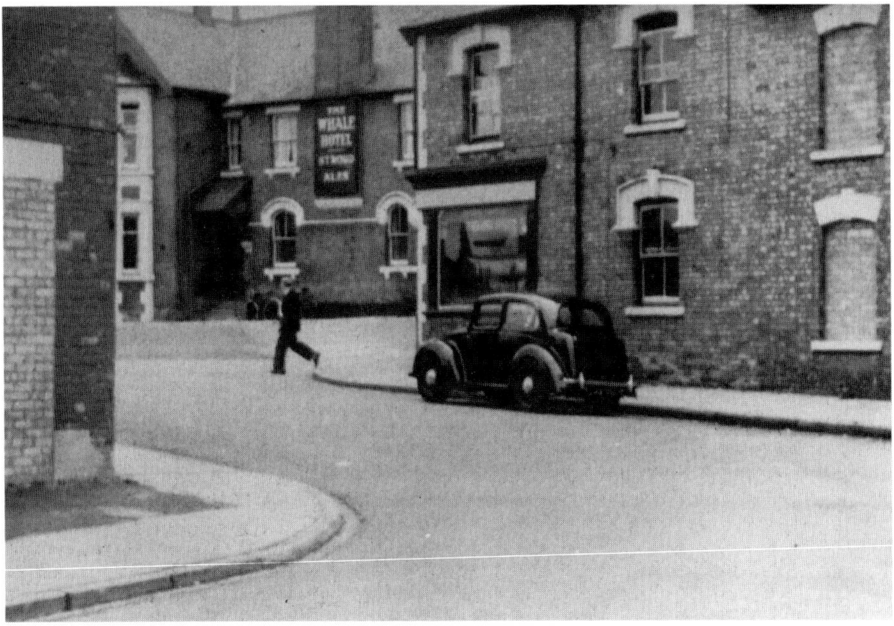

Oriel Street, *c.* 1950, looking towards the Whale Hotel and Corporation Street, with an off-licence on the corner.

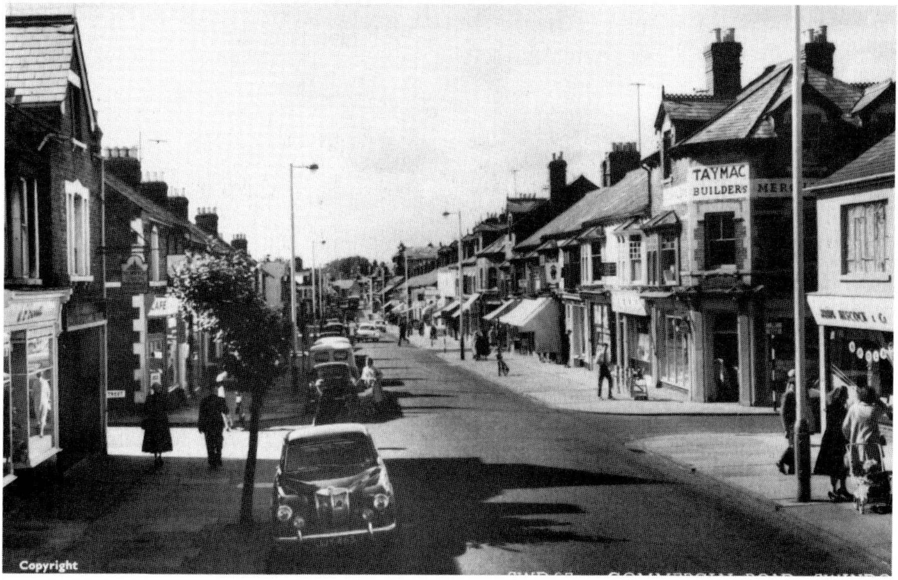

Commercial Road, *c.* 1960, looking north-west.

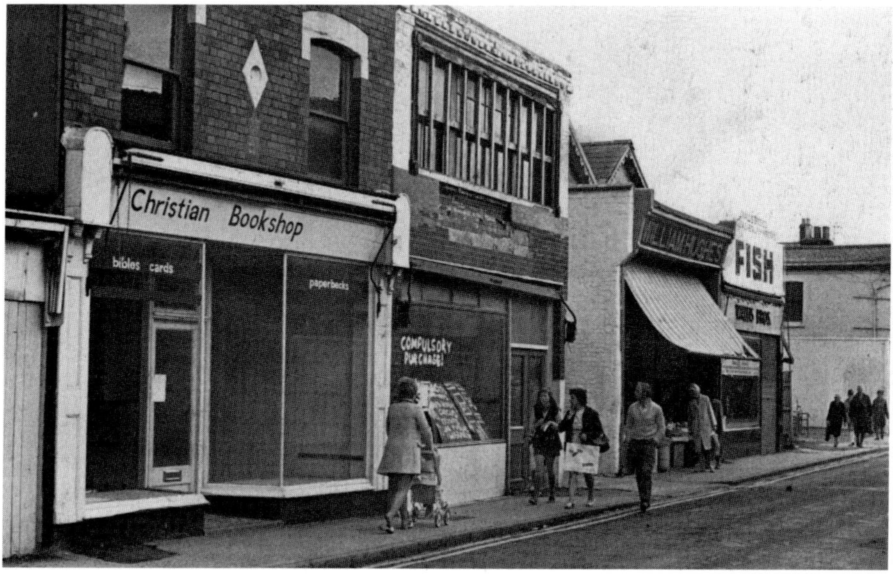

Cromwell Street, *c.* 1970. The closed shops are awaiting demolition. Still open are William Hughes, greengrocer, and Wallis Bros., fishmongers and poulterers.

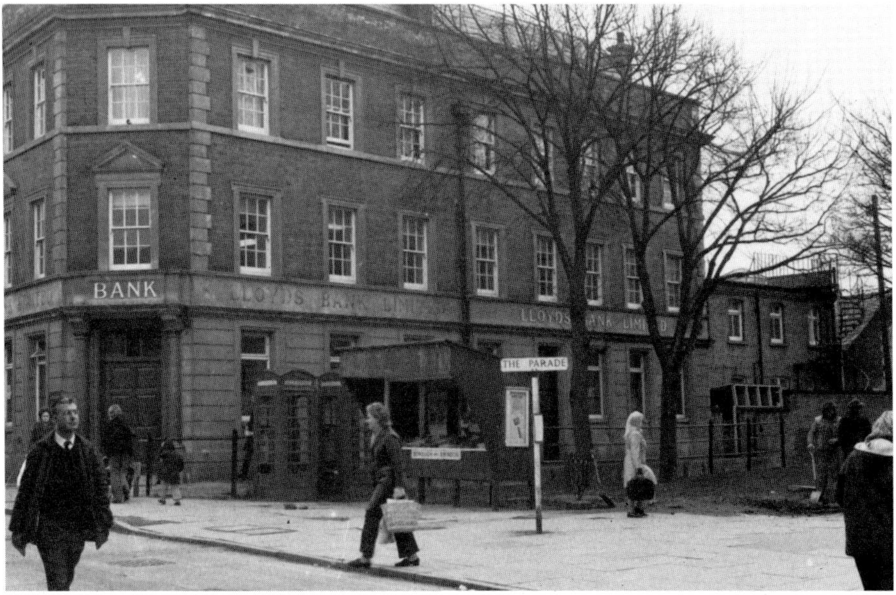

Lloyds Bank and The Parade (now Canal Walk), at the junction with Regent Street, *c.* 1968.

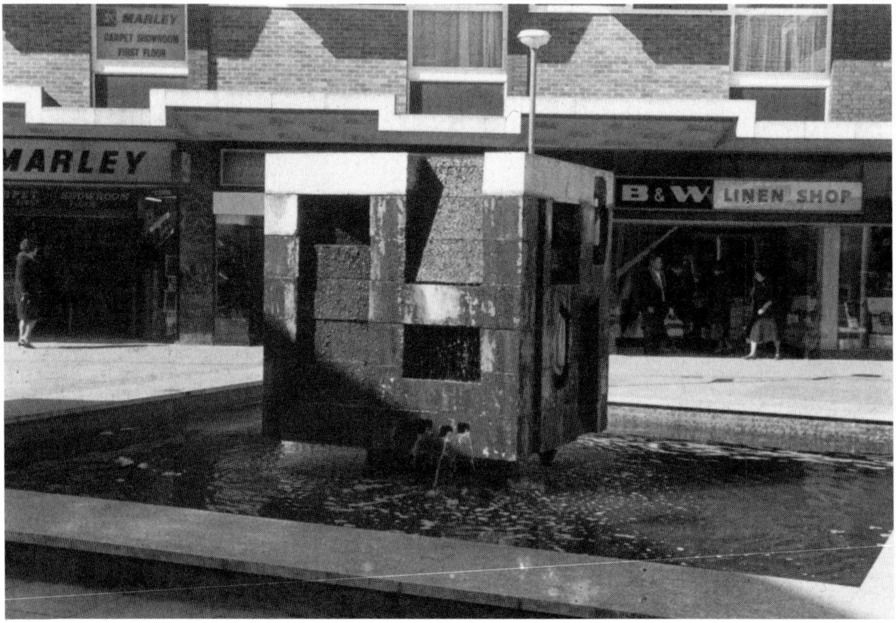

Water feature, The Parade, *c.* 1970. This modern 'sculpture' caused much adverse comment in its time. Eventually it was removed and the area paved over. In the background, shops include Marley Floors and B & W Linen Shop.

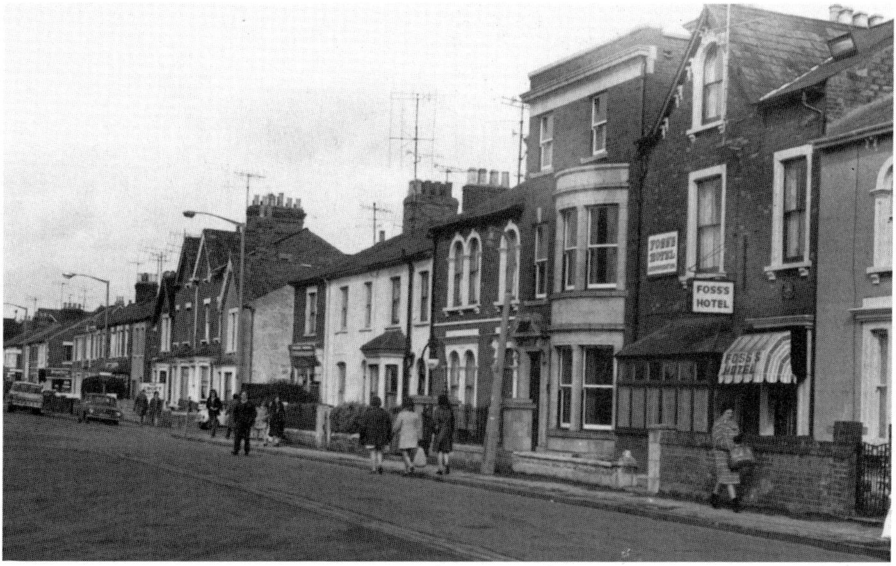

Wellington Street, looking north with Foss's Hotel and A.C. Priston, dentist, in the centre of the row of houses. All this area now lies under the new bus station/office development.

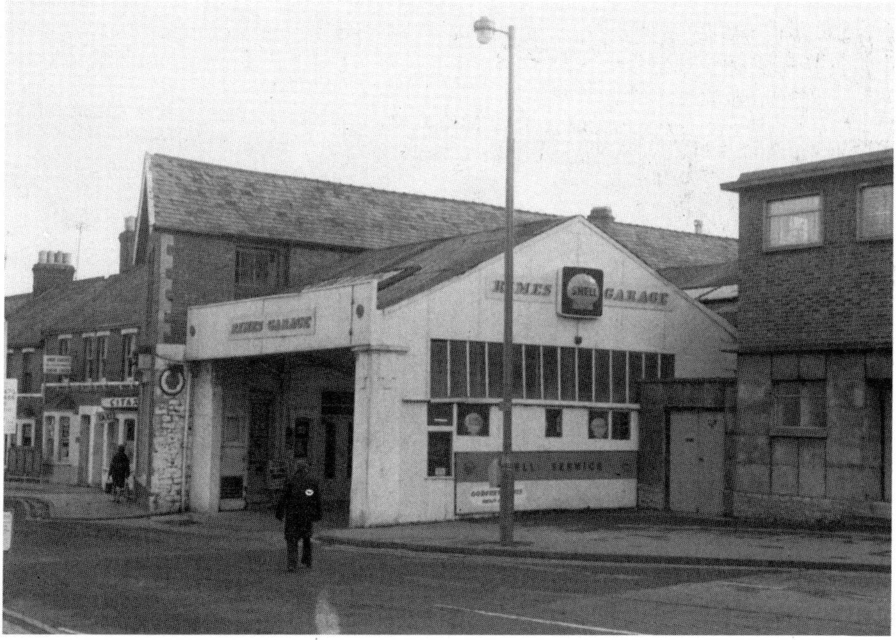

Rimes Garage, Princes Street, *c.* 1968. To the right is the recently built extension to the Methodist Central Hall. All these buildings were demolished for redevelopment of the town centre in the 1970s.

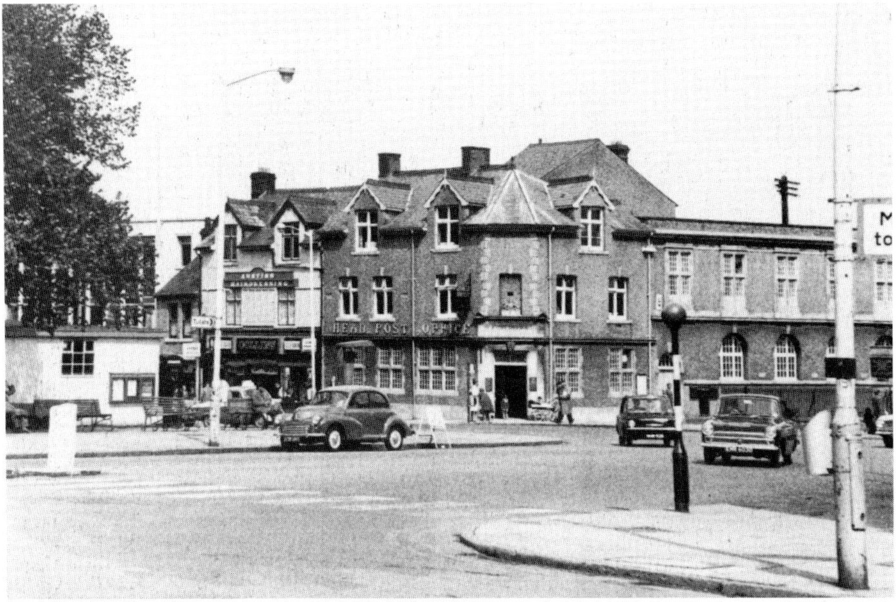

Head Post Office, Regent Circus, 1966. Built in 1900, it was demolished in the early 1970s to make way for modern offices and shops. The cast-iron letters on its façade were saved and subsequently repositioned on the new Head Post Office in Fleming Way.

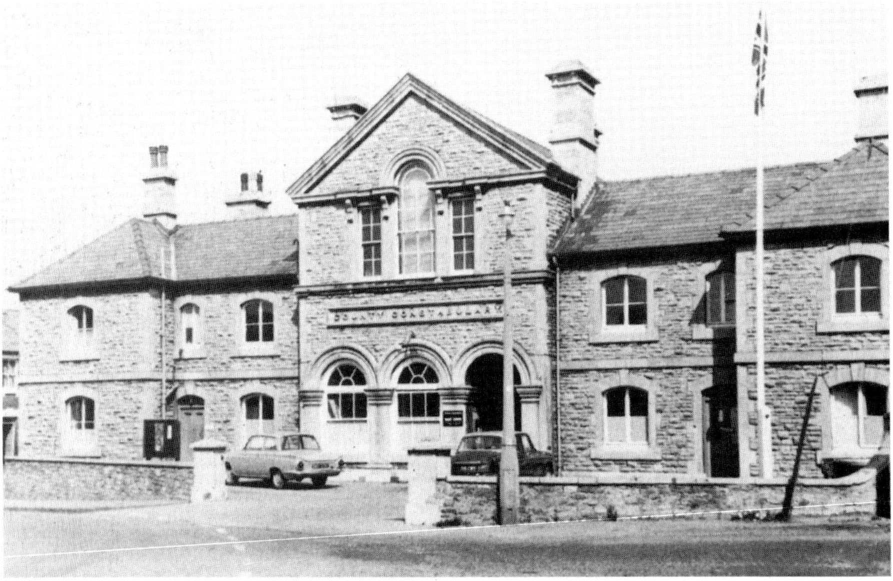

Police Station, Eastcott Road, 1966. Built in 1873 to replace the previous police station in Devizes Road, it was demolished in 1973 when the new divisional headquarters was opened in Fleming Way. Today residential flats stand on the site.

SECTION FOUR

Gorse Hill, Rodbourne, Moredon, Pinehurst, Haydon Wick & Kingsdown

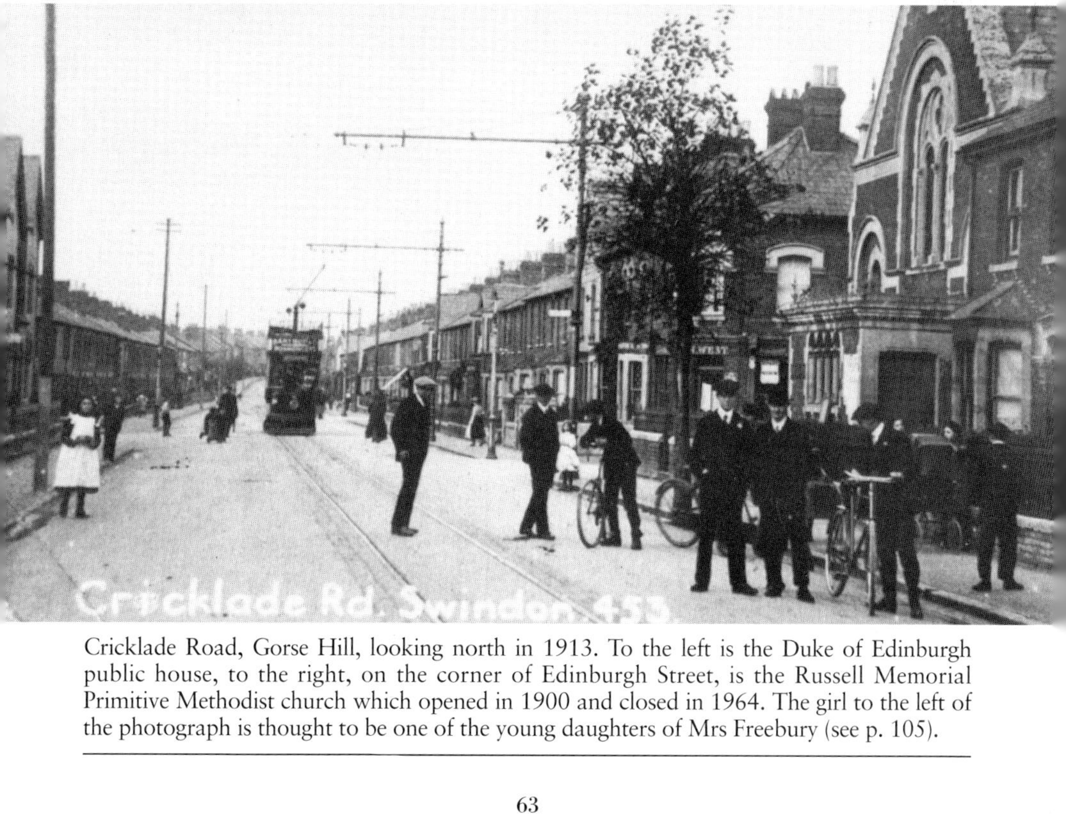

Cricklade Road, Gorse Hill, looking north in 1913. To the left is the Duke of Edinburgh public house, to the right, on the corner of Edinburgh Street, is the Russell Memorial Primitive Methodist church which opened in 1900 and closed in 1964. The girl to the left of the photograph is thought to be one of the young daughters of Mrs Freebury (see p. 105).

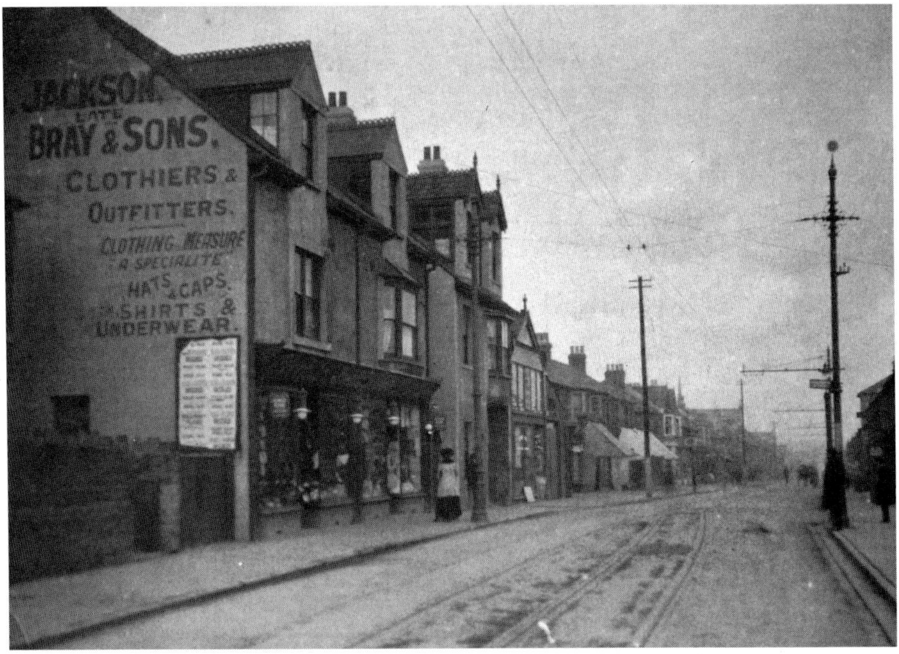

Cricklade Road, Gorse Hill, looking towards Ferndale Road, *c.* 1910. The shop on the left is J. Jackson (late Bray & Sons), clothiers and outfitters.

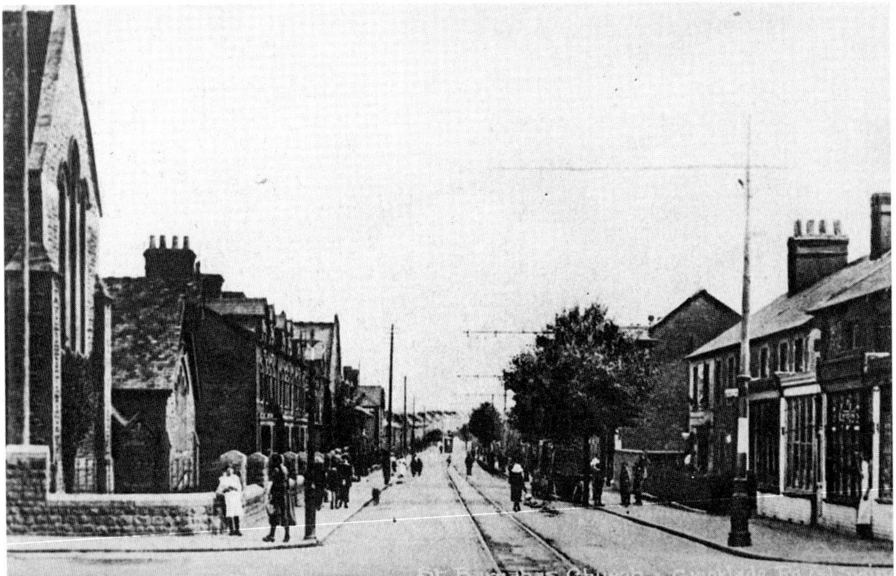

Cricklade Road, *c.* 1906, looking north from the junction with Ferndale Road and Chapel Street. St Barnabas church on the left was consecrated in 1886.

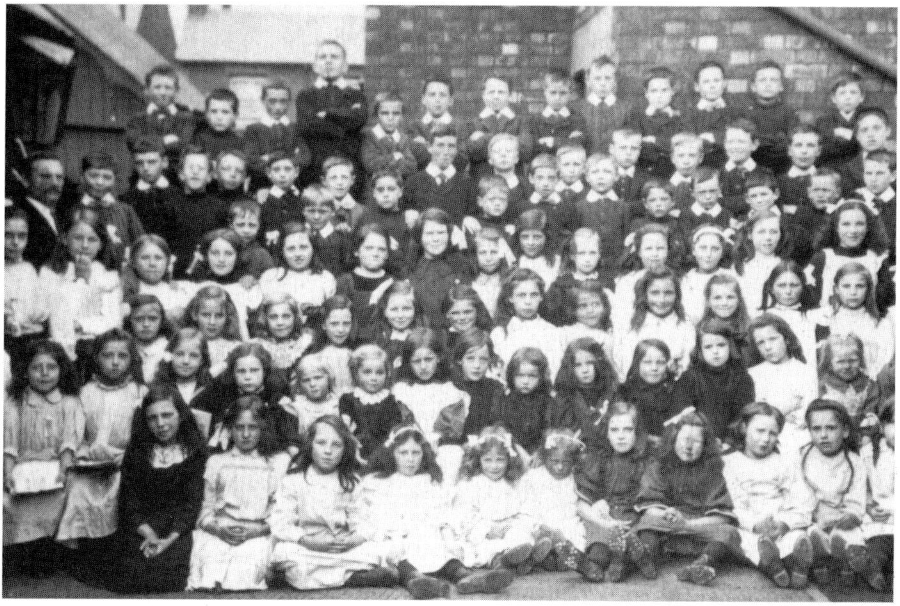

Gorse Hill School group, 1914. Some of these children are wearing hob-nailed boots!

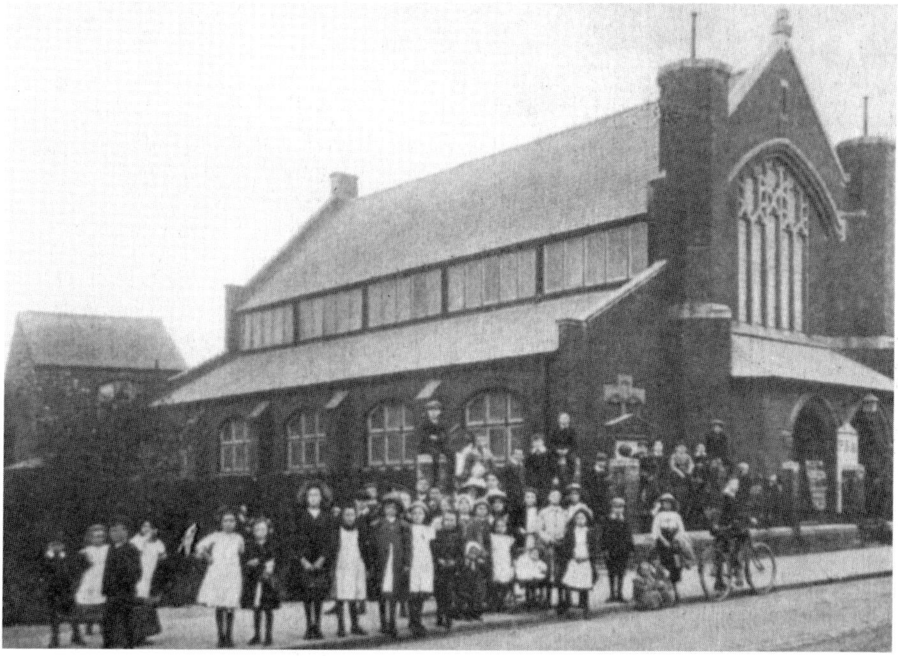

Baptist Church, Cricklade Road, *c.* 1910. Built in 1904 on the corner of Beatrice Street to replace the former chapel at the junction of Ferndale Road and Cricklade Road, it is still in use today.

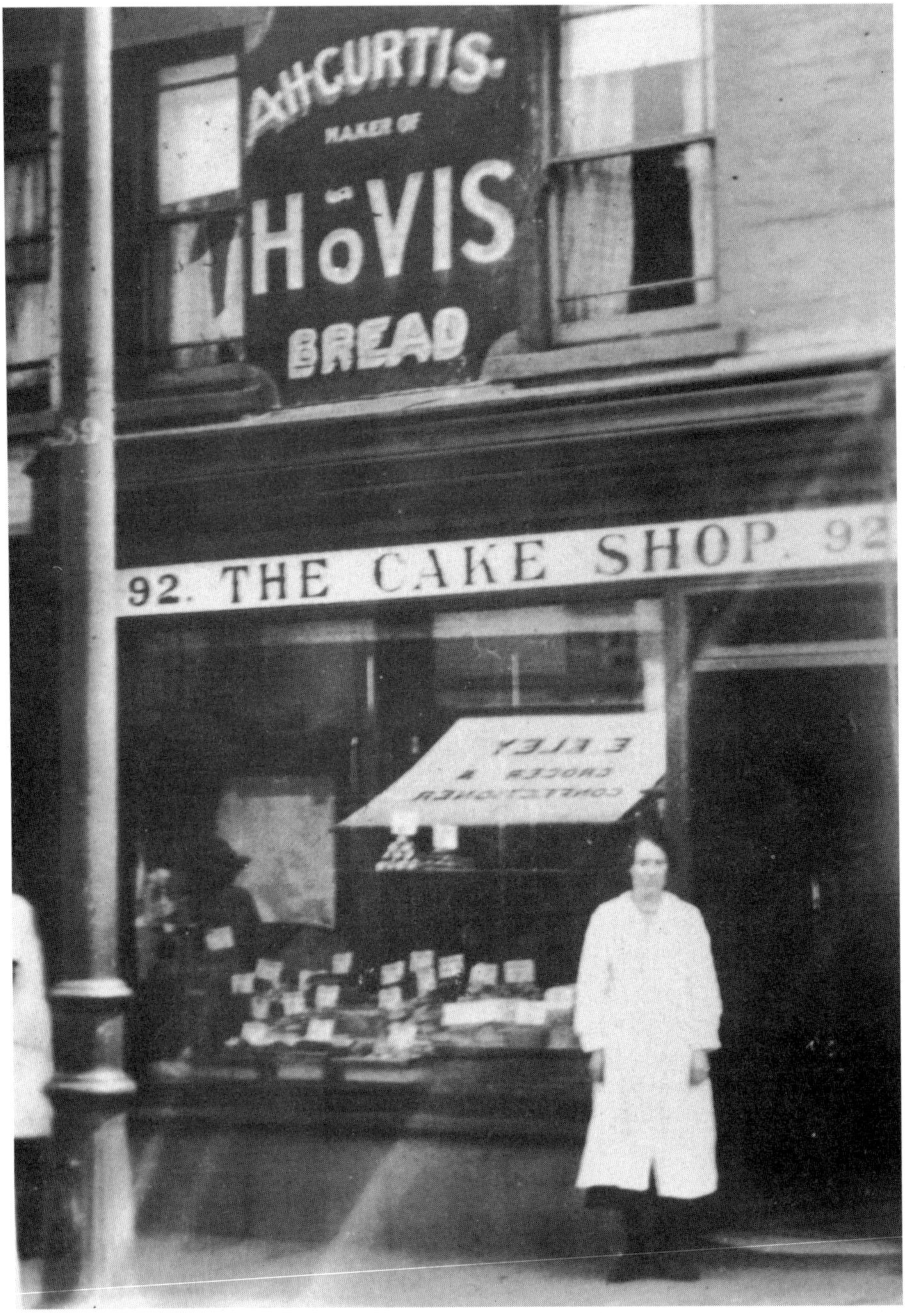

The Cake Shop, 92 Cricklade Road, *c.* 1925. The shop is now a take-away called Golden Nights. Note the reflection in the window of the premises of E. Eley, grocers, opposite, who later relocated to Manchester Road.

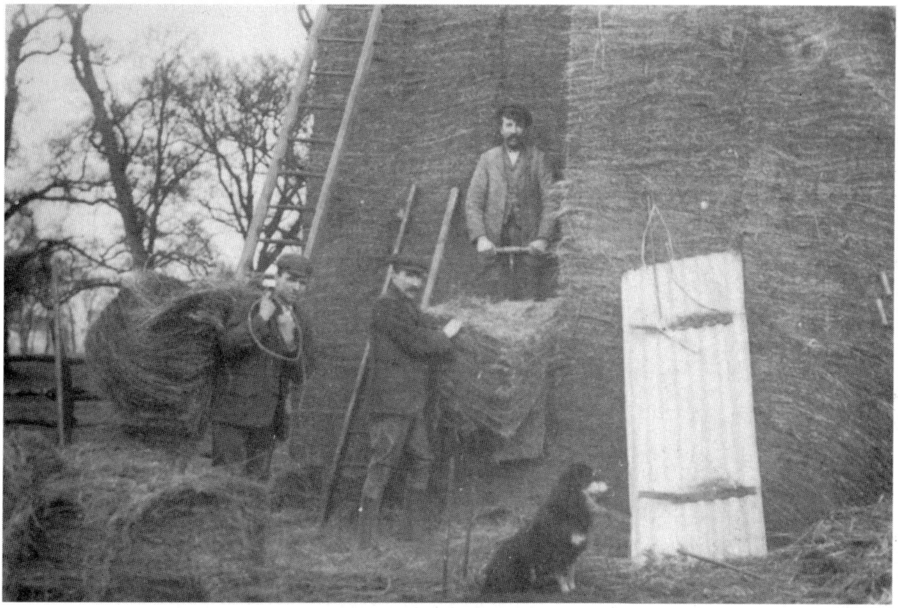

Cutting the hayrick at Lower Rodbourne Farm, *c.* 1920. Walter, Robert and Jim Hook ran the farm which their parents took over in 1882. The hayrick is on the present site of Bessemer Road school field.

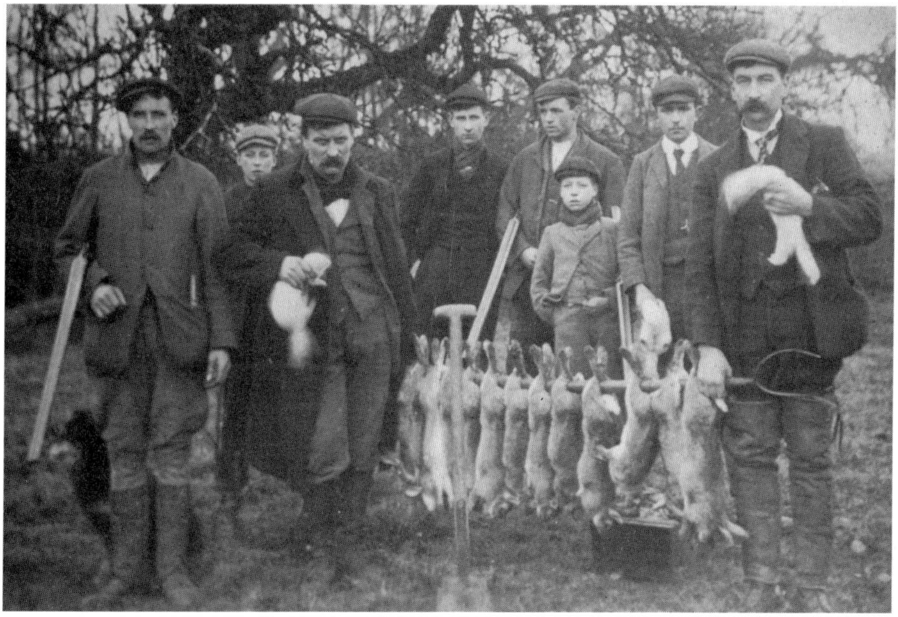

A shooting party at Lower Rodbourne Farm on Boxing Day 1905, including Jim Hook, extreme left, and Walter in the centre with the gun.

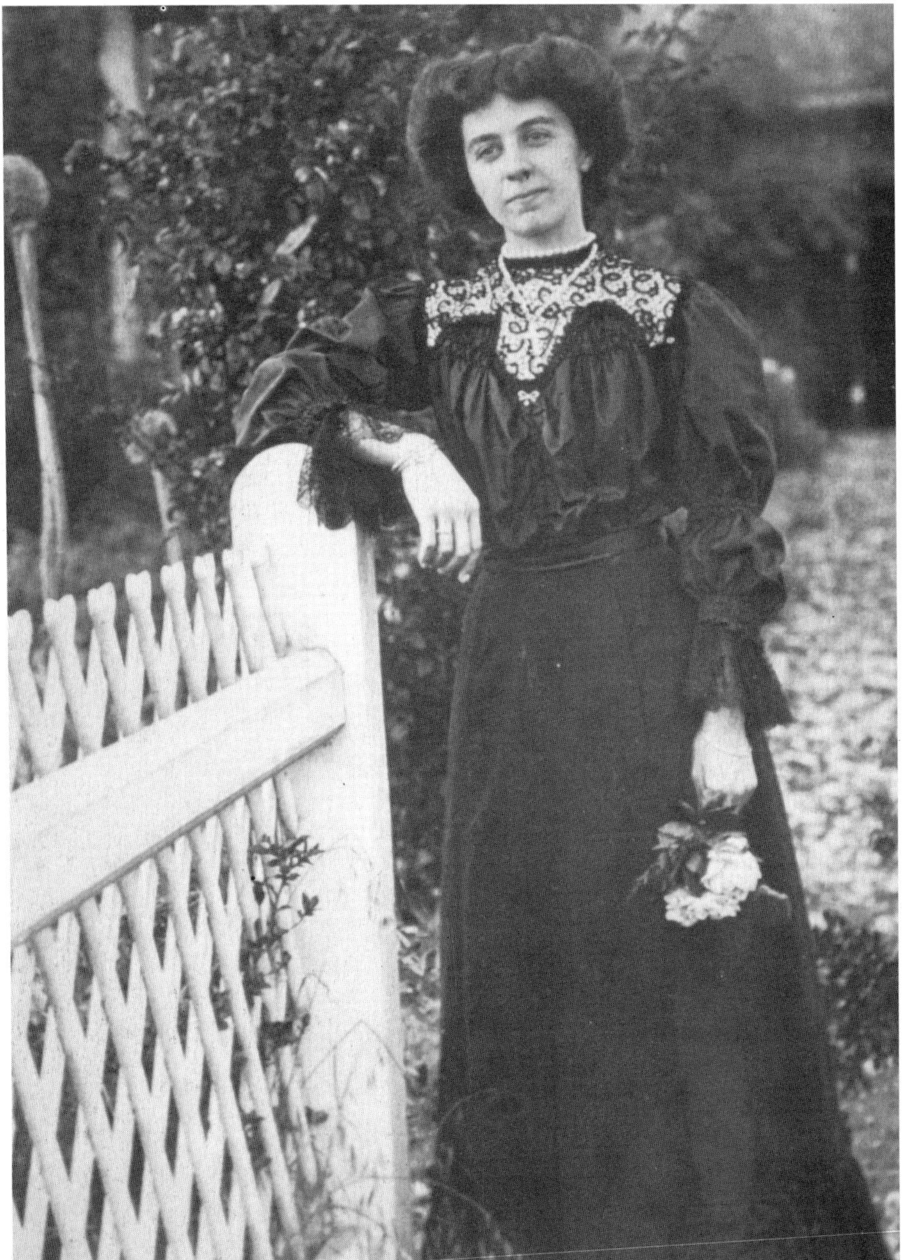

Mrs F.M. Watt (née Hook), pictured at the gate of Lower Rodbourne Farm on 6 August 1906. The gate was near a small bridge which crossed a stream in front of the farmhouse. At this time the postal address was Lower Rodbourne Farm, Rodbourne Cheney, near Swindon.

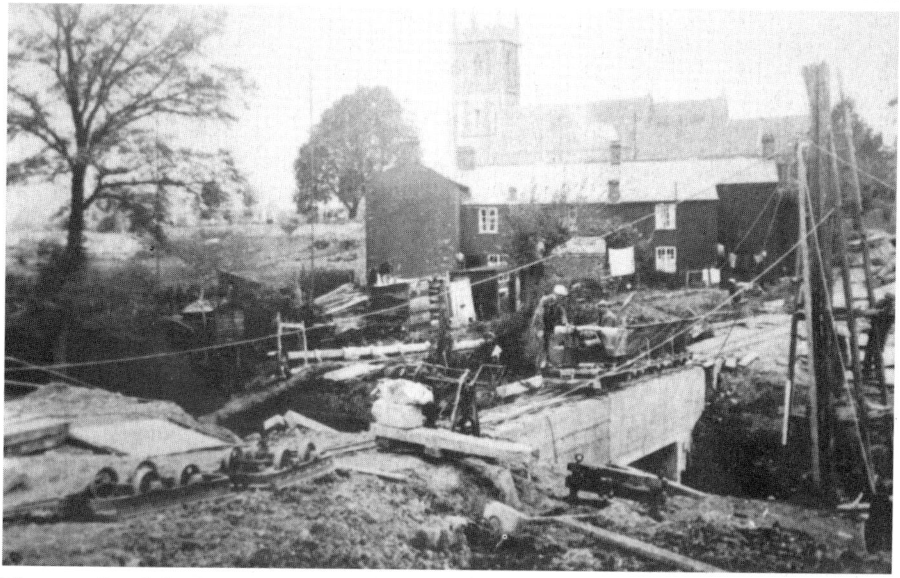

Vicarage Road, looking north, while under construction in 1935. In the background St Mary's church can be seen. This new road was built to improve communications and to bypass the old settlement of Rodbourne Cheney, which had been incorporated into the Borough of Swindon in 1928.

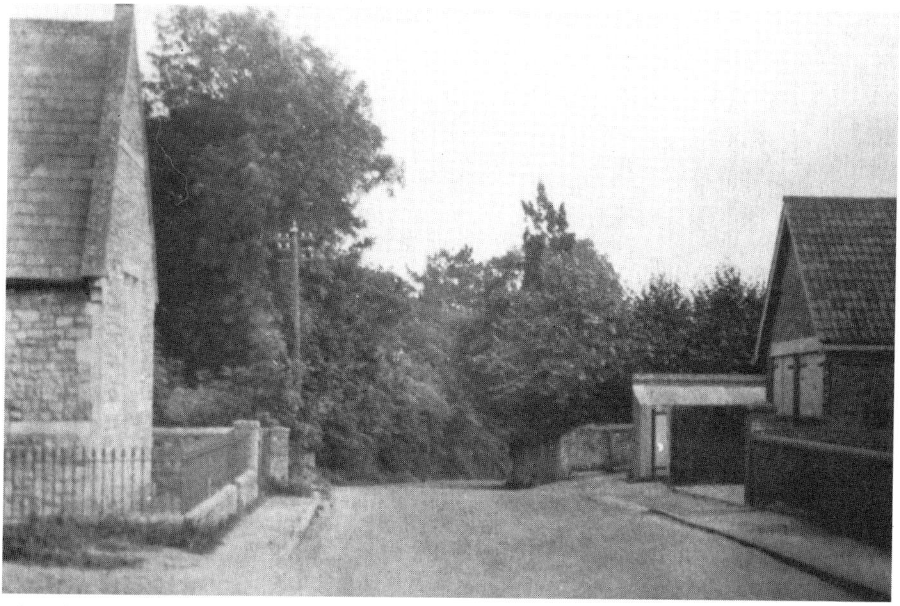

Church Road (now Cheney Manor Road), *c.* 1920. On the left is St Mary's Church Hall, once William Bowles Sunday School. This was rebuilt when Cheney Manor Road was widened and Vicarage Road built.

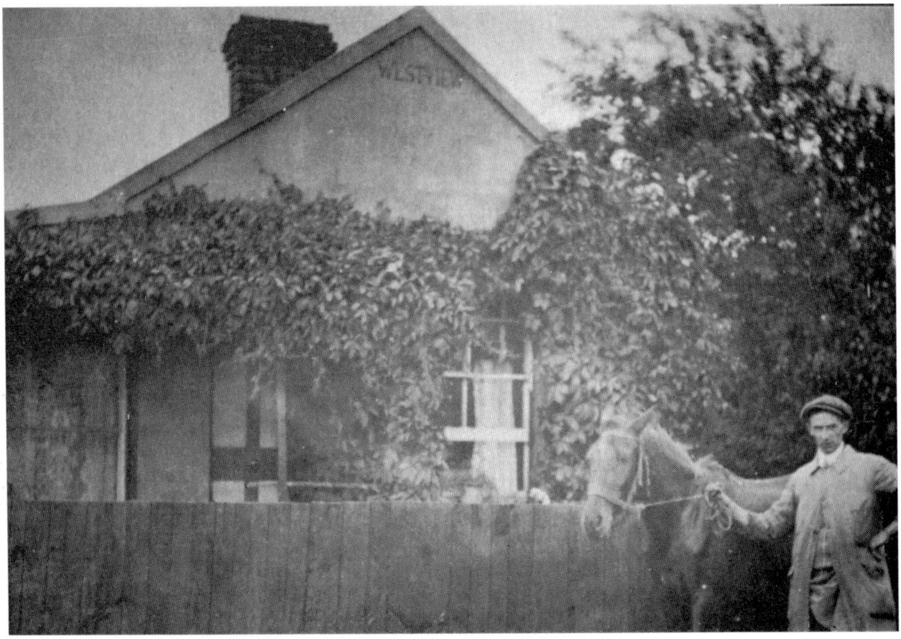

'Westview', Church Walk North, Rodbourne, with Mr E.H.G. Watt in front, in 1907. This stood approximately where Moredon Library is now.

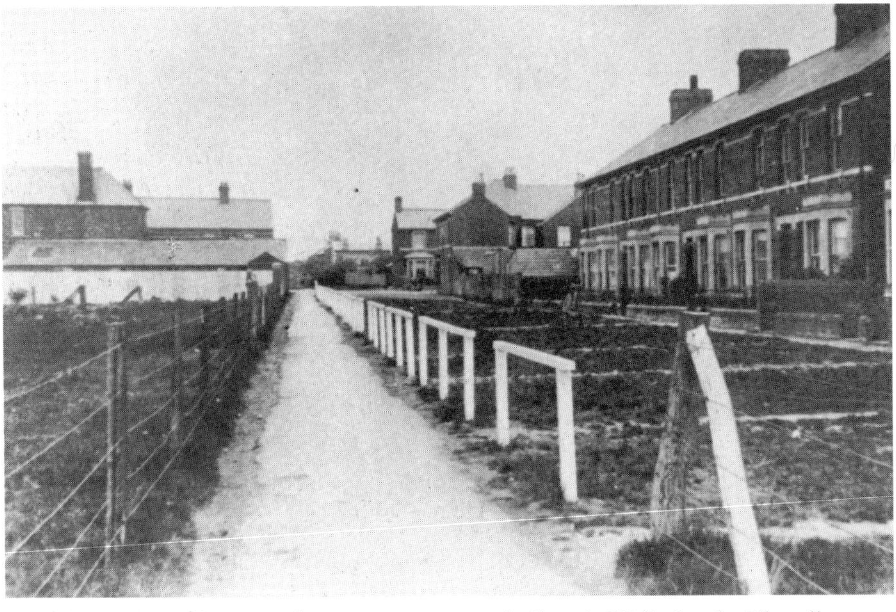

Church Lane, Rodbourne Cheney, now renamed Church Walk South. The allotment plots in front of the houses were used to provide the ground for the later roadway.

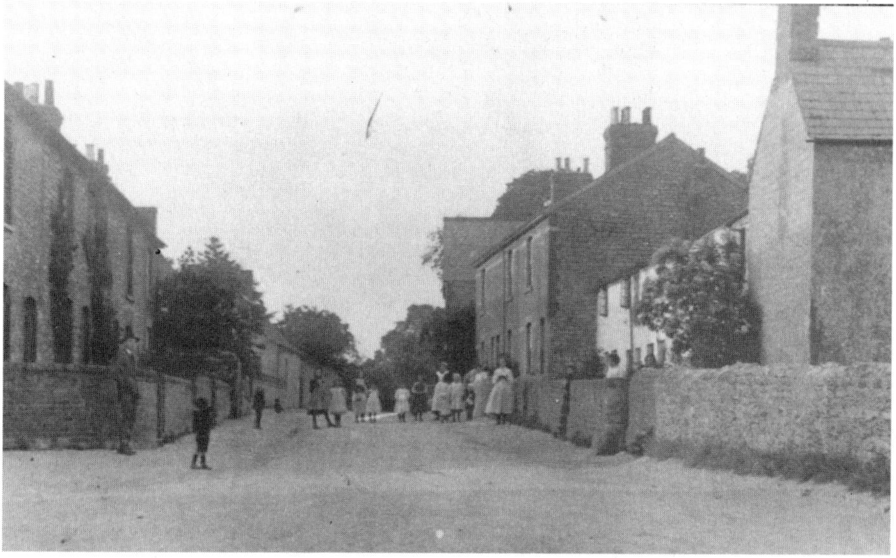

Moredon, near Swindon, *c*. 1908. This photograph was taken by a photographer from Halifax, Yorkshire, and is said to show the entire population of the village – with the exception of one man who did not come out of his house in time!

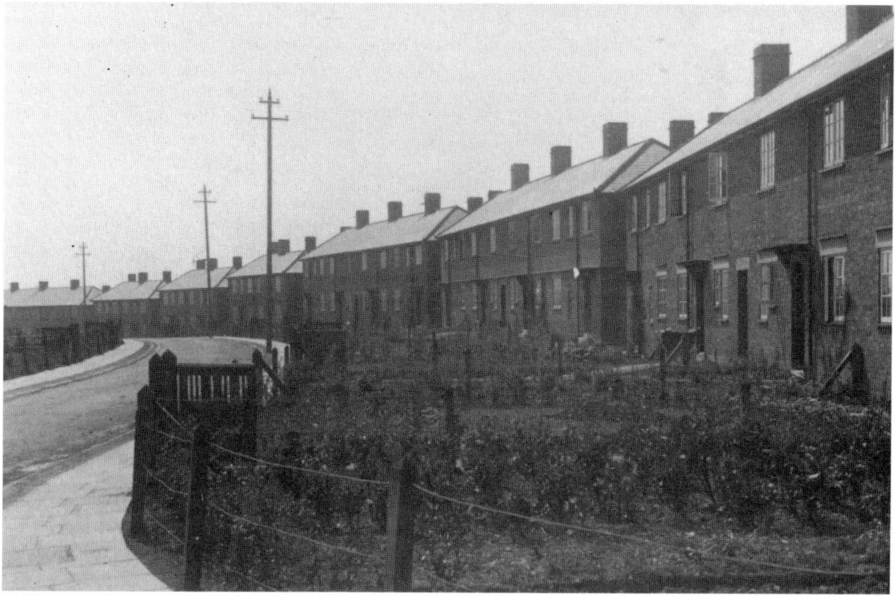

Linden Avenue, Pinehurst, viewed south from Whitworth Road, *c*. 1928.

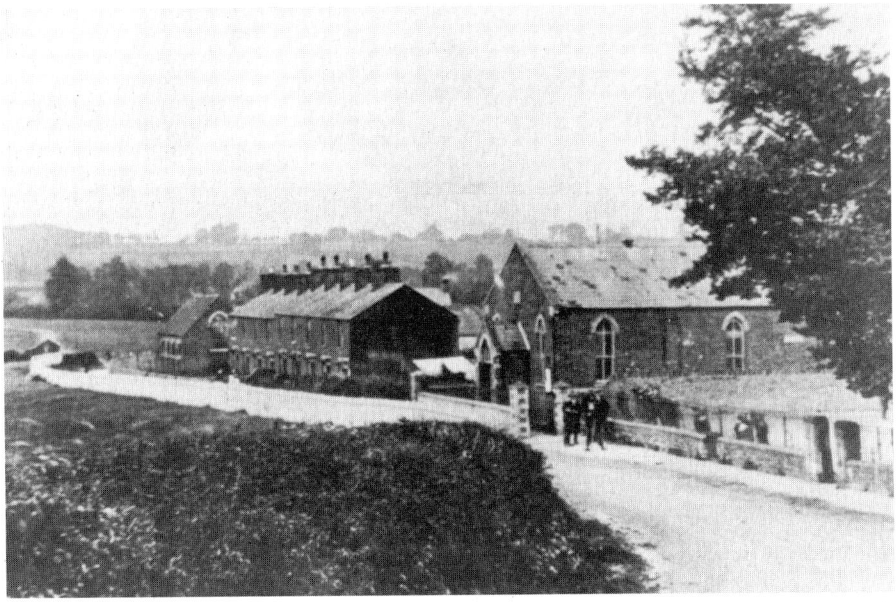

The Brow, Haydon Wick, 1916. At this time Haydon Wick was a hamlet in the parish of Rodbourne Cheney, which also included Moredon and Pinehurst. To the right can be seen the Wesleyan Methodist chapel, built in 1869, now used as a scout hut.

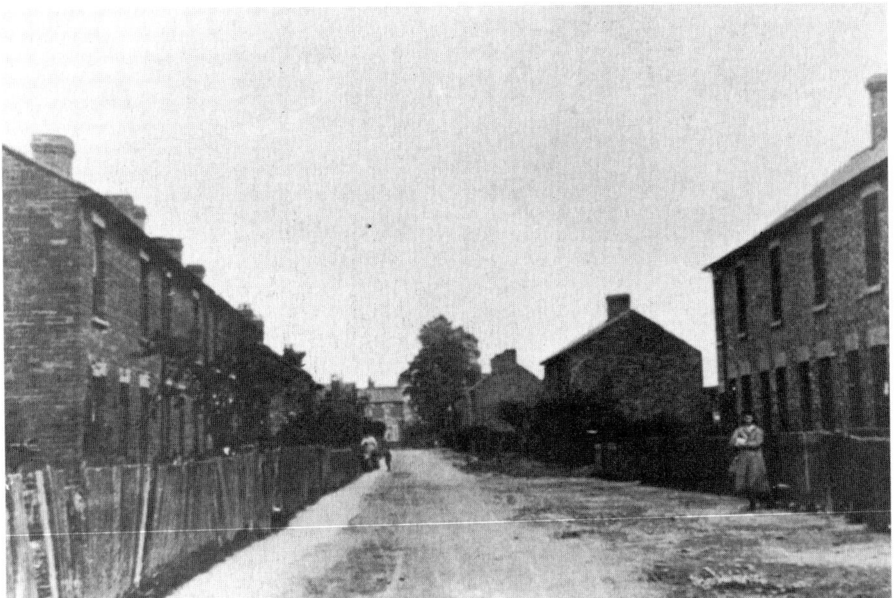

High Street, Haydon Wick, *c.* 1910, looking east from the junction of Blunsdon Road.

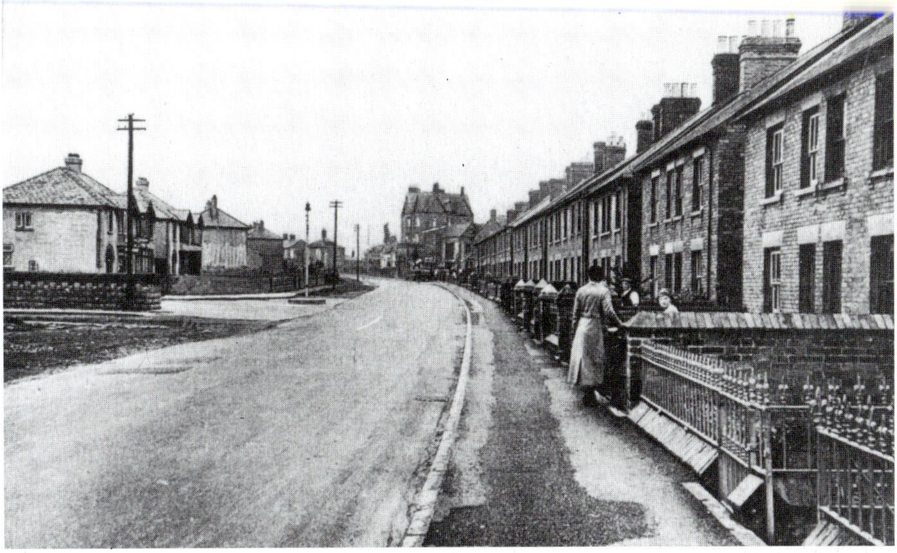

Kingsdown Road (now Beechcroft Road), looking east towards Boundary House, *c.* 1925.

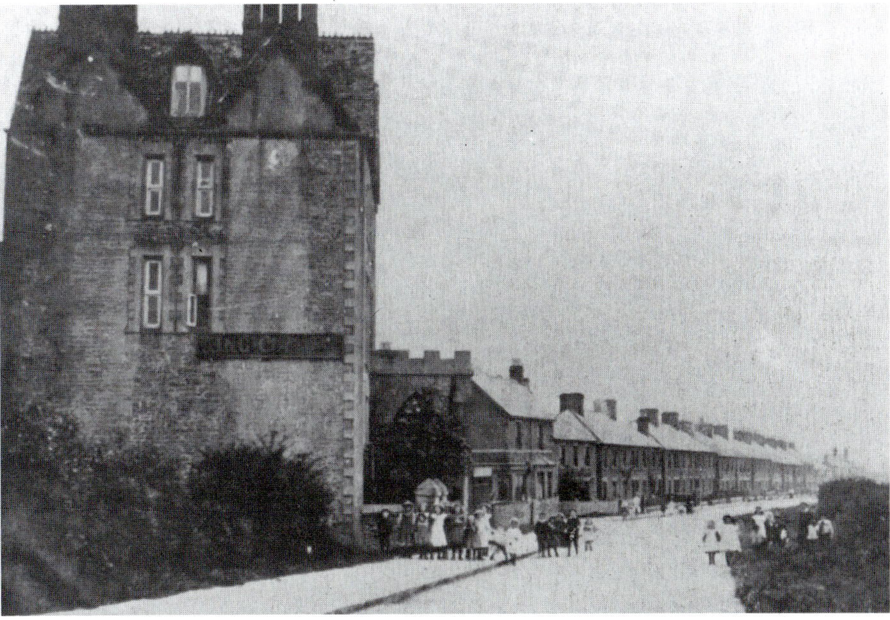

Kingsdown Road, looking west, *c.* 1910. To the left is Boundary House, built in 1894. Named after Boundary Cottage, which previously stood on the site, this was the last house of that period to pay rates and dues to Highworth rather than Swindon. When this photograph was taken it was the 'Napoleon' Carriage, Cycle and Motor Works of Messrs King & Co.

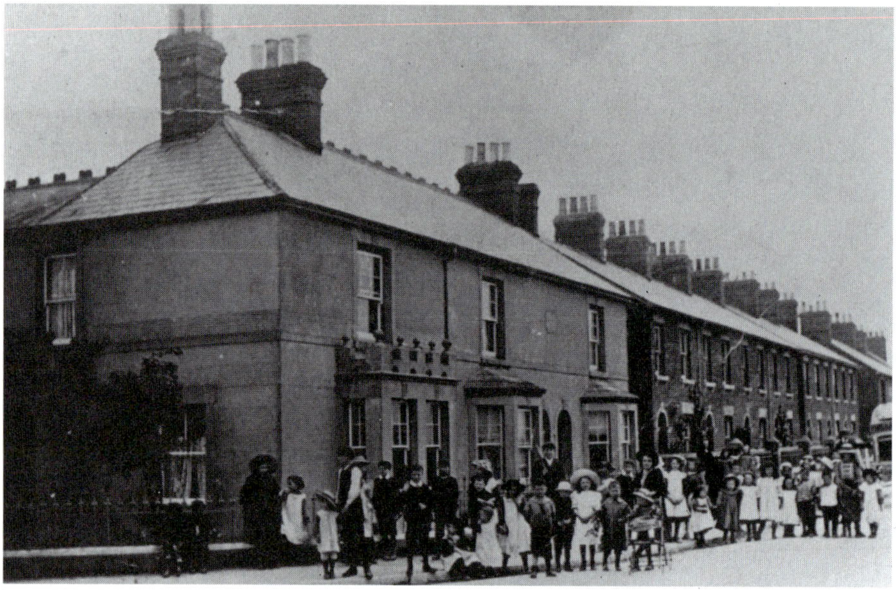

Cricklade Road, near the junction with Kingsdown Road, *c.* 1910.

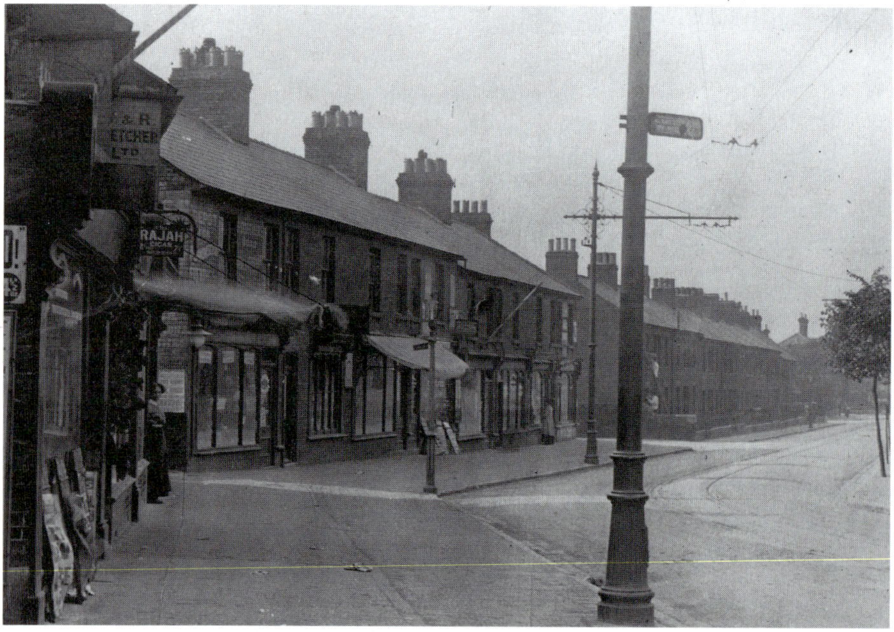

Rodbourne Road, looking north, *c.* 1905. The walls of the GWR Works are to the right. Note the tram stop sign on the cast-iron post.

SECTION FIVE

Churches, Chapels, Hospitals & Schools

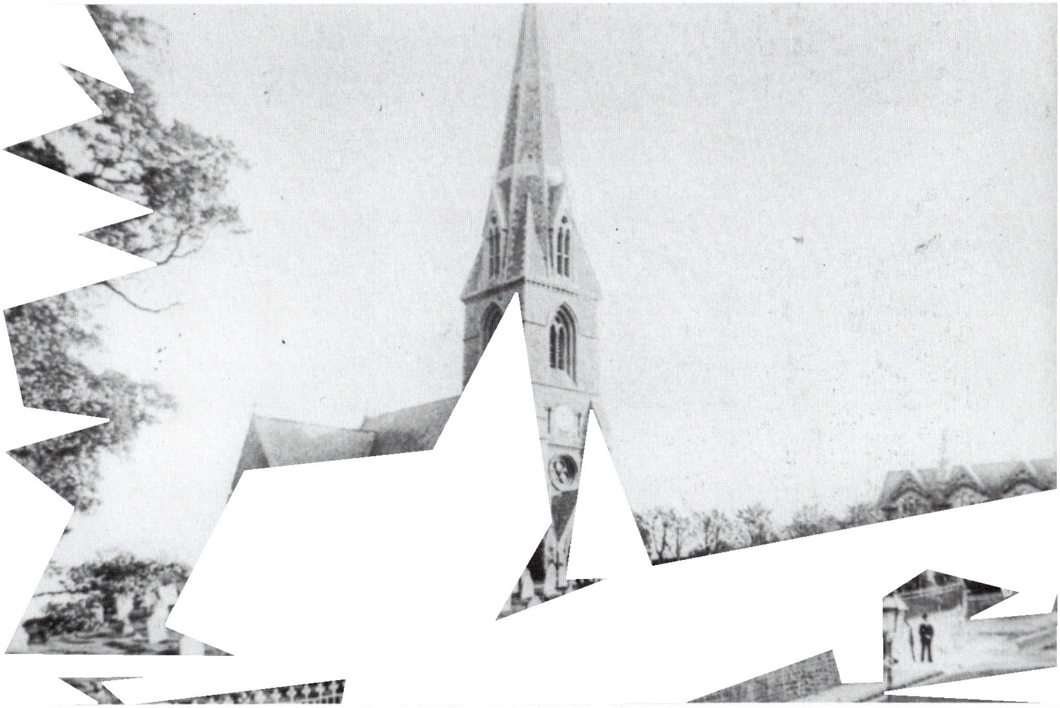

Christ Church, *c.* 1905, built to replace the ancient parish church of Swindon, Holy Rood, which, by the mid-1800s, had become too small for the rapidly expanding population of Old Town. This imposing building, designed by Gilbert (later Sir Gilbert) Scott, was dedicated in 1851. Its spire has dominated Swindon for nearly 150 years. Anderson's Hostel, to the right on the south side of the churchyard, are almshouses, erected and endowed in 1877 out of the proceeds of a bequest by a Mr Alexander Anderson for the benefit of the poor of Swindon. These dwellings have recently been completely renovated and have received a Borough of Thamesdown Civic Conservation Award.

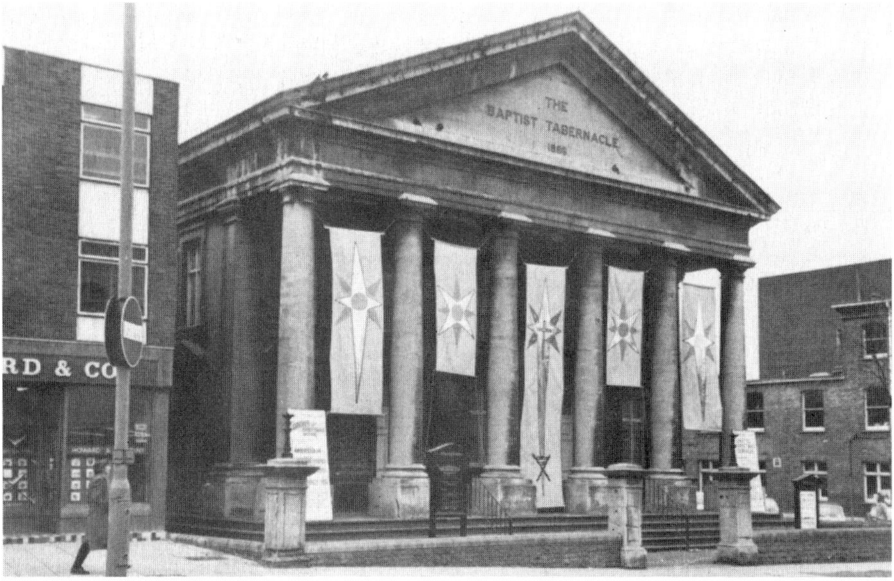

The Baptist Tabernacle in December 1971, decorated for a concert of Christmas music. The banners were made from hessian and foil by the Sunday school. The building was closed to public worship on 3 July 1977 and subsequently demolished in 1978. The Pilgrim Centre, which opened in 1990, now stands on the site.

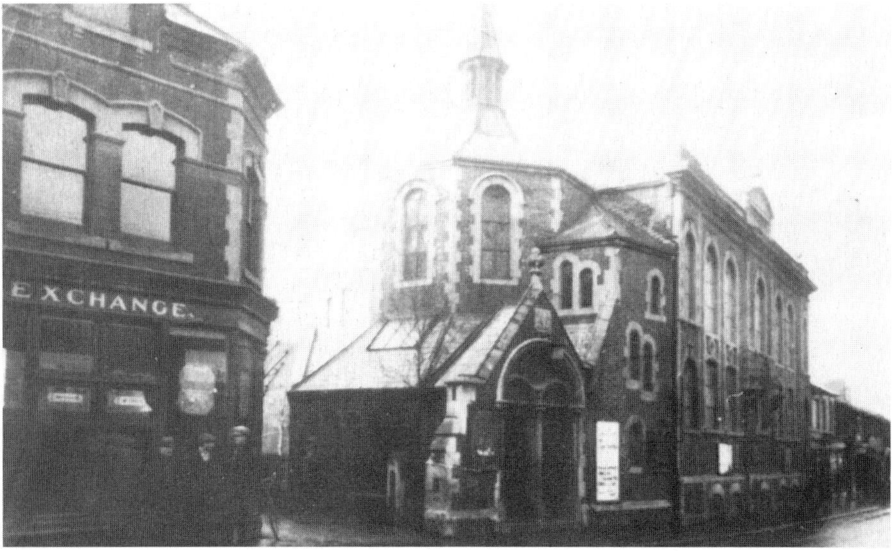

Primitive Methodist church, Regent Street, *c.* 1905. The original chapel on this site was built in 1849 and subsequently rebuilt and enlarged over the next thirty years to accommodate a congregation of around 600. In 1895 a large Sunday school was built behind the chapel. The chapel itself was demolished in 1957, but the old school building remained behind the new office block until 1992.

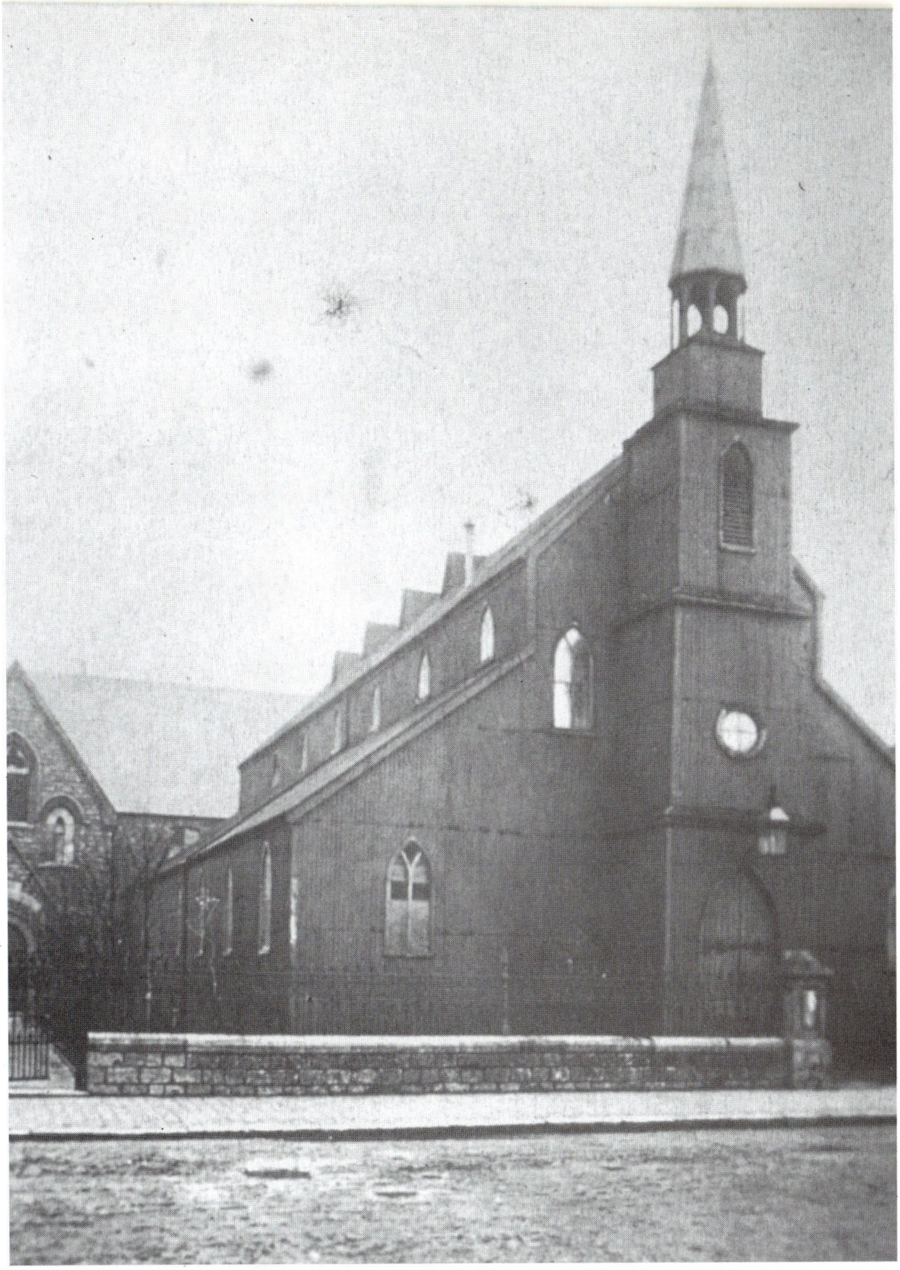

Congregational chapel, Sanford Street, *c.* 1885. The Pembroke chapel from Clifton, Bristol, a corrugated iron building, was dismantled, transported to Swindon and erected on this site in 1877. In 1894 a new chapel was built on the same site with accommodation for 550 (see *Swindon in Old Photographs (1)*, p. 78).

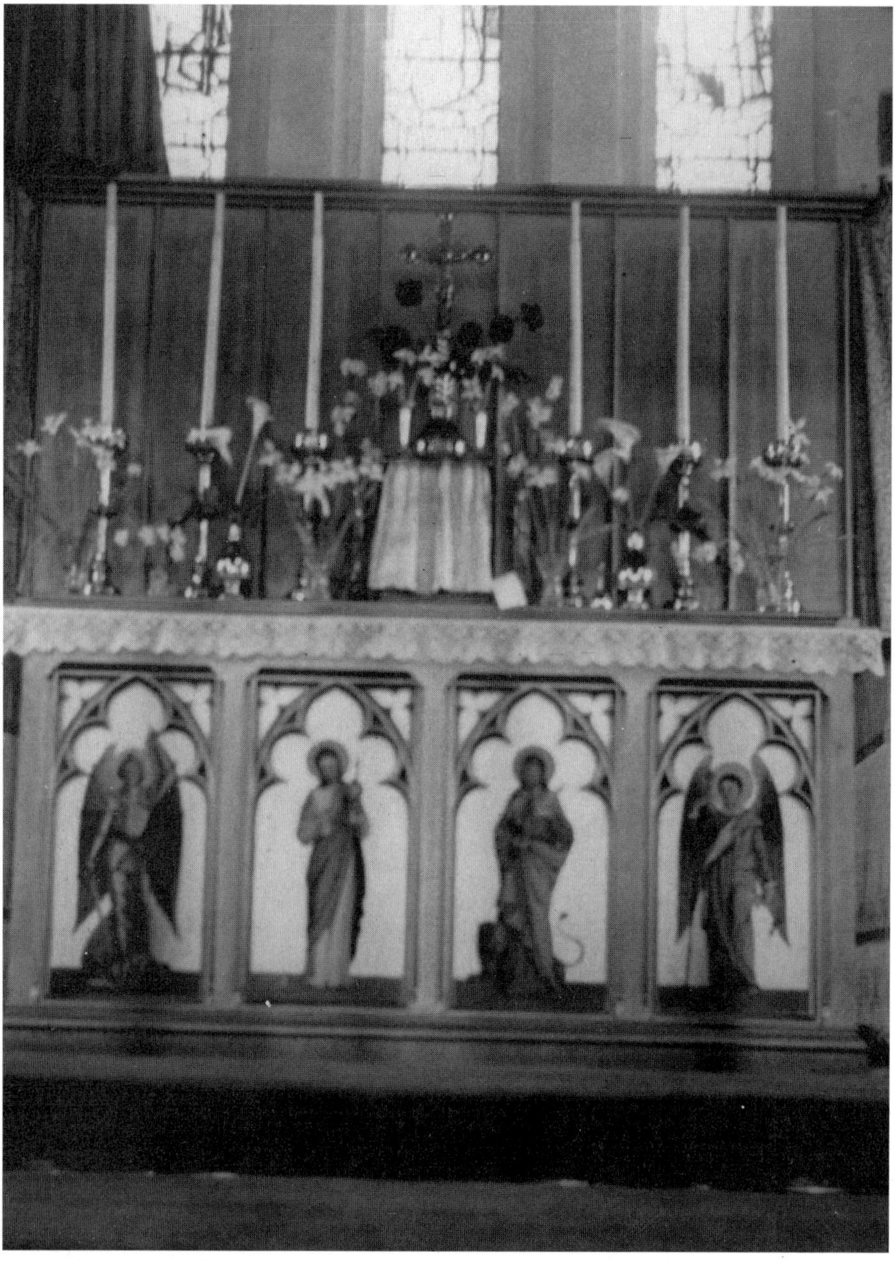

High Altar in St John's church, Aylesbury Street, *c.* 1950. The church of St John the Evangelist was built in 1883 as a daughter church of St Mark's. In 1956 it was closed and demolished shortly afterwards. The oak chancel screen, however, was saved and is now in St Luke's church, Newton Poppleford, near Sidmouth, Devon. See also *Swindon in Old Photographs (1)*, p. 81.

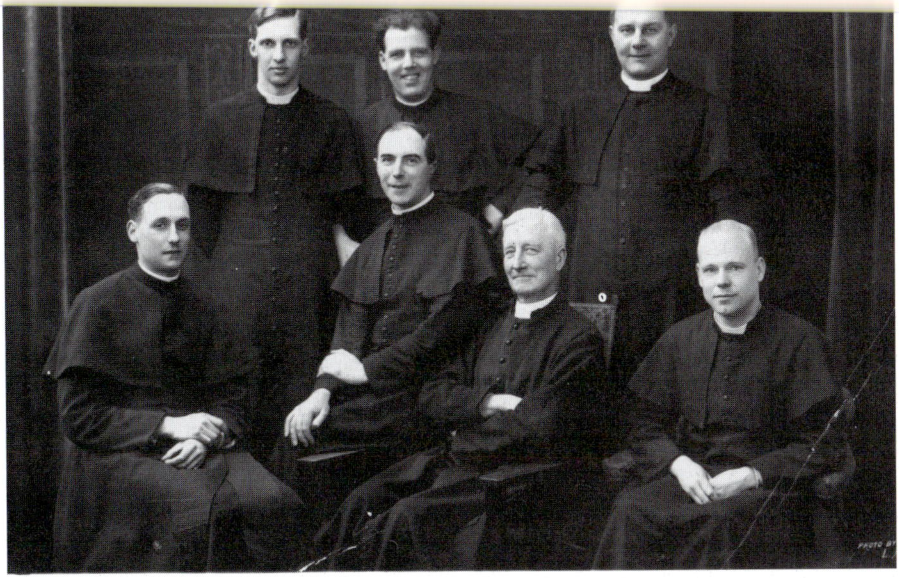

St Mark's parish staff, 1935. Back row, left to right: G. Suthers, J.C. Taylor, T.S.D. Barrett. Front row: J.M.E. Bagley, W.H.S. Taylor, Canon A.G.G. Ross, J.C. Tickner.

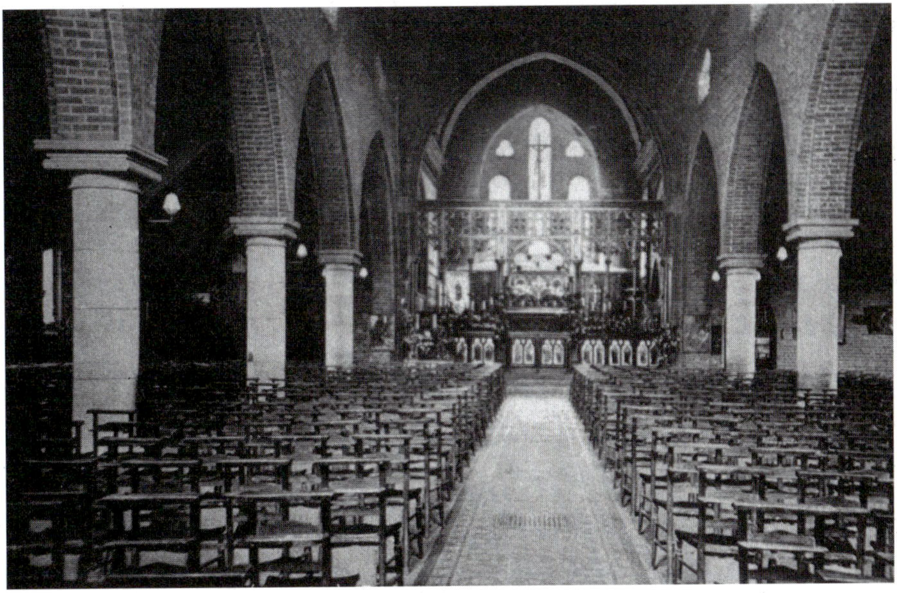

Interior of St Paul's church, Edgeware Road, *c.* 1910. Consecrated in 1881, the church was demolished in 1965 and Woolworth's store extended over most of the site. However, a small chapel of ease, St Aldhelm's, was built here for meetings and weekday services.

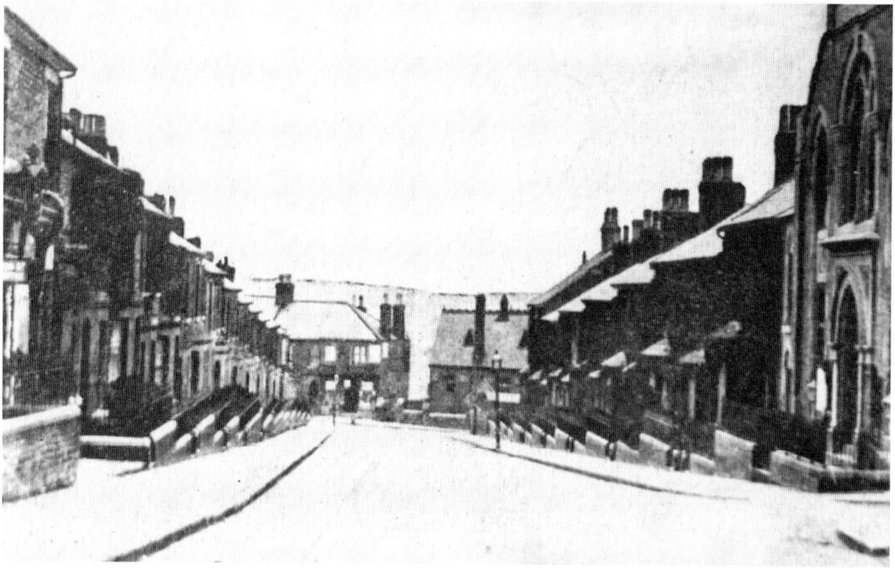

Clifton Street, looking north, *c.* 1910. The Primitive Methodist chapel to the right was erected in 1882 and subsequently enlarged in 1900 to provide accommodation for 360 people. It has since been demolished.

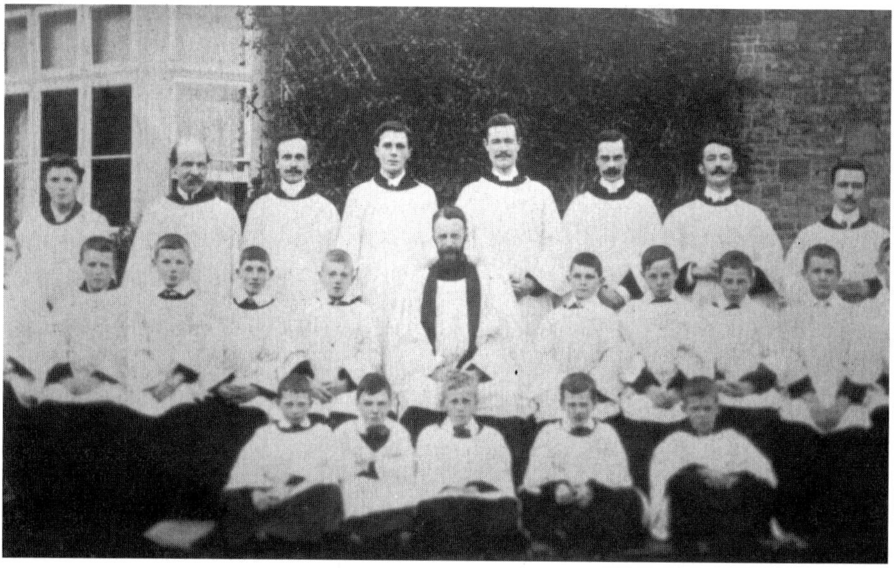

St Augustine's church choir, 1907. This photograph pre-dates the opening of the church of St Augustine's in Summers Street in 1908. Services were originally held in the Mission Room in Rodbourne Road, which then served as the Church Hall for many years. Daniel Gooch House (sheltered flats) now occupies the site. Canon W.B. Harvey was the vicar at this church until his death in 1931.

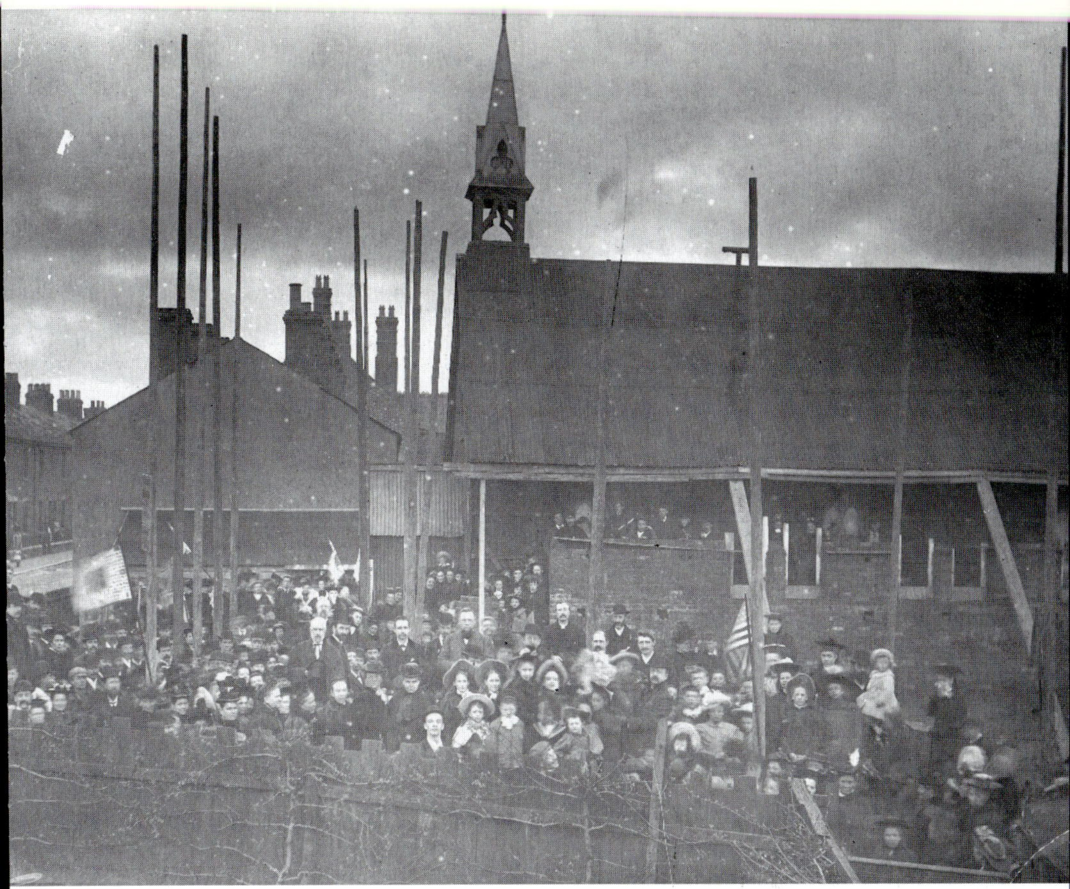

Percy Street chapel, Even Swindon, 1898. Photographed from a back first-floor window of a house in Rodbourne Road. An iron chapel with accommodation for 200 was built here in 1877. The picture shows the new building that was being erected which, when opened, increased accommodation to 450. The chapel was closed around 1956 and the Rentaset office (now Shaftesbury Centre of Great Western Enterprise Ltd) was built on the site. The brick chapel building, however, is still visible from Morris Street car park. In the background can be seen the chimney stack of Even Swindon Club.

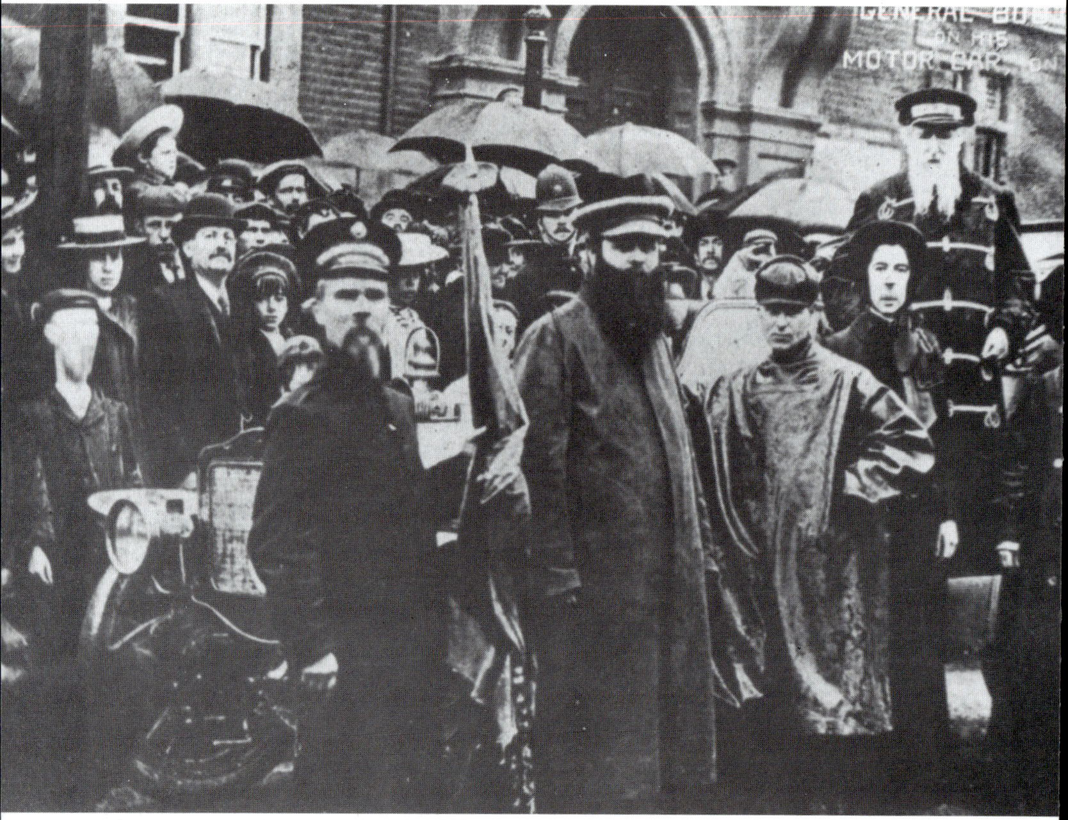

General William Booth, founder of the Salvation Army, outside the main entrance of the Town Hall on Saturday 5 August 1905. He was visiting Swindon on one of his Motor Tours which had begun the previous year, when Rolls Royce was founded. General Booth, who was then 76 years old, is the white-bearded gentleman standing in the car to the right of the picture. His son, Bramwell Booth, is the heavy-bearded gentleman in the centre of the picture. The next day a large audience filled the Queen's Theatre for a special service at which General Booth gave an address.

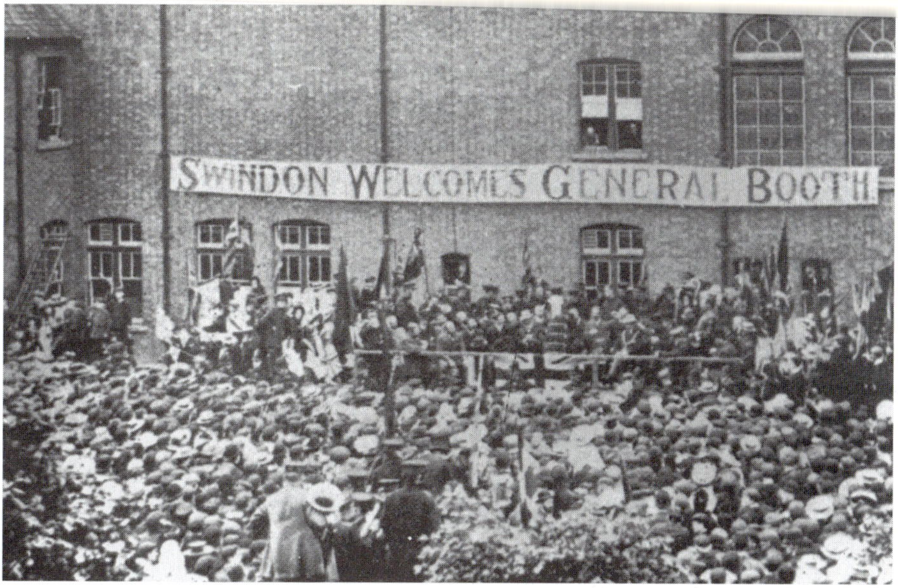

Crowds are gathered outside the rear of the Town Hall to greet General Booth of the Salvation Army during his visit in 1905. The Central Library now stands where the large group is congregated.

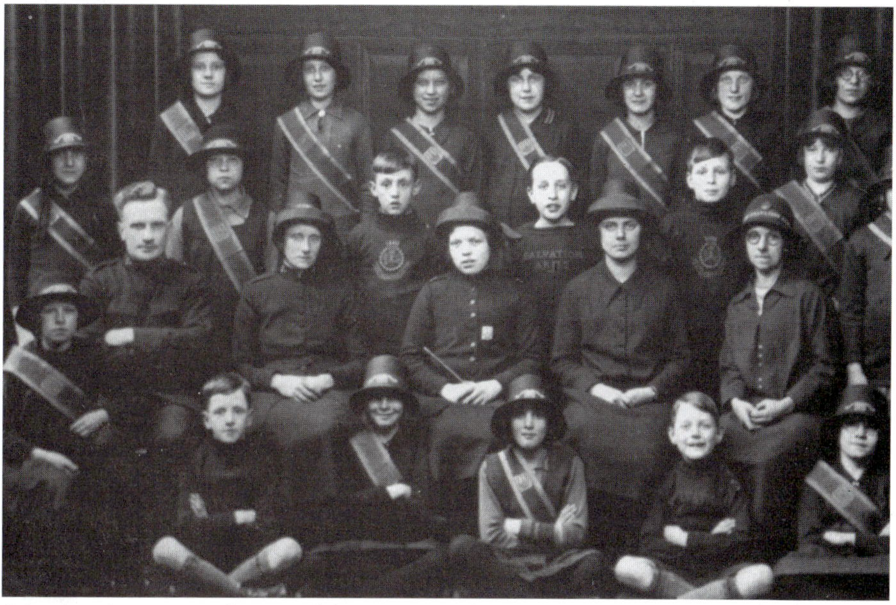
Salvation Army, Swindon Citadel Young People's Singing Company, *c.* 1930. Back row, left to right: -?-, -?-, Doris Draper, Elsie Allen, -?-, Vera Allen, Vera Haines. Middle row (standing): Peggy Davis, -?-, -?-, John Snook, Ken Eatwell, -?-, -?-. Seated: -?-, -?-, Olive Snook (née Matthews), ? Bullock, Mrs Davis, -?-. Front row: Jesse Jones, -?-, -?-, -?-, -?-.

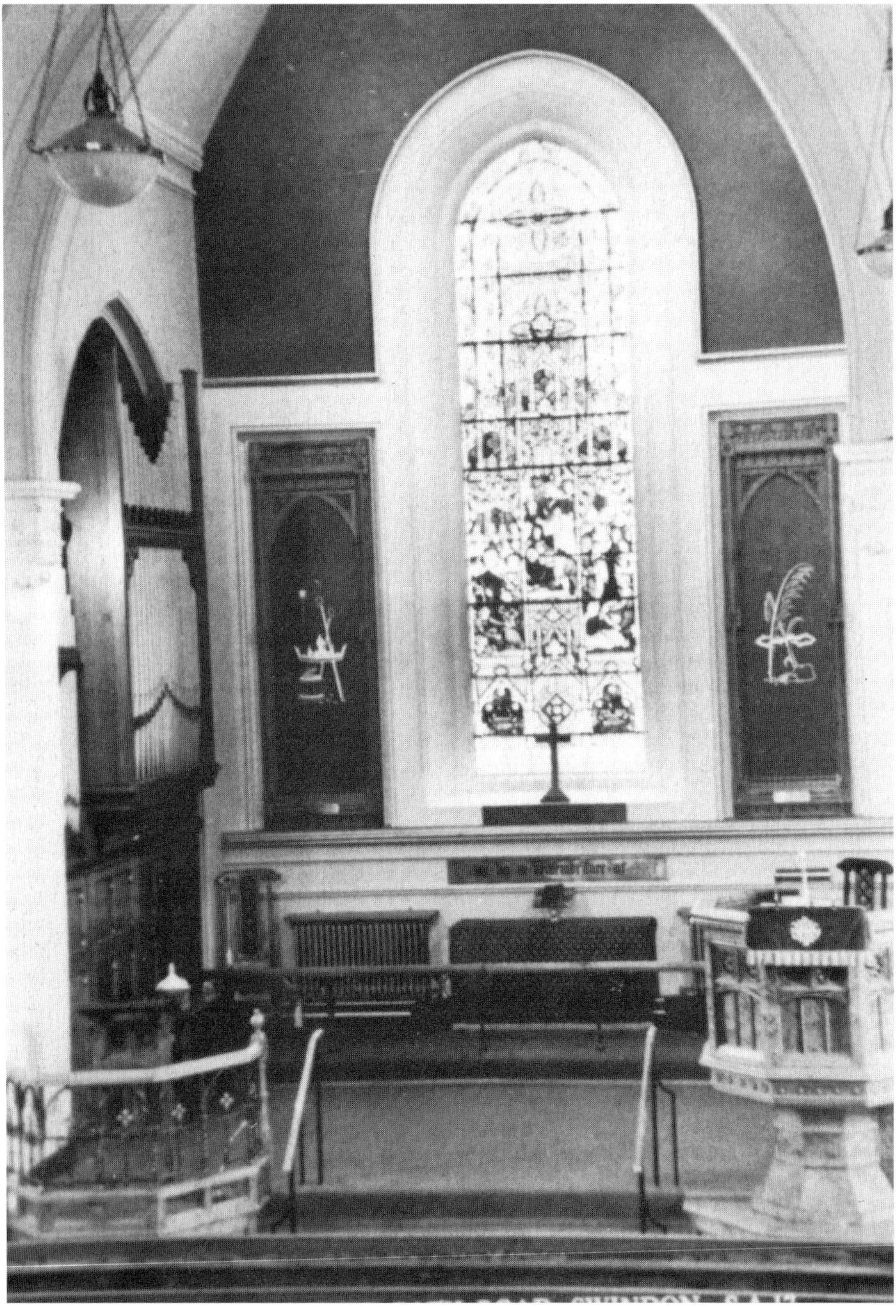

Interior of Wesleyan Methodist church, Bath Road, *c.* 1925. Opened in 1880 to replace former 'Octagonal' chapel in the Planks (see *Swindon in Old Photographs (2)*, p. 74) with accommodation for 800, the church was renovated and extended in the 1970s.

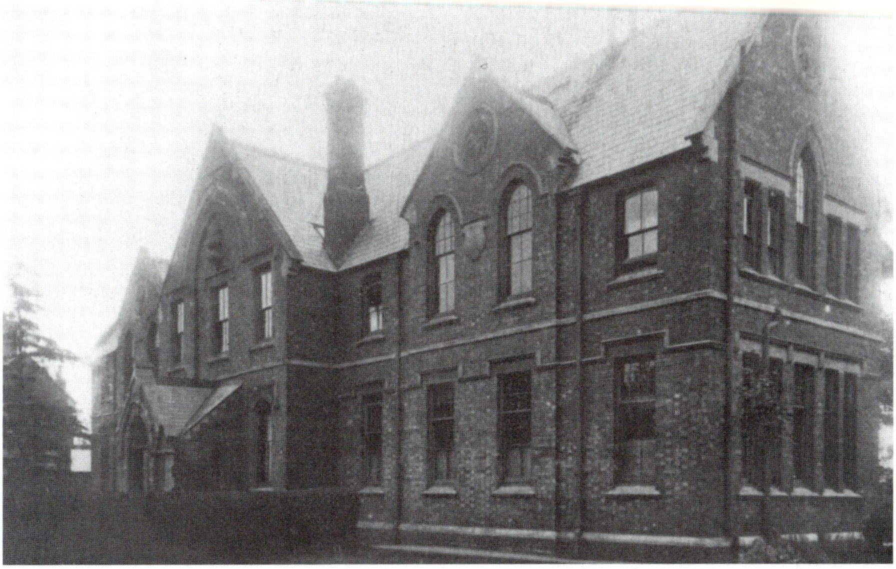

Victoria Hospital, Okus Road, 1913. The hospital was built in 1887/8 on land given by A.L. Goddard as a memorial for Queen Victoria's Golden Jubilee, and opened in September 1888. It was extended in 1904, and again in 1923 and 1930.

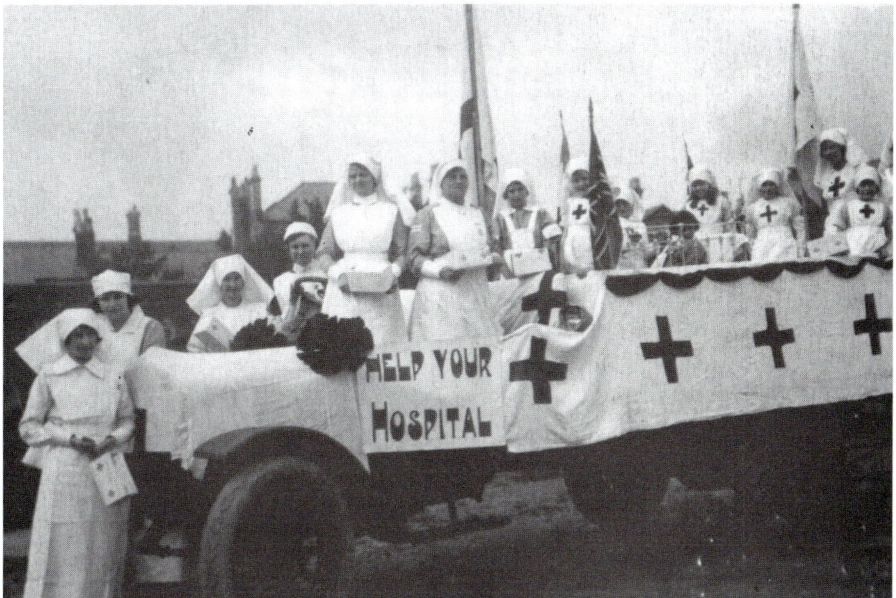

Victoria Hospital Carnival, an annual fund-raising event to support this hospital which depended on voluntary subscriptions. The date is unknown but the lorry is of 1920s vintage. (Photograph by Fred Palmer of Cromwell Street)

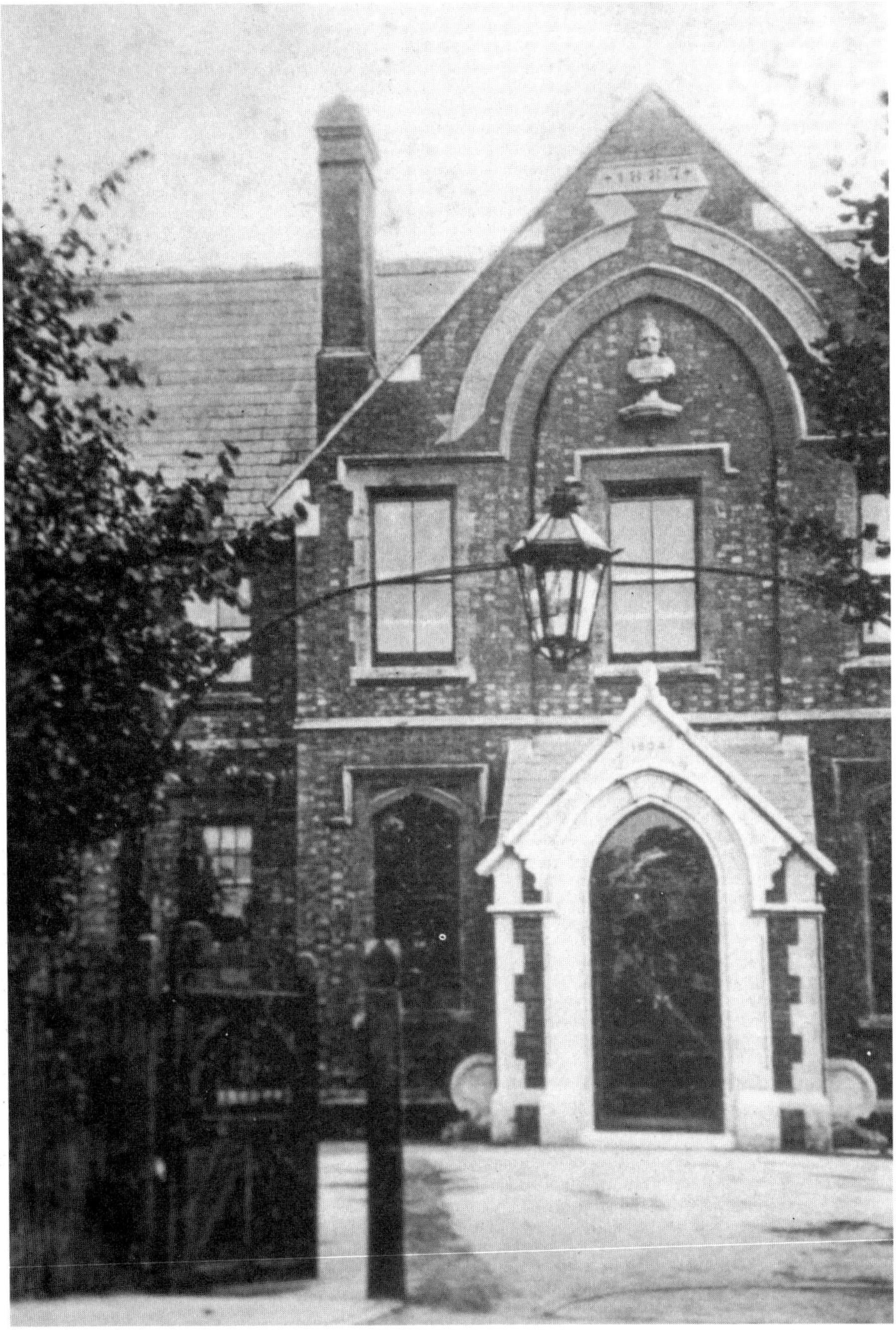

Main entrance to Victoria Hospital, Okus Road, *c.* 1910. Note the ornate lamp over the gate.

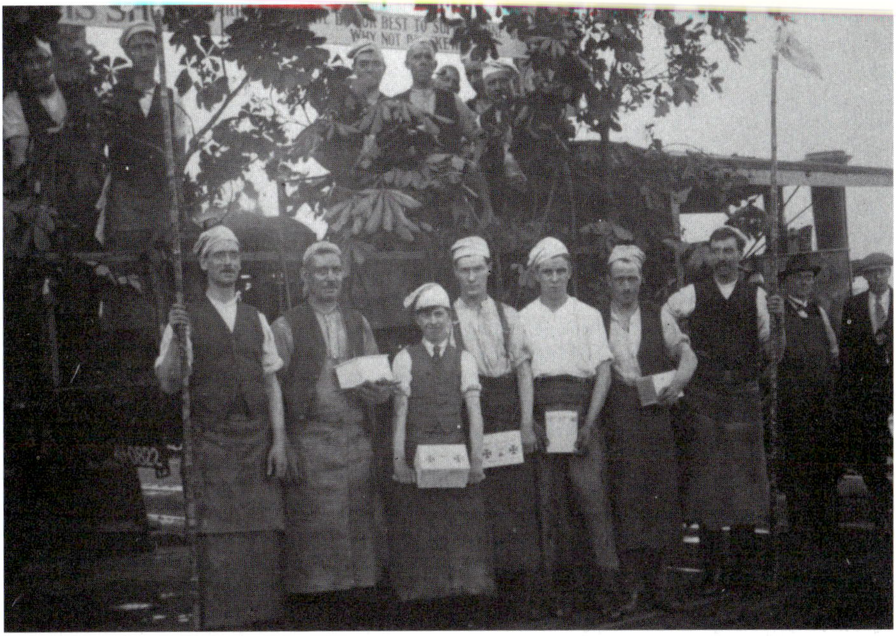

Victoria Hospital Expenses Fund, *c.* 1920. Aproned men stand in front of a steam traction engine and trailer with collecting boxes at one of the hospital carnivals. Local hospitals depended on these events and collections for much needed funds.

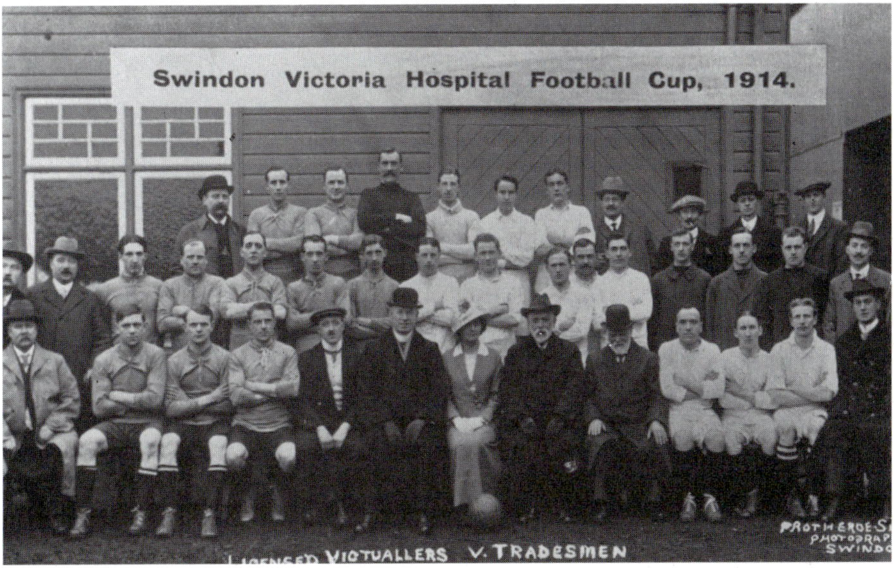

Swindon Victoria Hospital Football Cup, 1914. Teams of the Licenced Victuallers and Tradesmen pose for the camera. The hospital received a great deal of support for its fund-raising activities from the local population.

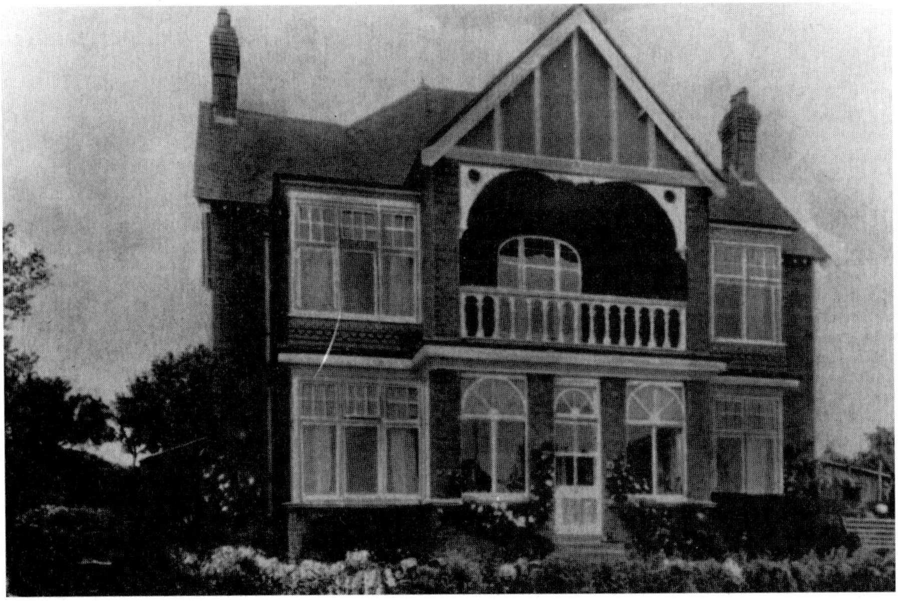

St Catherine's School, 67 Westlecott Road, *c.* 1928. A private boarding and day school for girls, and kindergarten for boys and girls, it is advertised as 'splendidly situated on the edge of Old Town, overlooking the downs and 503 feet above sea level'. It closed as a school in 1960 and is now a private residence.

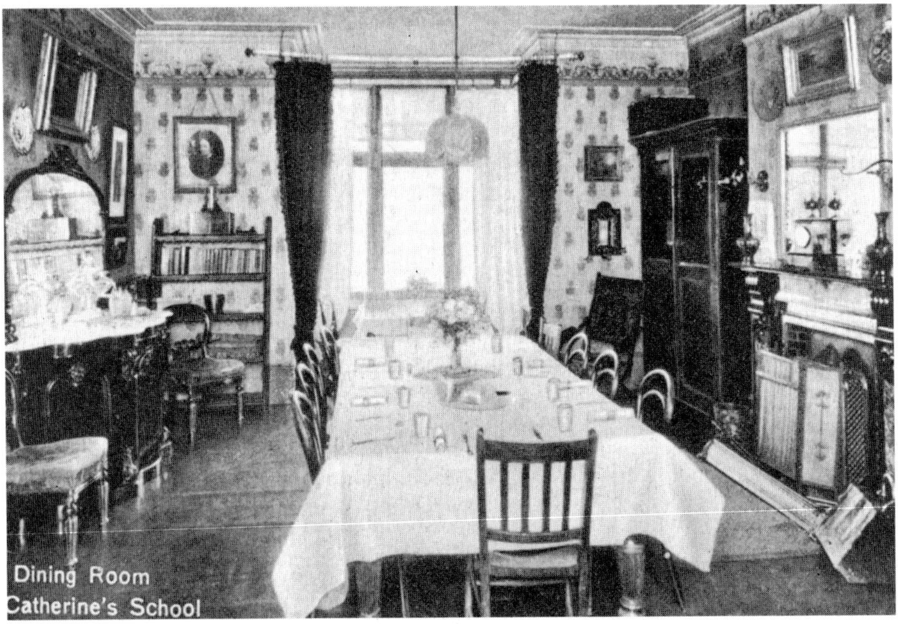

Dining-room at St Catherine's School, Westlecott Road, *c.* 1928.

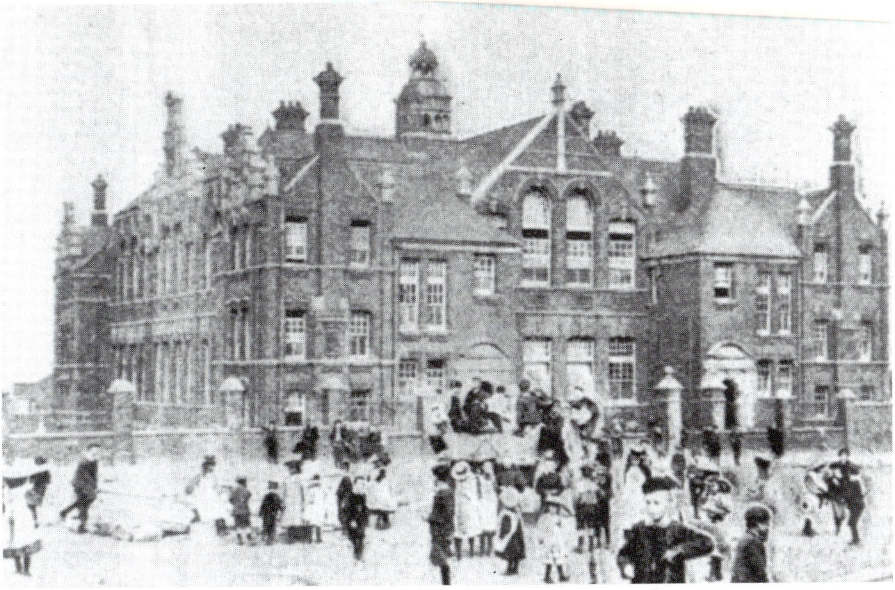

Clarence Street School, *c.* 1898. Although of inferior quality, this photograph shows the newly built school in 1897. At this time Euclid Street had not been completed. The school opened with 235 boys and 115 girls.

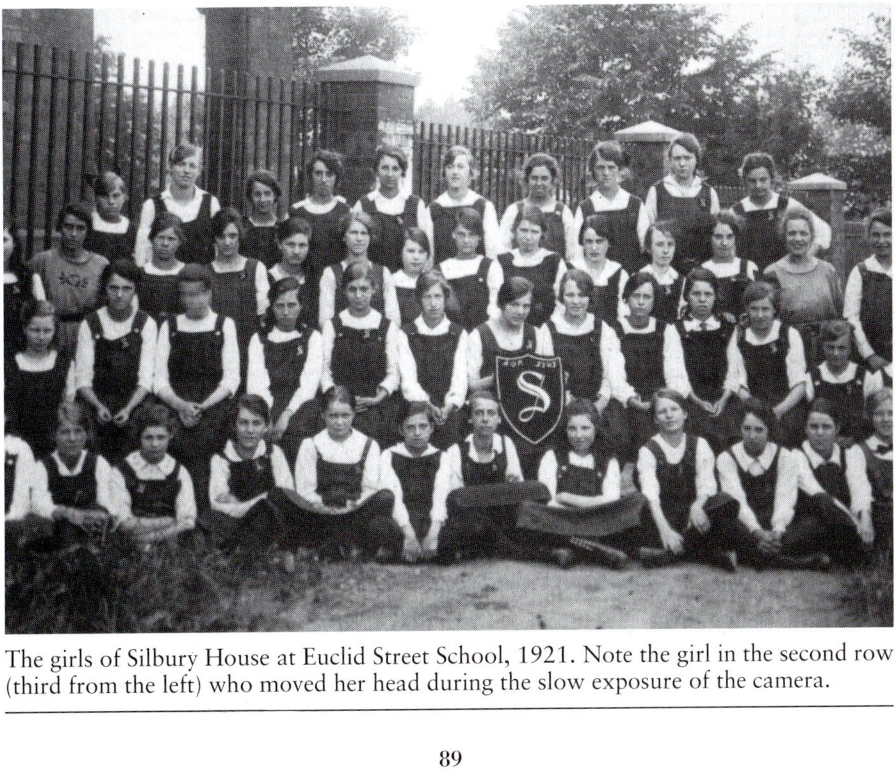

The girls of Silbury House at Euclid Street School, 1921. Note the girl in the second row (third from the left) who moved her head during the slow exposure of the camera.

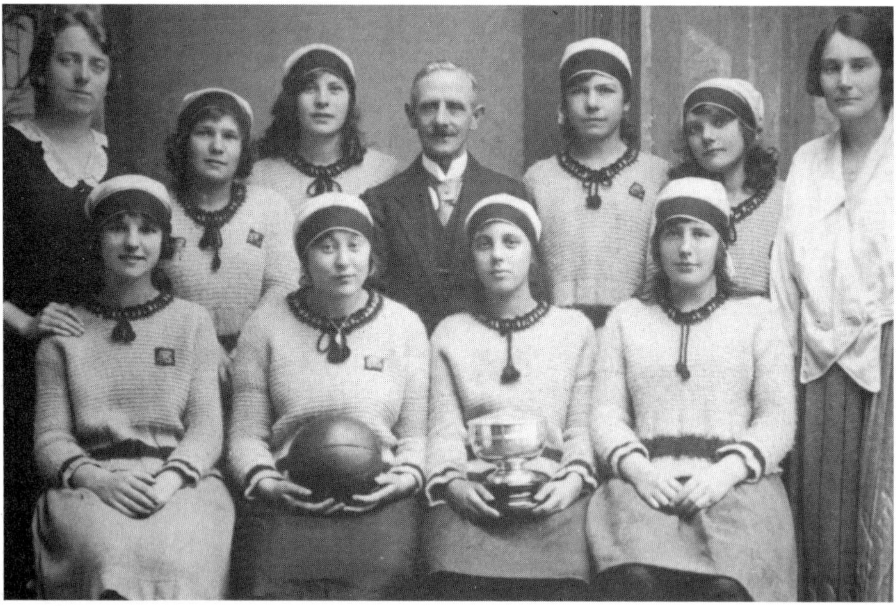

Ferndale Road School Netball Team, 1922/3, with the headmaster, Mr 'Dapper' Dutton, so nicknamed because he allegedly used a dap (plimsoll) instead of a cane.

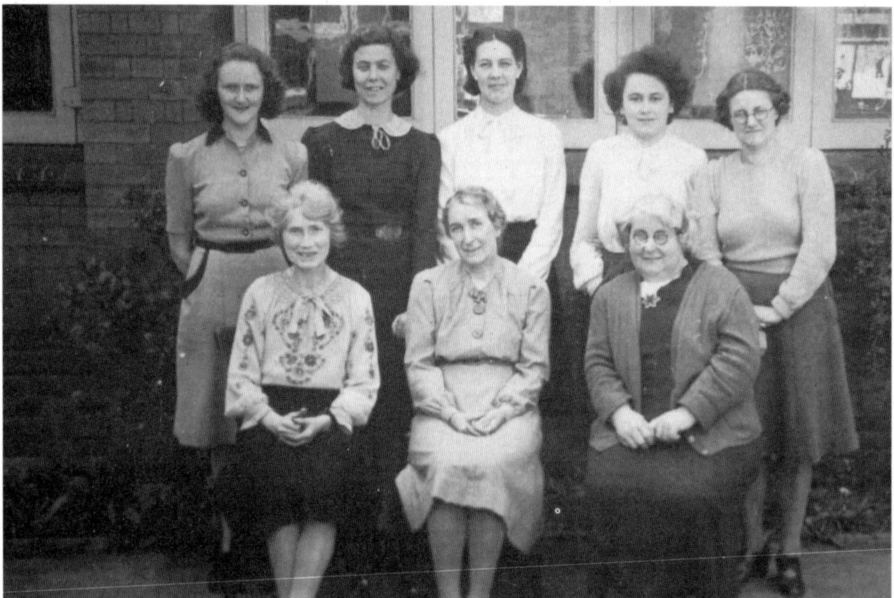

Ferndale Road Infants School staff, 1949. Back row: Miss Killa, Miss Swallow, Miss Dracup, Miss Davies, Mrs Parsons. Front row: Miss Walling (deputy head), Miss Minnes (head), Miss Hill.

SECTION SIX

The Co-operative Movement

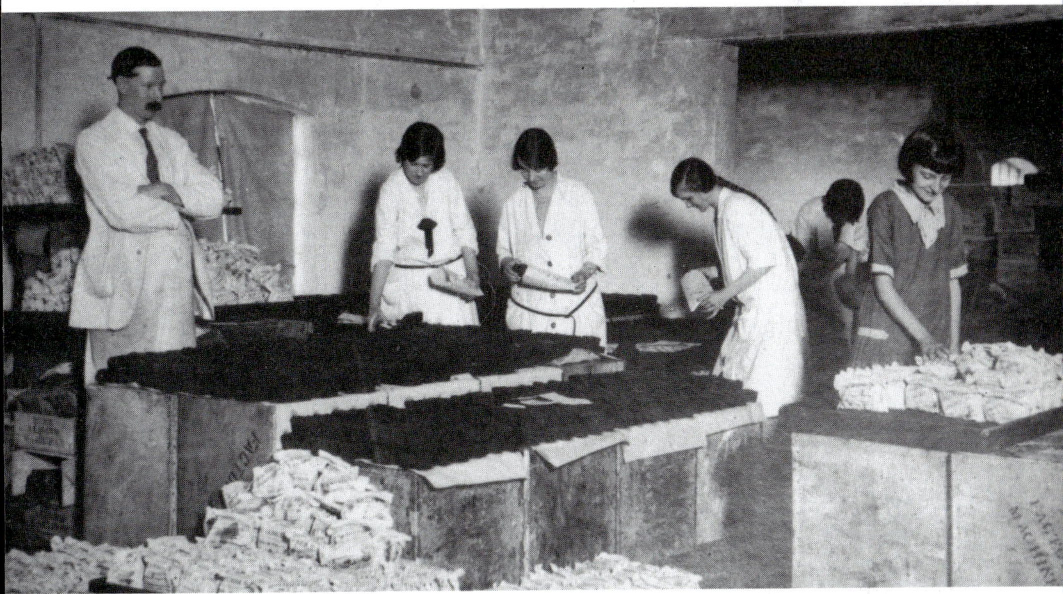

Cakes for the Children's Fête, Swindon Co-operative Provident Society bakery, Henry Street, *c.* 1925. The Provident Co-operative Society had the annual contract to supply the cake for the famous Children's Fête in the mid-1920s (the Co-op had previously shared the contract with a Mr Monk, the High Street baker, in the early years of the century). Oval cake tins were made especially to accommodate the ½ lb cakes and to obviate the task of cutting slabs into slices (see p. 125). The recipe for the fruit cake is said to be an exclusive secret recipe devised by the foreman at the Henry Street bakery, Mr Frank Hudd. This photograph shows Mr Hudd, on the left, supervising the 'bagging-up' of the fête cakes by his staff prior to loading the crates for transportation to GWR Park. The ladies are, left to right: Nell Stanton, Amy Oliver, Doll Lewington, Vi Hudd, Blanche Hudd. Wages at the time were 10s. a week of 48 hours at the age of 14 increasing to 34s. a week at the age of 21.

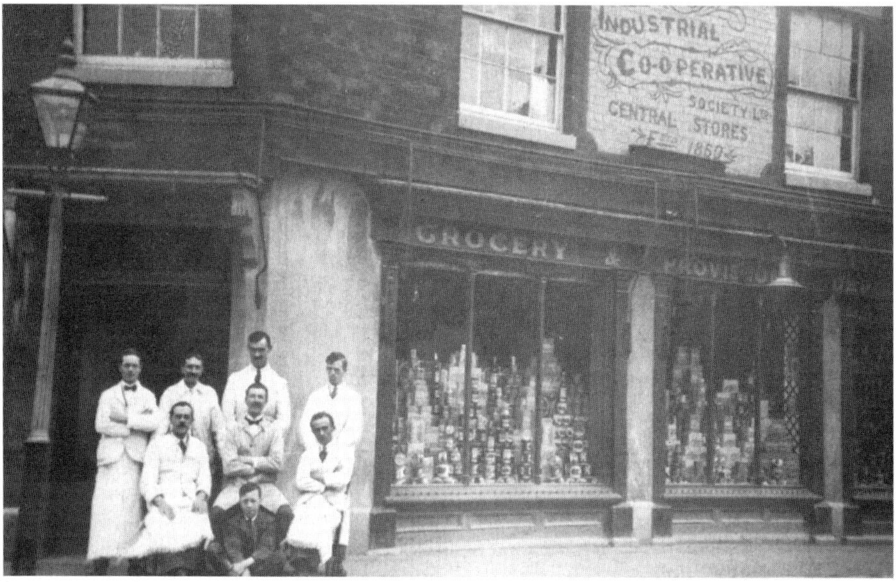

New Swindon Industrial Co-operative Society Ltd, central grocery, drapery, hardware and footwear departments, 10–13 East Street, *c.* 1922. The cash office was on the extreme right (not in picture) with the warehouse and general offices on the first floor.

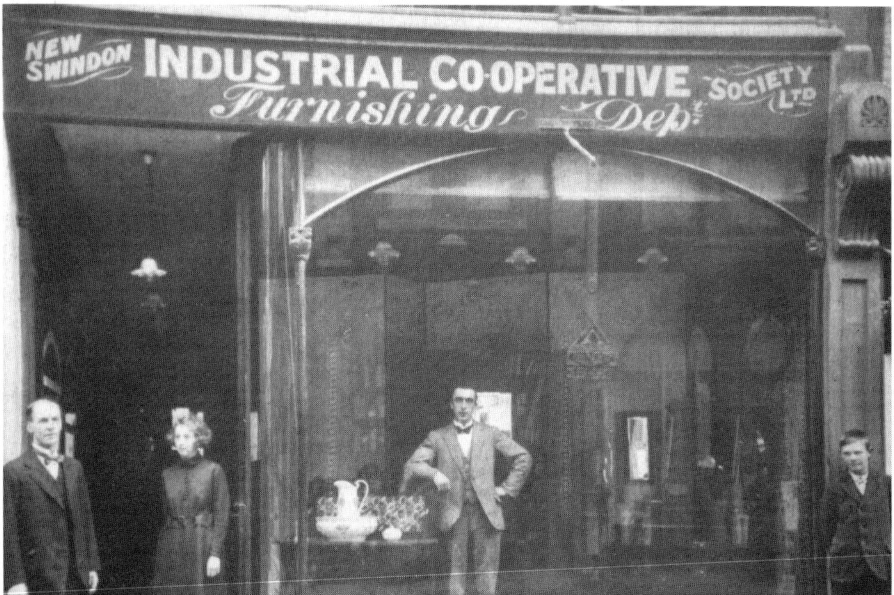

New Swindon Industrial Co-operative Society Ltd, furnishing department, 81 Regent Street, *c.* 1925. The lady assistant is Miss Hilda Jones. The site of these premises is now part of the Marks and Spencer's store.

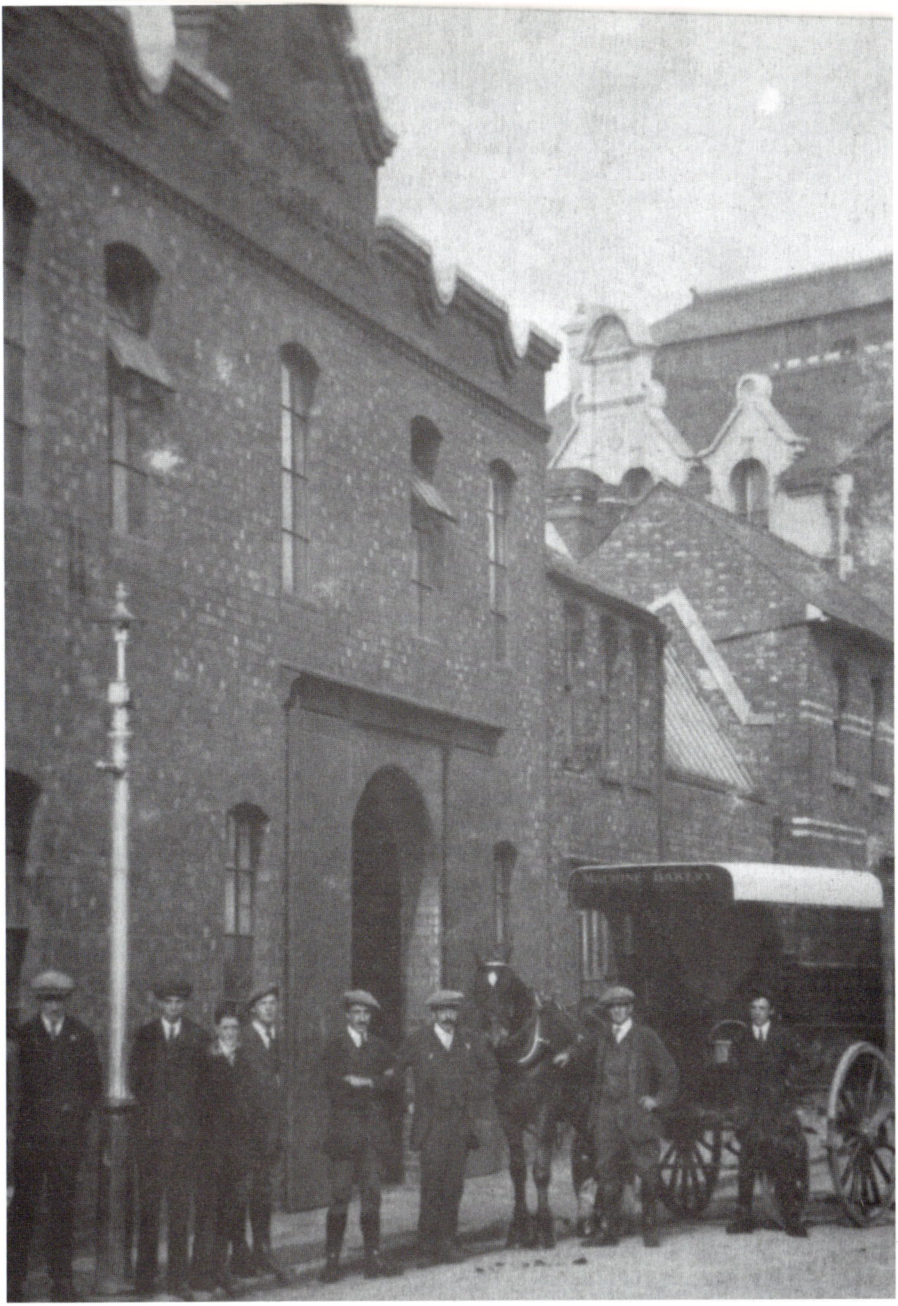

John Street, looking towards Fleet Street, *c.* 1910. To the left is the New Swindon Co-operative Society stables, opened in 1908. Delivery vans, like the one in the photograph, were also kept there. The façade of the YMCA in the background is still visible today.

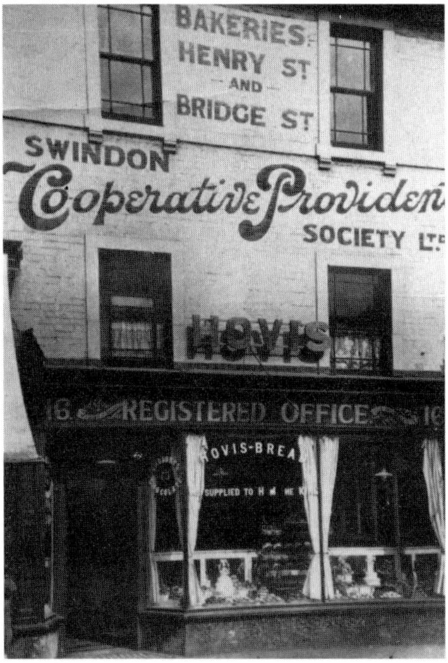

Registered Office, Swindon Co-operative Provident Society Ltd, 16 Fleet Street, *c.* 1920. Now Bernards furniture store. The frontage facing Bridge Street was, and still is, more impressive.

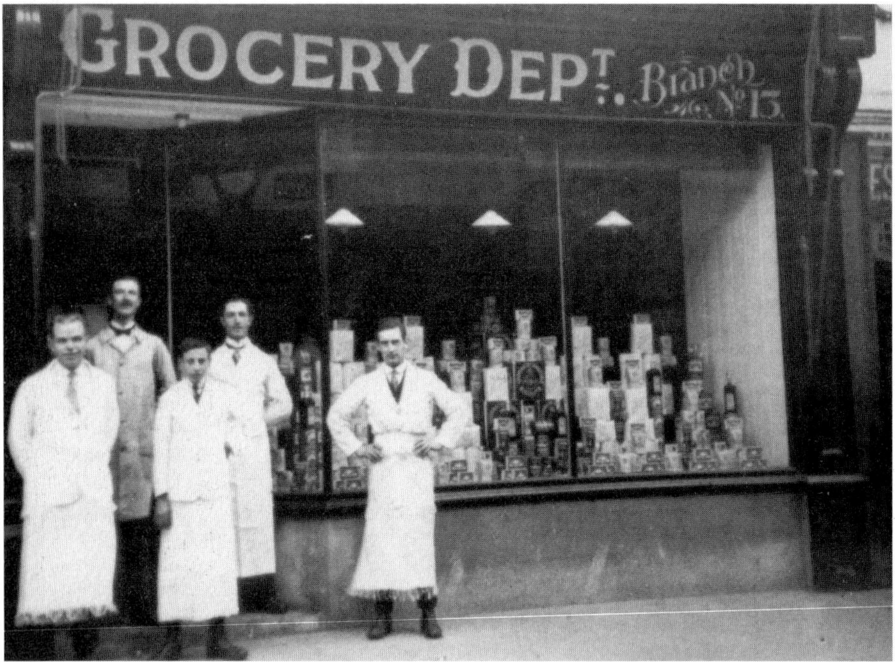

No. 13 branch, grocery department, New Swindon Industrial Co-operative Society, 12 Fleet Street, 1925. This was opened on 21 June 1921. The manager, Mr Evry, is standing in the doorway, and Mr F. Nash is on the right.

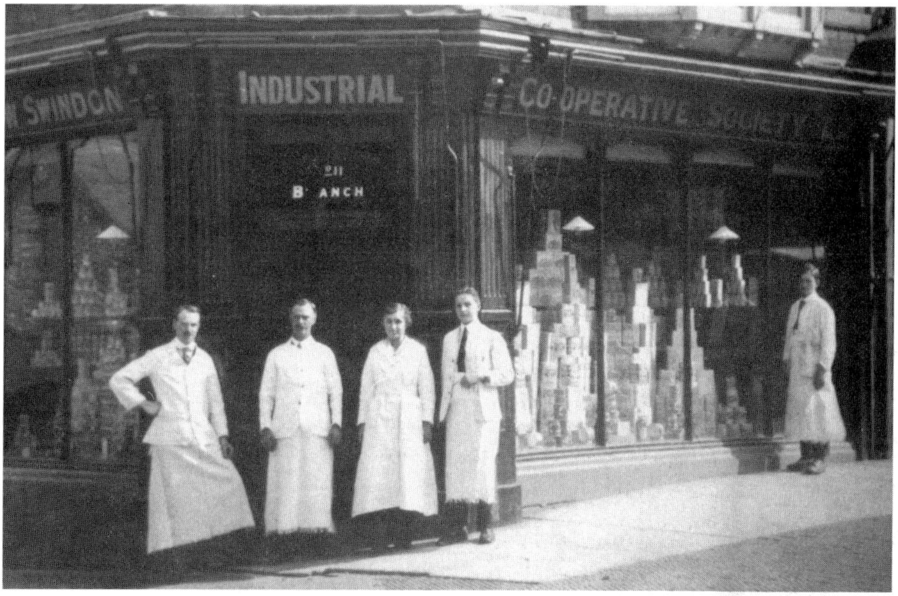

No. 11 branch, New Swindon Industrial Co-operative Society, 101 Commercial Road, *c.* 1918. This was opened in September 1916, but because of wartime conditions no opening ceremony was performed. Situated on the corner of Granville Street, these premises are now used by the National & Provincial Building Society.

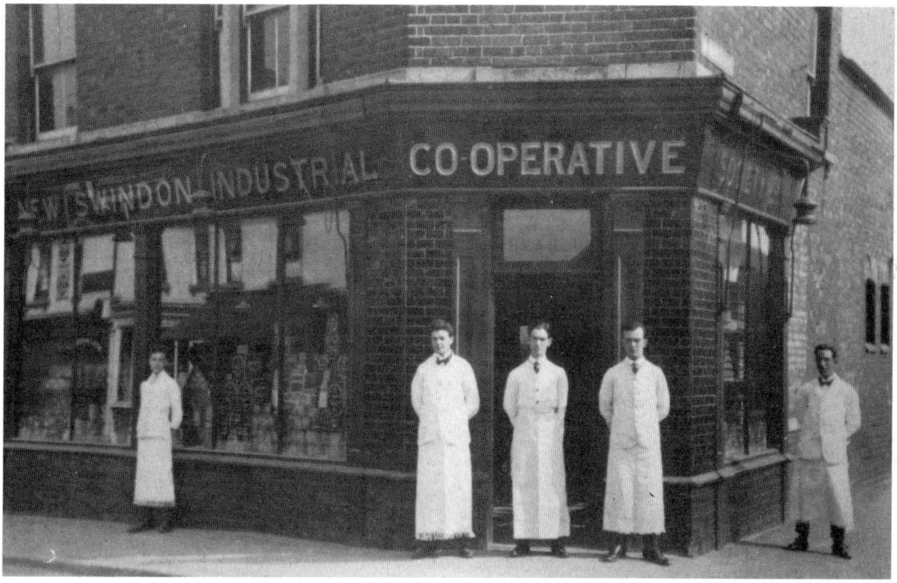

No. 2 branch, New Swindon Industrial Co-operative Society, 2 Rodbourne Road, 1912. This branch was moved from the opposite side of Rodbourne Road in 1911. It is still a Co-operative Society shop today.

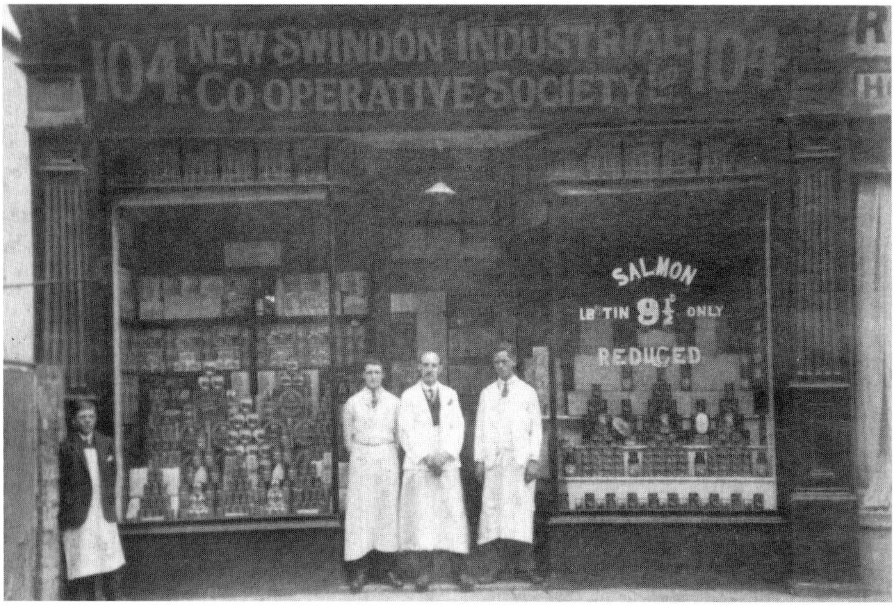

No. 8 branch, New Swindon Industrial Co-operative Society Ltd, 104 Victoria Road. Opened in 1914, it moved to Devizes Road in 1925. The site of the shop is now occupied by public toilets.

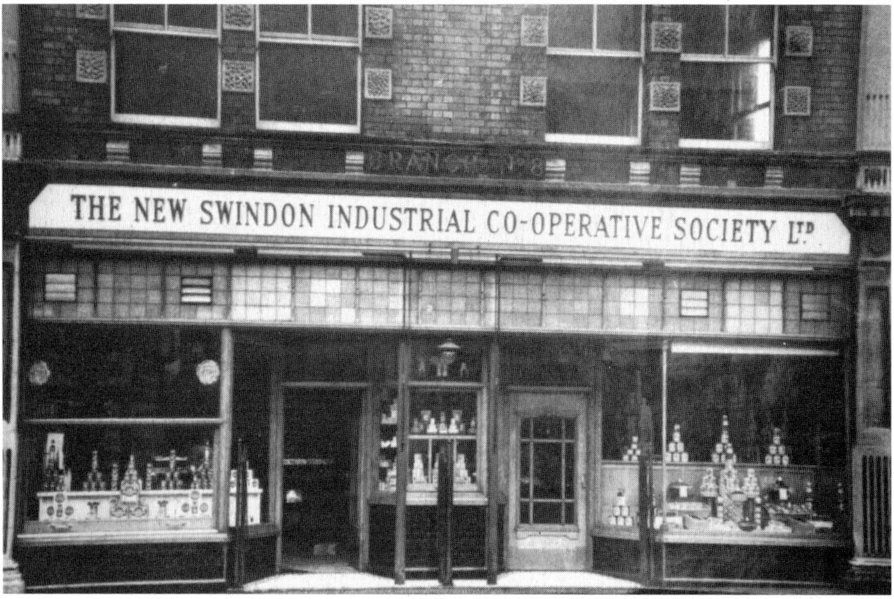

No. 8 branch, New Swindon Industrial Co-operative Society Ltd, 4 Devizes Road, Old Town. It was opened on 21 March 1925 to replace the store in Victoria Road. Today it is Mr Ashcroft's pine furniture store.

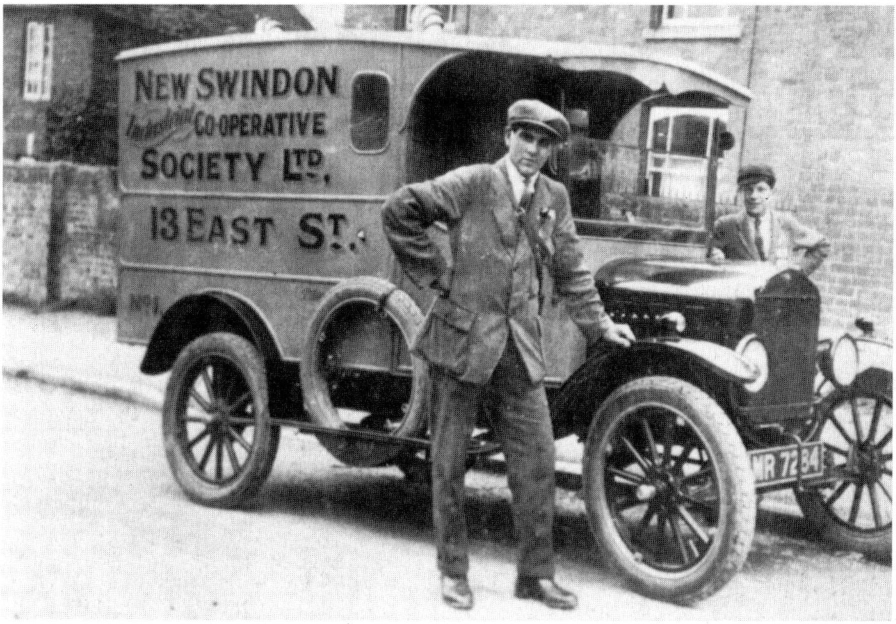

New Swindon Industrial Society Ltd delivery van, No. 1, *c.* 1920. Groceries could be delivered 'to your door' right up until the 1960s.

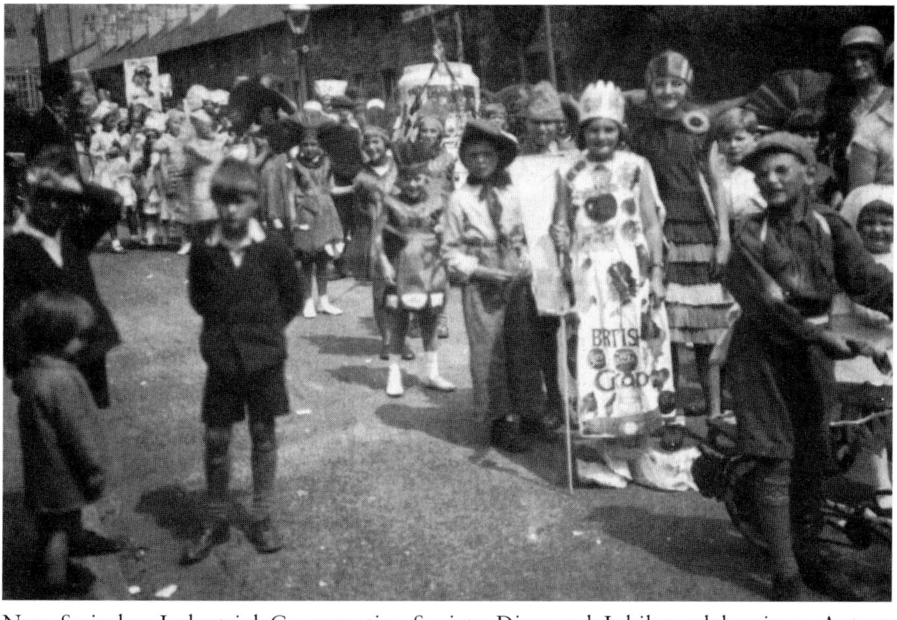

New Swindon Industrial Co-operative Society Diamond Jubilee celebrations, August 1921. This was the children's fancy dress procession during the exhibition week. This view looks east along Bathampton Street towards the Mechanics Institute.

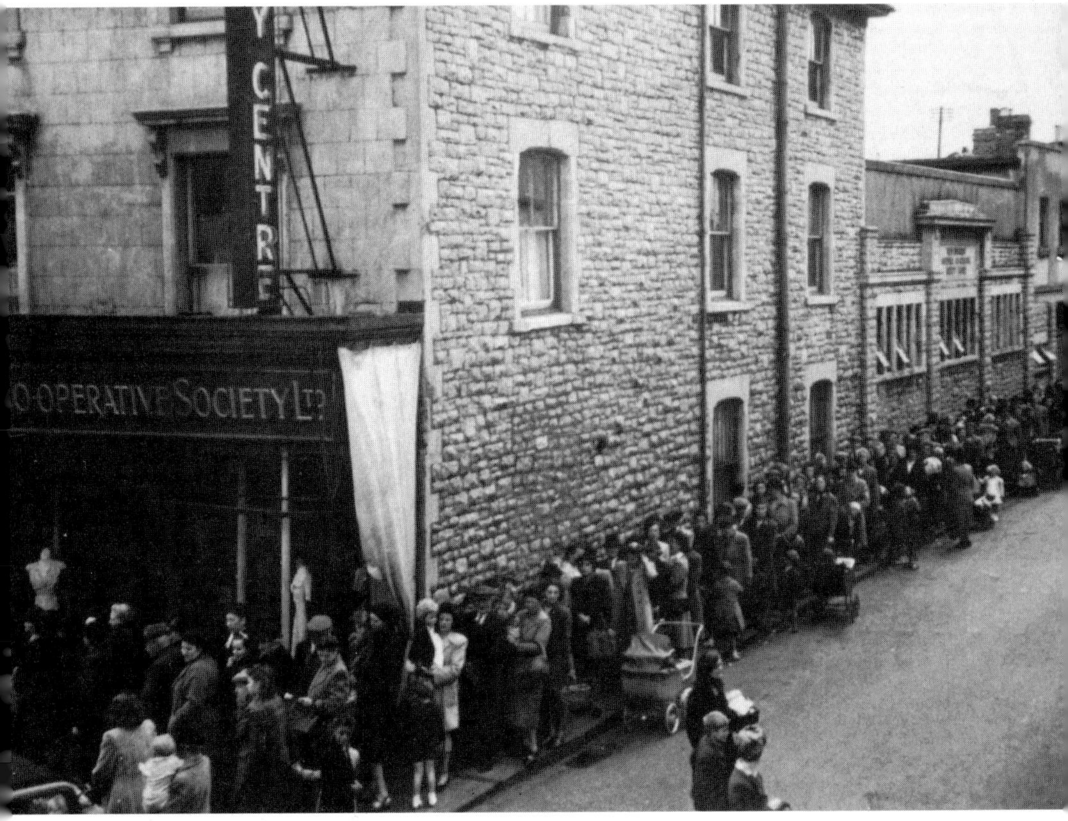

Queuing for dividend, from the New Swindon Industrial Co-operative Society offices at 57 Fleet Street around the corner into Queen Street, June 1949. Dividend was paid to members twice yearly, in June and December, at a few pence for each pound spent in the society's shops. This extra cash was useful to help with summer holidays and Christmas extras. The buildings shown above were later demolished and a new departmental store and office complex, Fleetway House, was built on the site. The Co-op vacated these premises in the 1980s and the store has recently been re-opened as a Kwik Save supermarket.

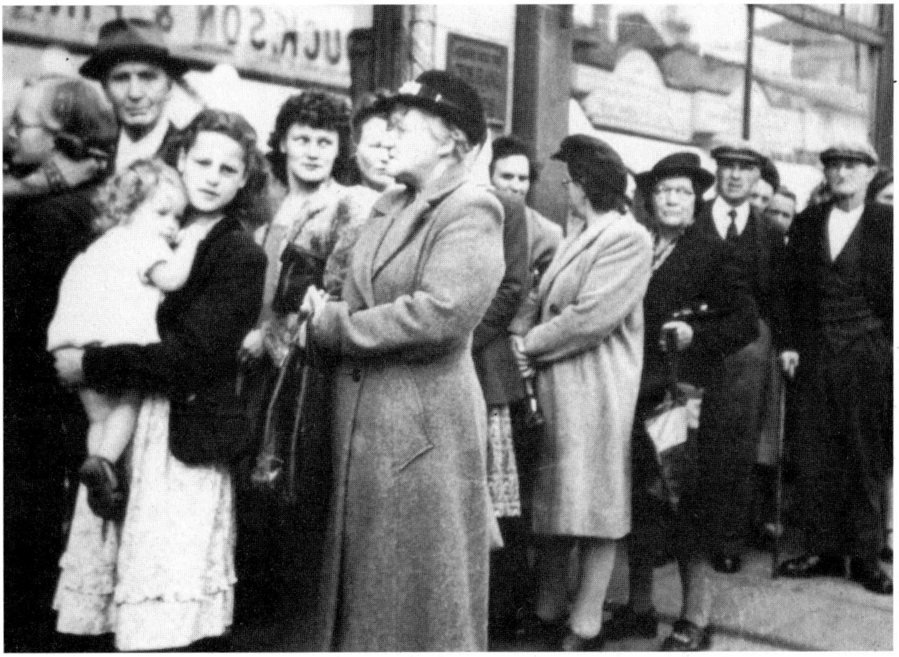

Patient queue of Co-op members awaiting a dividend payout, Queen Street, 1949.

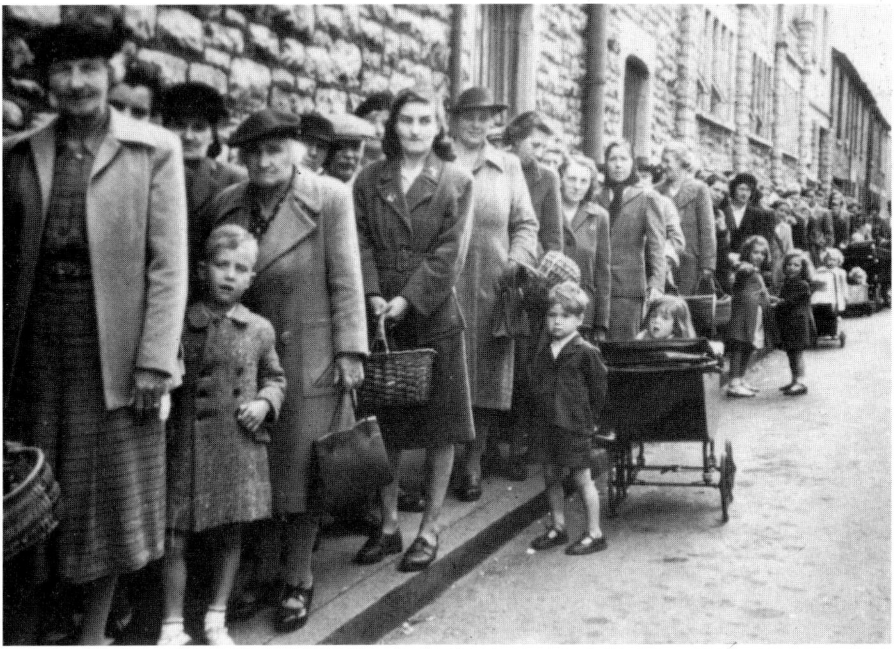

Dividend queue, Queen Street, 1949.

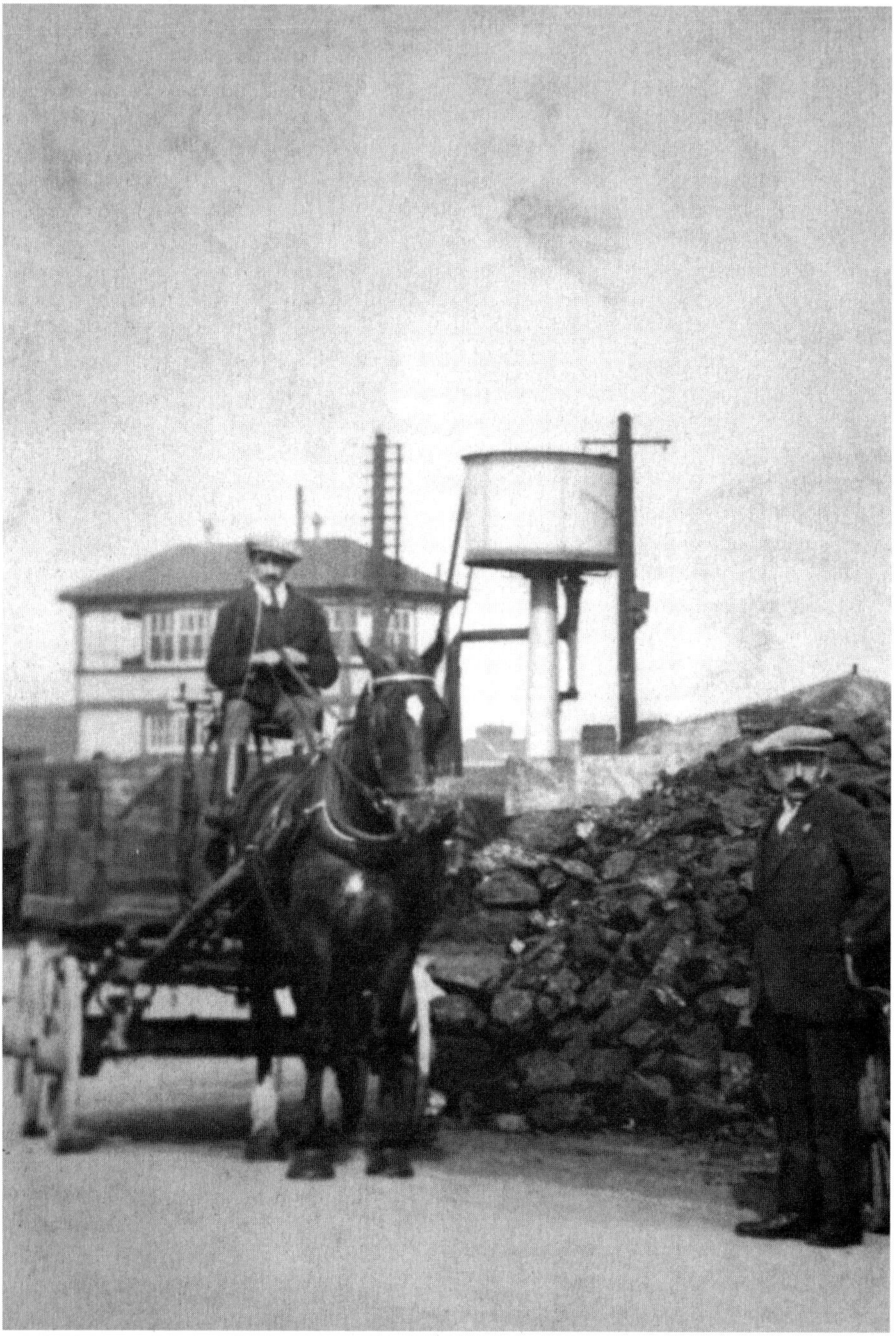

Co-operative Society coal wharf at the GWR transfer off County Road, *c.* 1910. On the left is Mr J. (Bill) Bright, and on the right is Mr Bill Church.

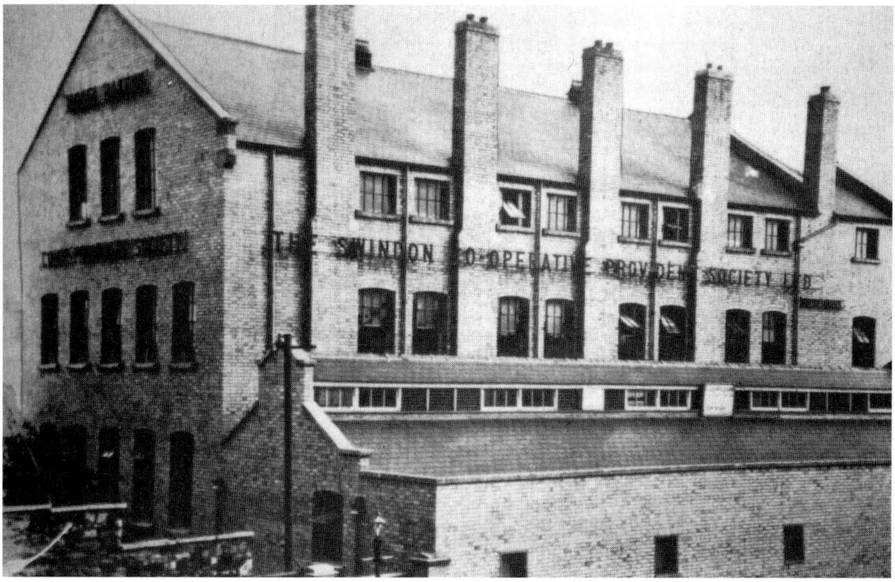

Swindon Co-operative Provident Society model bakery, Station Road, *c.* 1925. The Society's Henry Street premises could not cope with the demand by the early 1920s, so it purchased land in Station Road from the GWR in 1923 and built this large bakery (the Henry Street bakery was converted into a confectionery bakery). The building was demolished when the area was redeveloped in the 1970s.

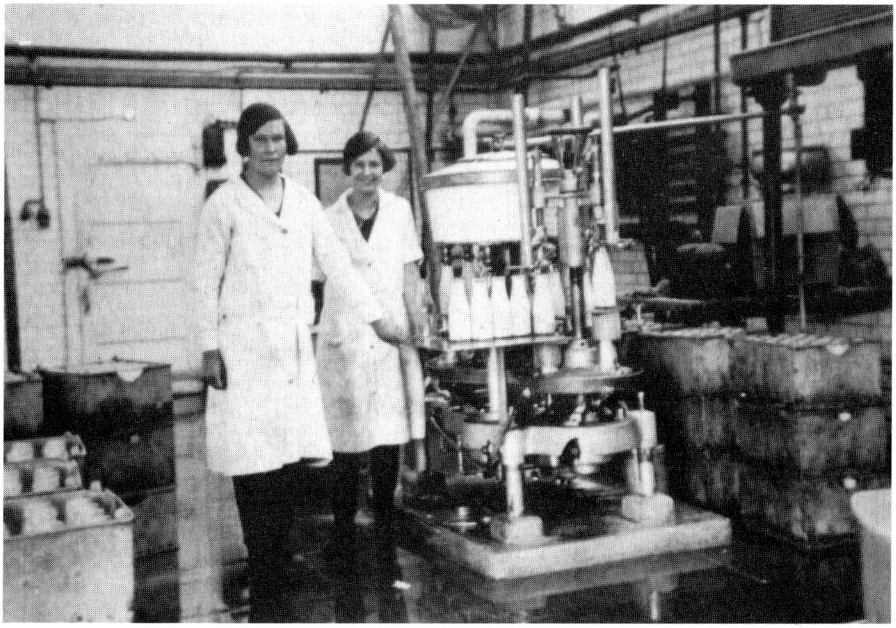

Co-operative Dairy, Colbourne Street, *c.* 1925.

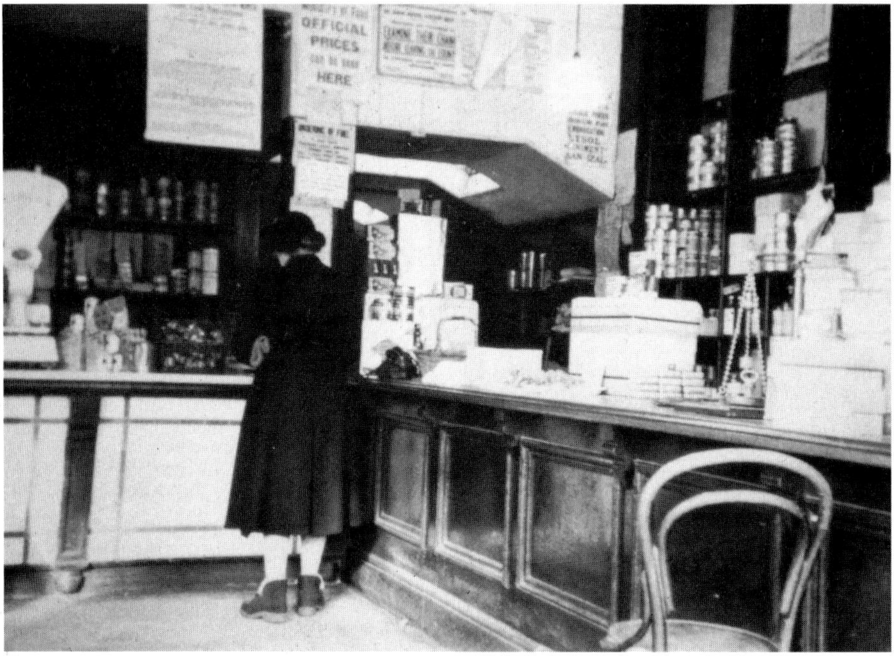

Interior of No. 11 branch, New Swindon Industrial Co-operative Society Ltd, Commercial Road, during the Second World War. Note the galaxy of posters from the Ministry of Food and the sparse shelves.

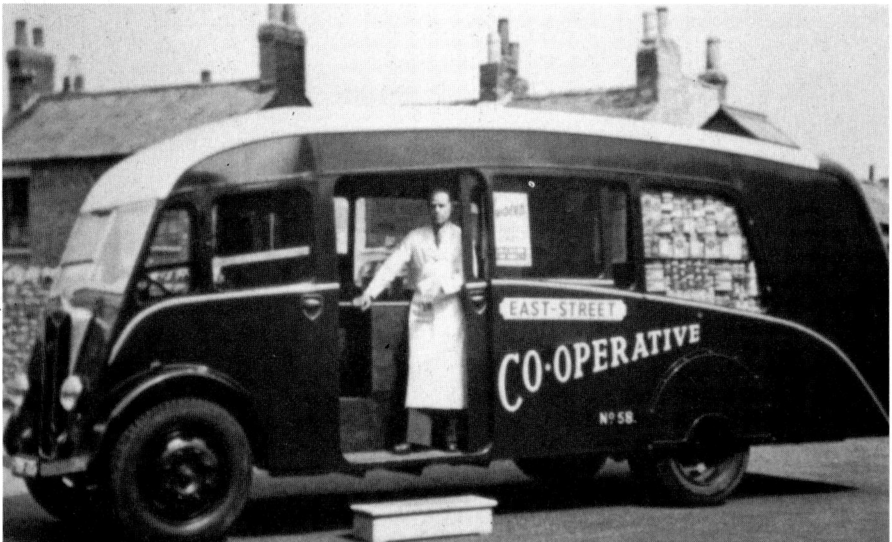

East Street New Swindon Industrial Co-operative Society delivery van No. 58, Colbourne Street warehouse, *c*. 1950.

SECTION SEVEN

People & Events

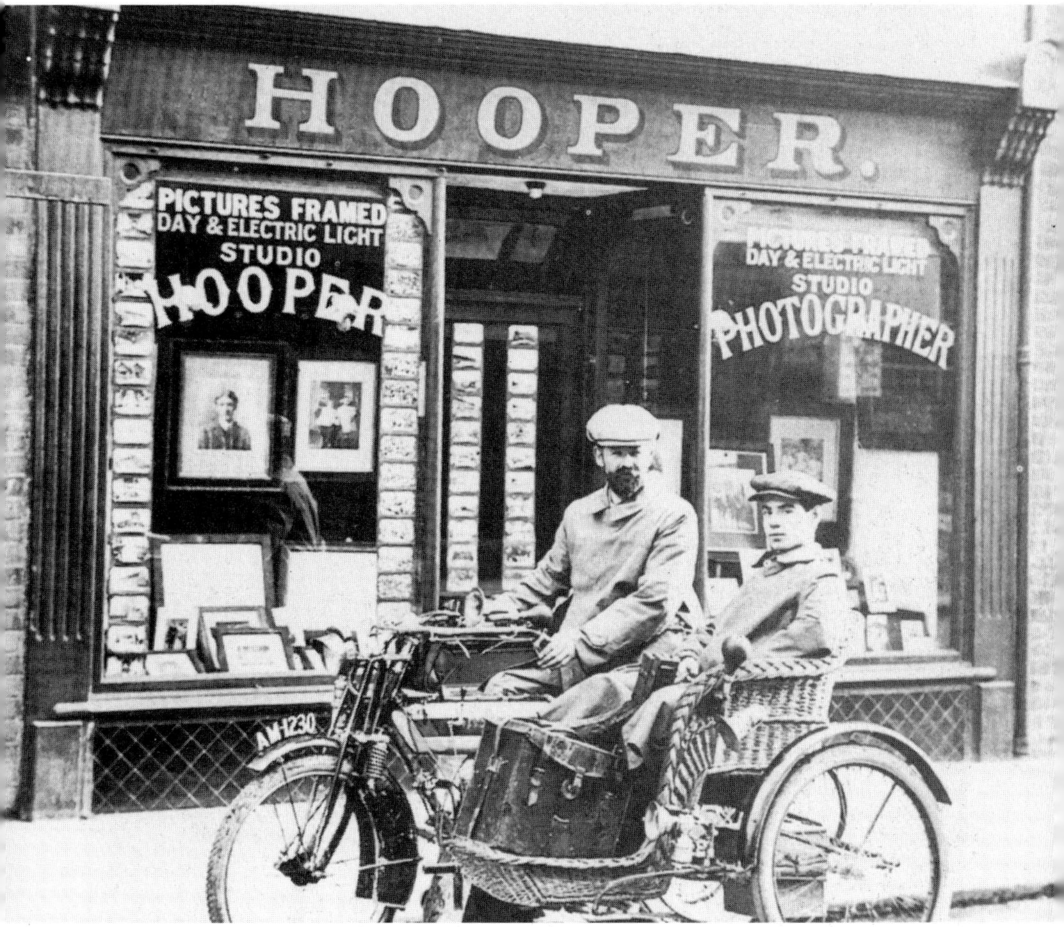

William Hooper, photographer, pictured on his motorcycle outside his studio at 6 Cromwell Street, *c.* 1912. With him, in the wicker sidecar, is Charles Ireland, his apprentice.

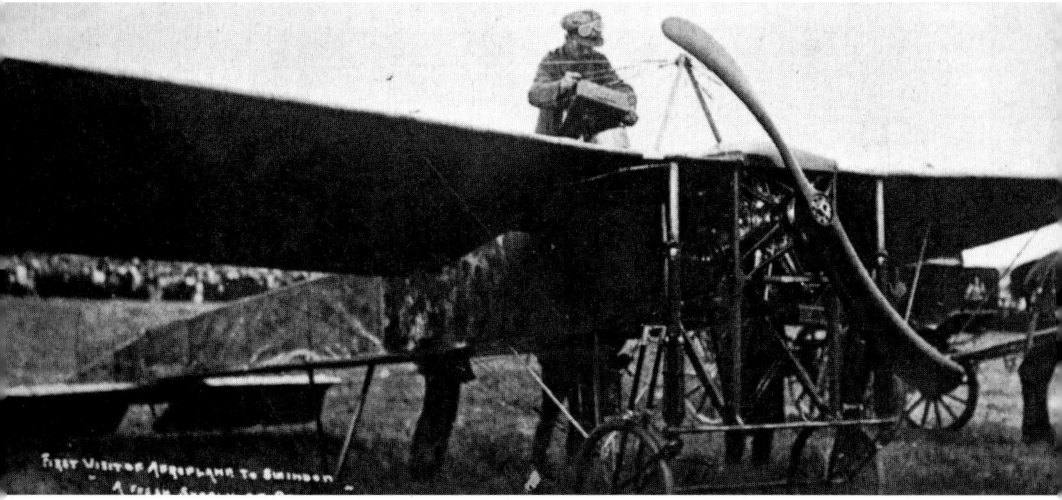

'A fresh supply of petrol.' The first aeroplane to land in Swindon, 27 July 1912. M. Salmet, a French pilot, who had given a two-day flying display at Cirencester, landed his aircraft at Pipers Corner, Coate Road, where he was welcomed by the mayor, G. Brooks, and deputy mayor, T. Butler. After refuelling, the intrepid aviator performed a display of aerobatics for the crowd of 30,000 who had flocked to see him and his flying machine. He completed the day by giving a lecture to a crowded house at the Empire Theatre. See also *Swindon in Old Photographs (1)*, p. 116.

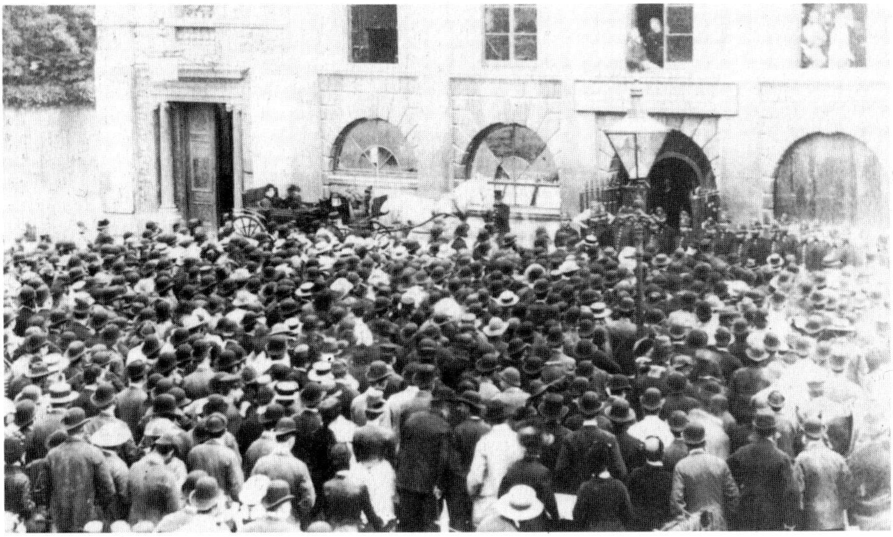

Declaration of the poll for the General Election, June 1886, Market Square, Old Town. This was for the Cricklade and North Wilts. Constituency as Swindon did not have its own MP until 1918. Elected to represent the division was Nevil Story Maskelyne, Liberal Unionist. The other candidates were B.C.F. Costello and Sir John Bennett. In the background is the (Old) Town Hall, built in 1852, and to the left, the Corn Exchange, added in 1866.

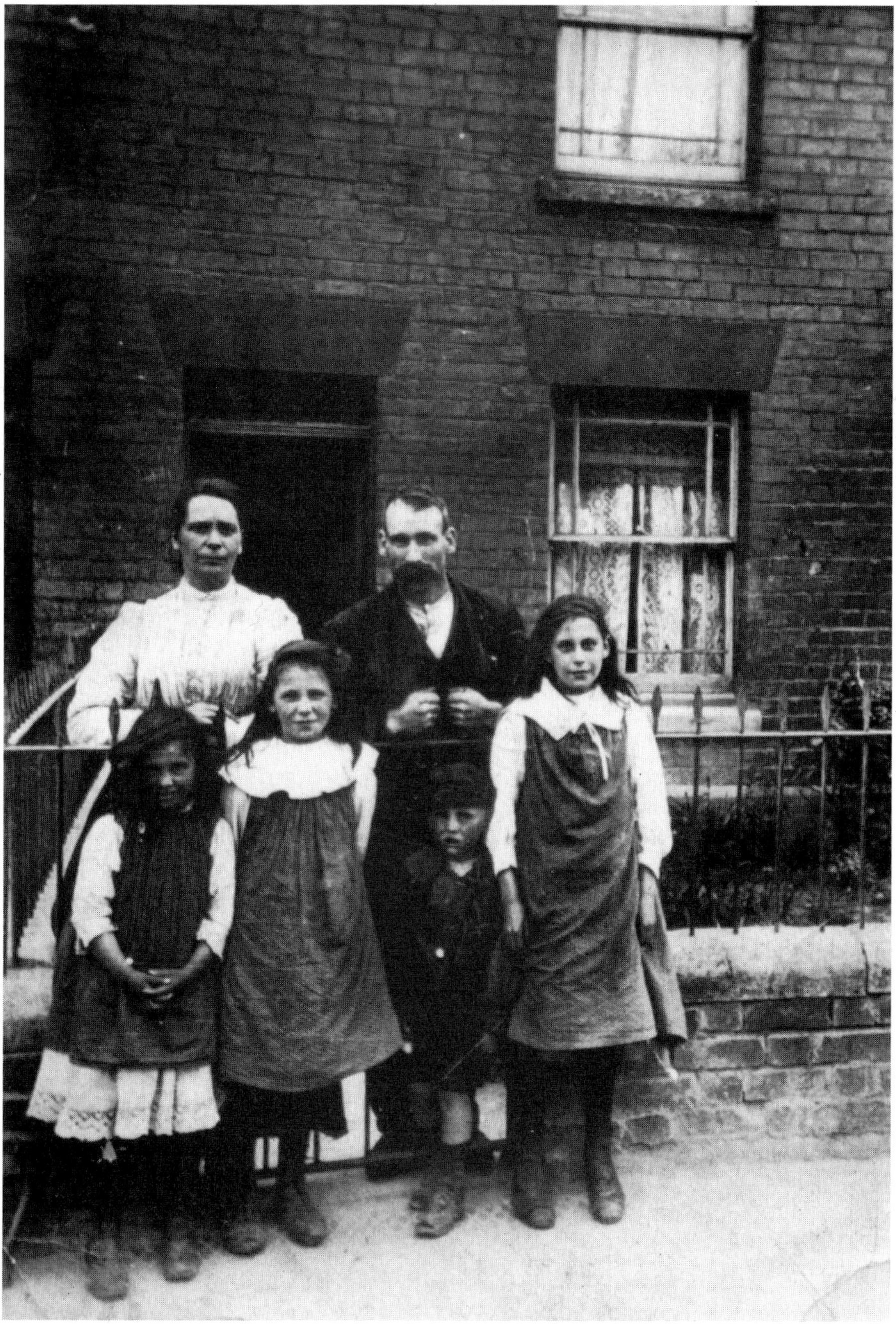

Mr & Mrs Freebury, with their children, Doris, Hylda, Fred and Gladys, outside their terraced home, 171 Cricklade Road, in 1912.

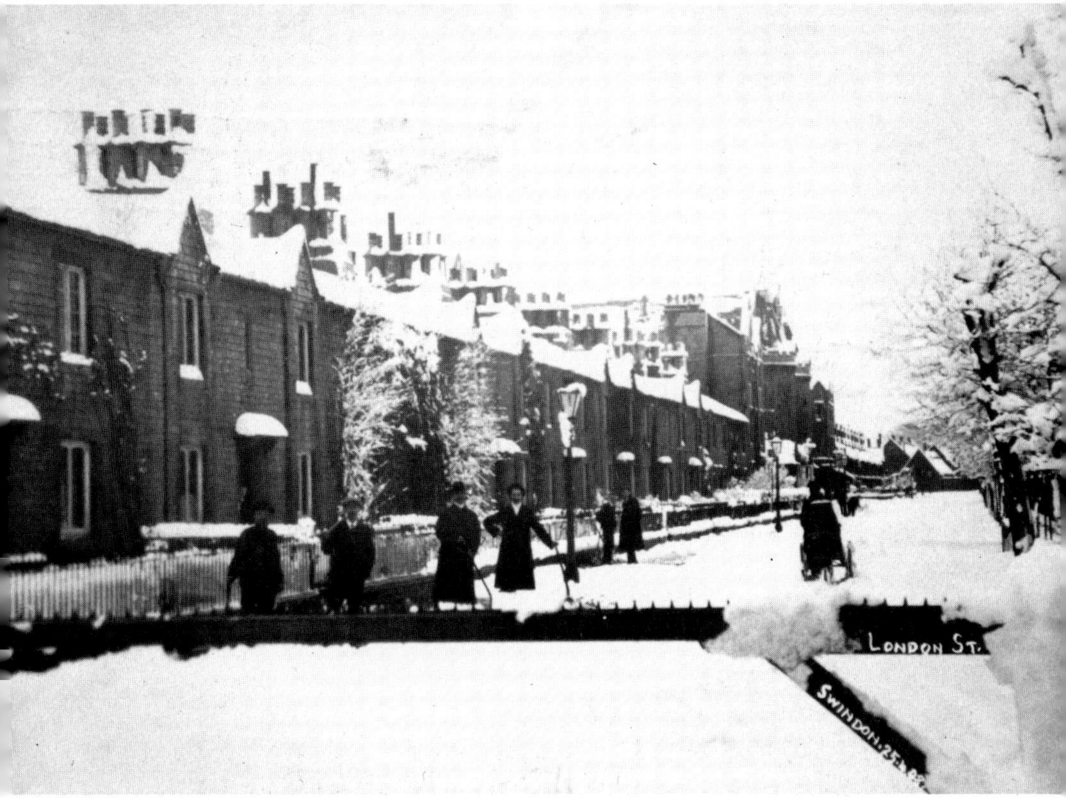

London Street, looking west towards Mechanics Institute, after the freak snowfall on Saturday 25 April 1908. Swindon had 15 inches of snow. The football match at the County Ground had to be called off and the cold weather deterred fans from going to London for the Cup Final, where Newcastle United were playing Wolverhampton Wanderers at Crystal Palace. Seventeen trains had to stop at Swindon (the first at 3.00 a.m.). Snow halted the Corn Exchange clock so the trams did not run on time. There were drifts up to 6 ft deep. Swindon butchers could not deliver and many country families went without their accustomed Sunday roast. Gutters collapsed and trees split under the weight of the snow. It was the worst snowfall reported since the memorable blizzard of January 1881. The Swindon weekly newspaper contained the following item: 'On Sunday the local Corporation, with its customary enterprising activity, sought all the unemployed lurking in the holes and corners of Swindon and put them to sweeping away snow. But the sun entered into the competition and, if rumour be true, cleared more snow in one hour than the unemployed did in 12.'

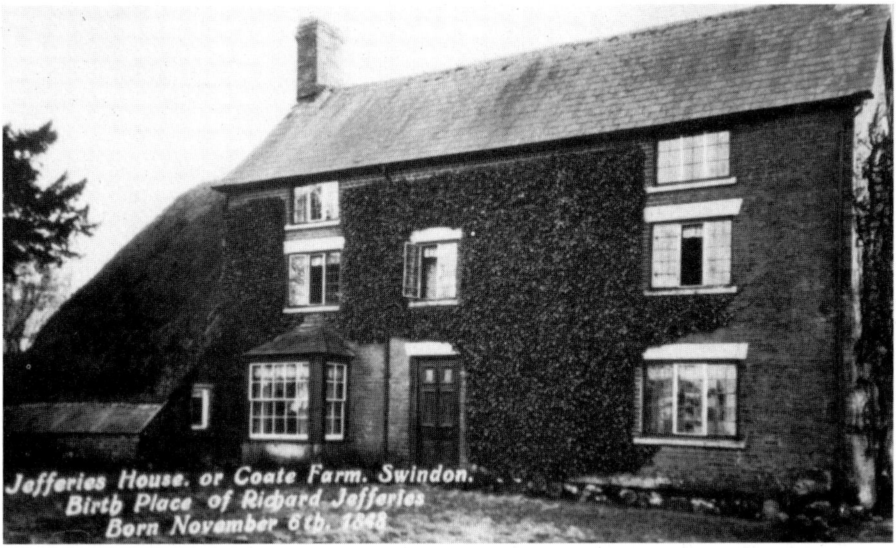

Coate Farm, birthplace of Richard Jefferies (1848–87), *c.* 1905. Richard Jefferies, author and poet, became a reporter on the *North Wilts Herald* and first became well known with a 4,000-word letter to *The Times* about the plight of Wiltshire agricultural workers. After his marriage in 1874 he moved nearer to London where he completed his most famous work, including novels *Hodge and his Masters* (1880) and *Bevis, The Story of a Boy* (1882).

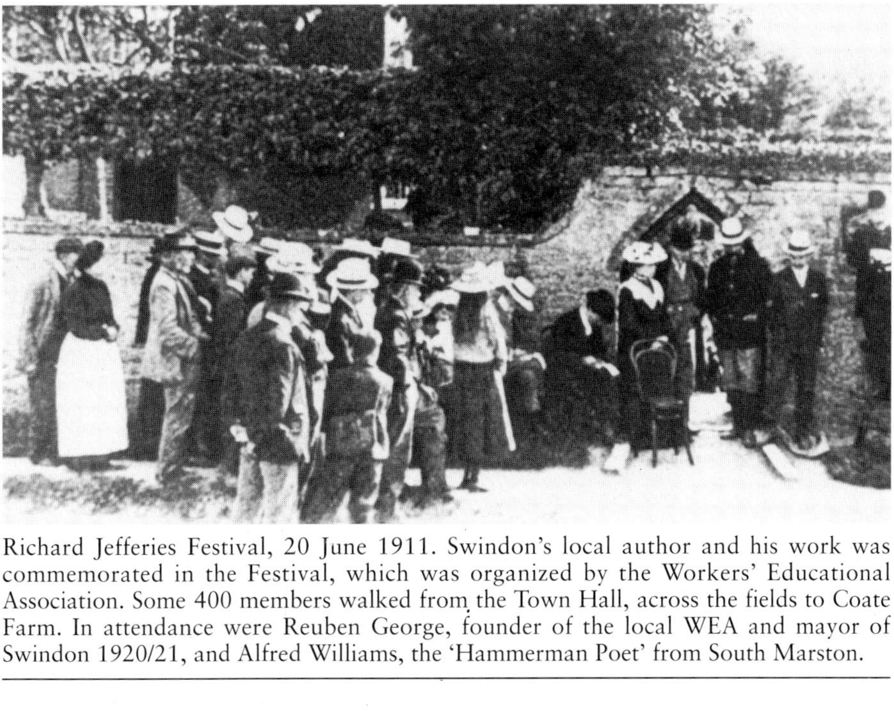

Richard Jefferies Festival, 20 June 1911. Swindon's local author and his work was commemorated in the Festival, which was organized by the Workers' Educational Association. Some 400 members walked from the Town Hall, across the fields to Coate Farm. In attendance were Reuben George, founder of the local WEA and mayor of Swindon 1920/21, and Alfred Williams, the 'Hammerman Poet' from South Marston.

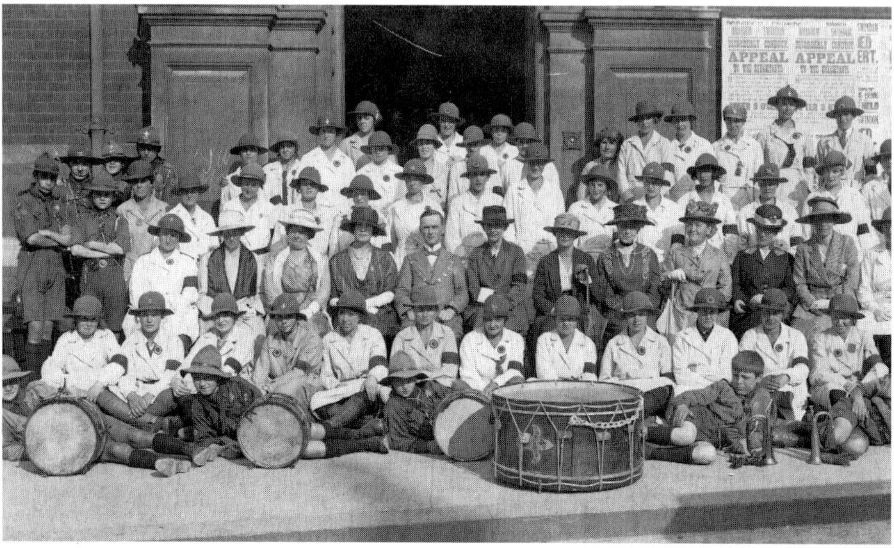

Boys and girls of uniformed youth organizations gathered outside the entrance to the Town Hall in July 1919 during the celebrations to mark the peace treaty which was signed on 28 June 1919 to formally end the First World War. At the centre of the group is the mayor, C.A. Plaister. The proclamation on the Town Hall notice-board in the right background, however, adds a sombre note (see p. 109).

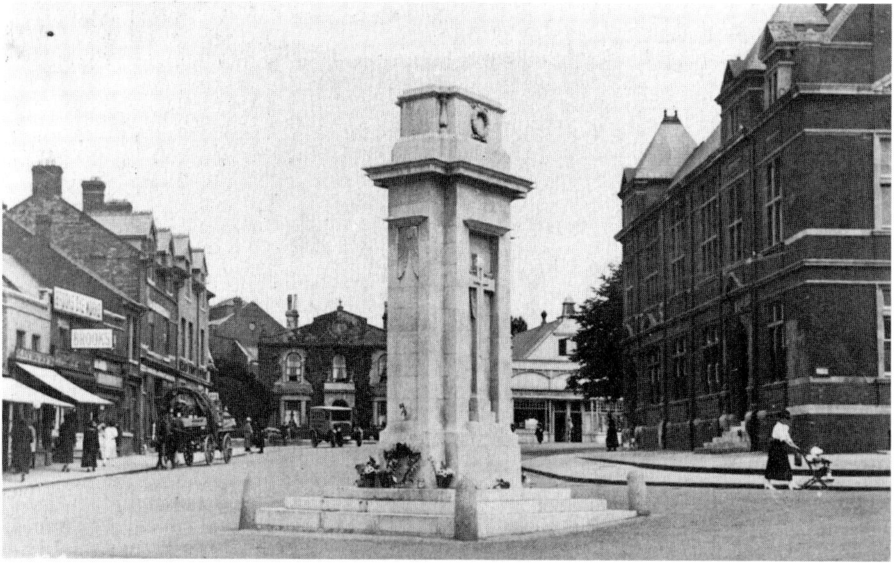

Cenotaph and Town Hall, *c.* 1925. In the left background are Dr Lavery's large villa and Bristol Tramways & Carriage Co. waiting rooms (formerly The Picture House cinema). The doctor's house – he had a joint practice with Dr Holland – was demolished in the late 1920s and the Regent Cinema built on the site.

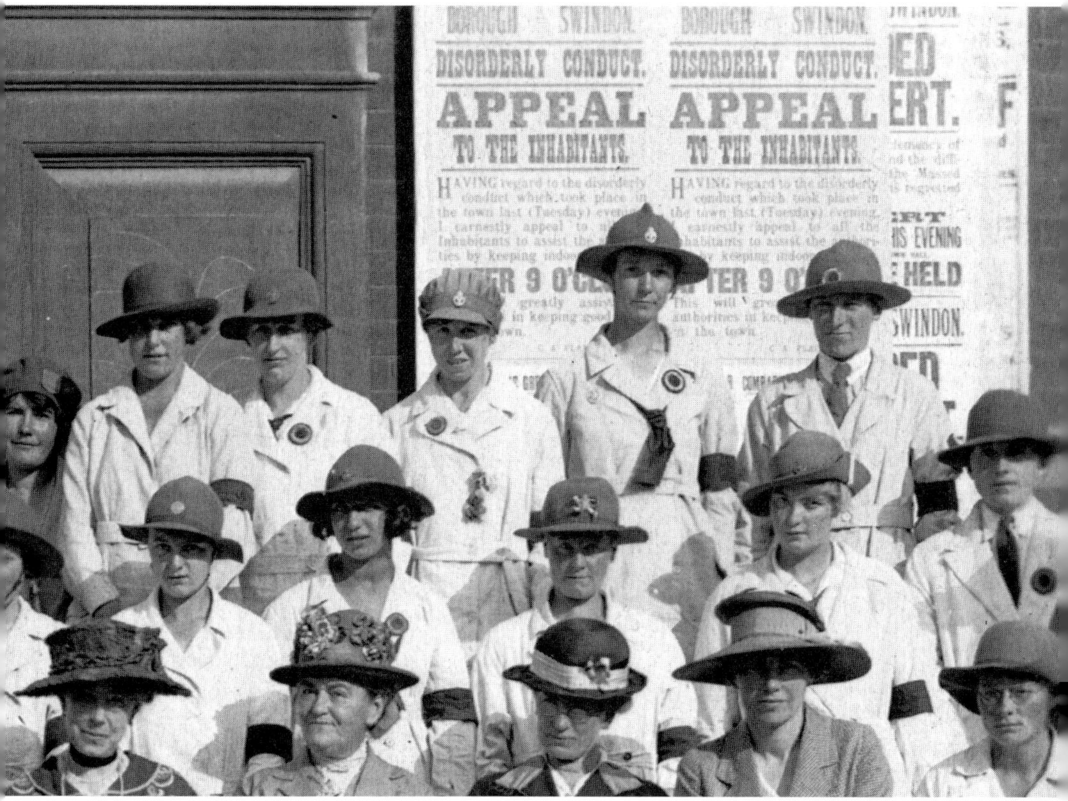

Curfew Over Swindon! The notice on the Town Hall reads:

DISORDERLY CONDUCT: APPEAL TO THE INHABITANTS. Having regard to the disorderly conduct which took place in the town last (Tuesday) evening, I earnestly appeal to all the inhabitants to assist the authorities in keeping indoors AFTER 9 O'CLOCK. This will greatly assist the authorities in keeping good order in the town. C.A. Plaister (Mayor).

'Peace Celebrations' to mark the official end to the First World War were fixed in Swindon for Saturday, 19 July 1919, with festivities continuing into the following week. A 50-ft flag-pole, complete with a large 'Peace Flag', was erected to the north-west of the Town Hall for the celebrations. During a procession on Monday evening, 21 July, an ex-soldier made an inflammatory speech in which he criticized the Council for spending £200 on a new flag-staff while ignoring the plight of the many disabled ex-servicemen in the town. Incited by this fiery oratory, men rushed to the flag-staff, cut the shrouds and attempted to pull the pole out of its concrete foundations. The police were also helpless to prevent petrol being brought up, the flag-pole set alight, and finally brought down, surrounded by a singing and dancing crowd. The charred remains were carried down Regent Street in procession and thrown across the tram-rails at the Centre. Monday's disturbances became Tuesday's riot with the Labour Exchange and shops in the town centre having their windows smashed and looted. On Wednesday (23 July) the mayor issued the appeal shown above and the Swindon Trade Union organizations and ex-servicemen formed a picket that evening that patrolled the town until after midnight to prevent violence from flaring up again.

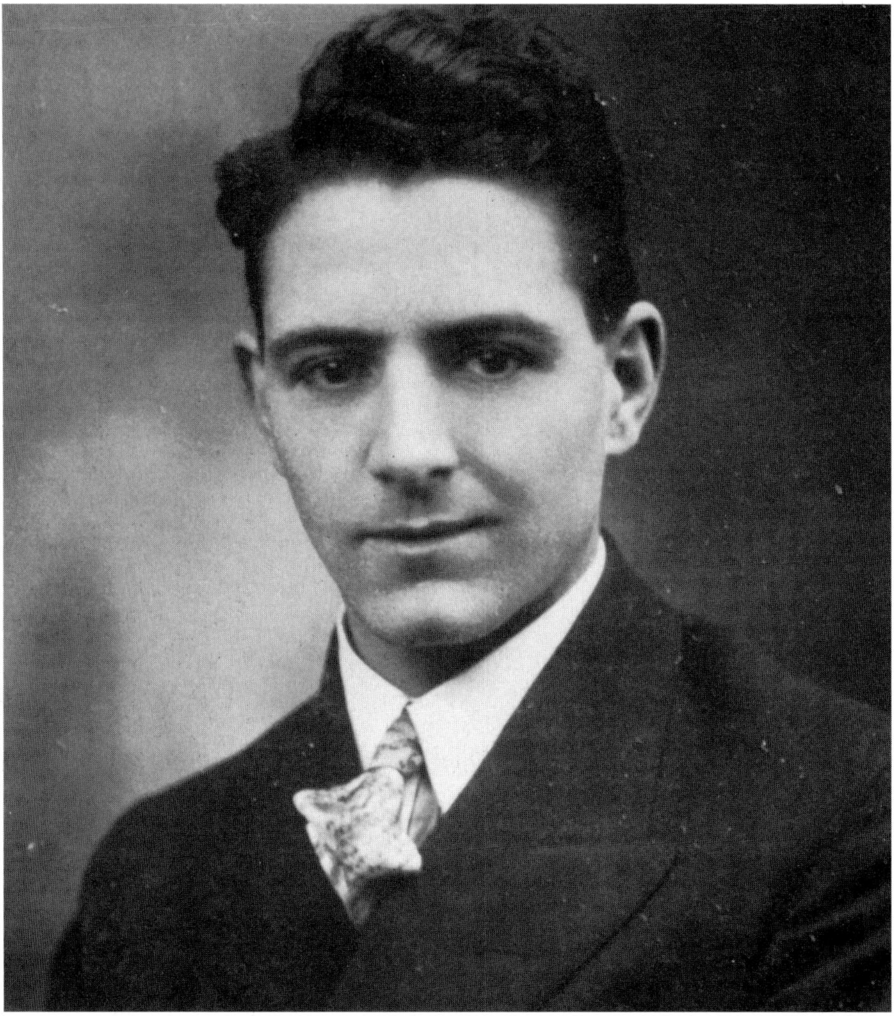

This photograph by L.C. Maylott of Faringdon Road is of Tom Williams in 1926. Born in Blaenavon in Wales, Williams started work at the age of 13 with woodworking machines in the local mines. Like many others in the Depression, with no likelihood of work he decided to leave for better opportunities. He walked from Wales to Swindon doing odd jobs and sleeping rough along the way. He reached Swindon late on a Friday afternoon, and seeking employment at Colbourne's timber yard in County Road was told there was a possibility if he returned on Monday morning. He slept in the shelter at Ferndale Road Recreation Ground over the weekend and was indeed offered employment. There followed many years working for the company, including the war years when he also served in the Civil Defence. In later years he worked for the local builders, Pope Brothers, as a wood machinist. Being a typical Welshman he enjoyed singing and was a well-known local soloist in competitions and Mayor's Balls in nearby towns. He was also a soloist at the Christ Church centenary celebrations. After retirement from work he sang with the Railway Veterans Choir.

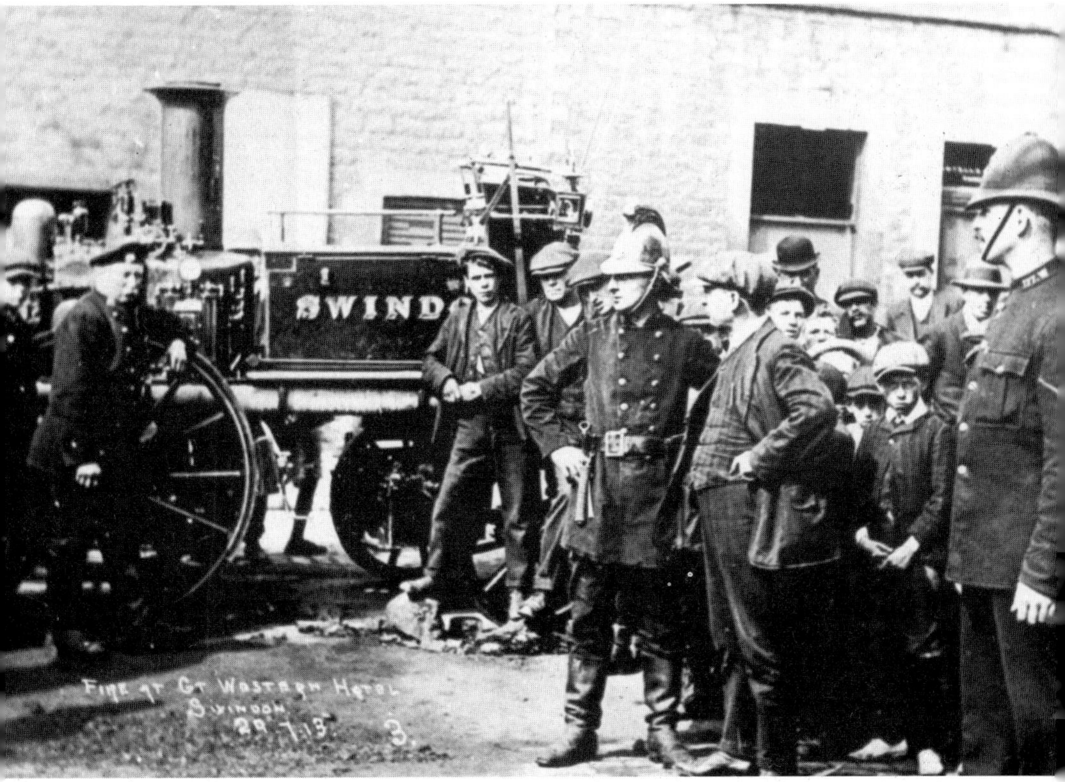

Fire at Great Western Hotel, Station Road, on 29 July 1913. The alarm was raised at 4.45 a.m. and the Swindon Fire Brigade was summoned to fight the fire which had broken out in the hotel's garage. Despite the effort of Captain J.N. Jefferies and his men, the garage could not be saved as it was soon well ablaze. Explosions could be heard over a wide area as the petrol tanks of the motor cars in the garage exploded. Eventually the roof collapsed and the brigade concentrated its efforts in trying to save the hotel itself and neighbouring properties. The brigade finally brought the fire under control by 8.15 a.m. but little remained of the two motor cars and other vehicles that had been in the garage except a few piles of twisted metalwork. The amount of damage was estimated at £2,000.

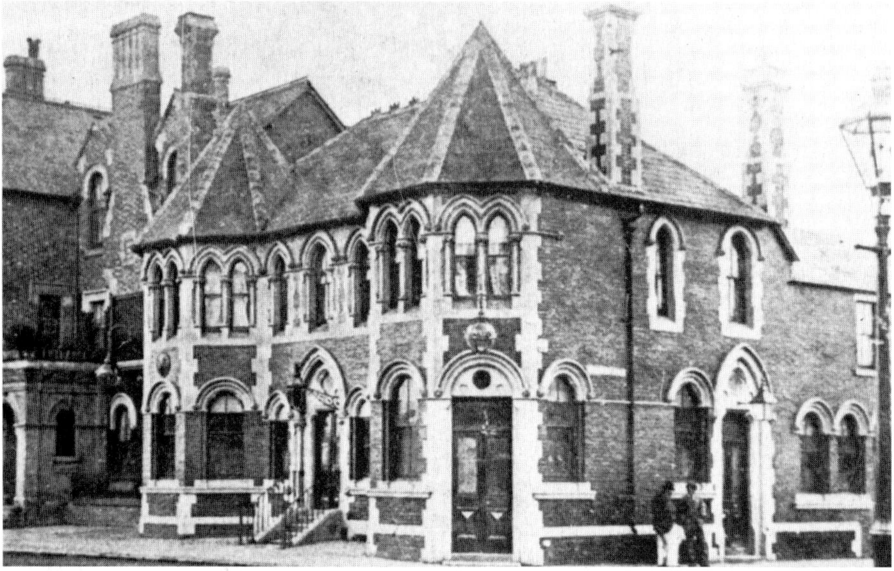

Great Western Hotel, Station Road, *c.* 1905. Built in 1870 with stables added two years later, the building was extended in 1904 with a large east wing of residential accommodation. For a while it was called the Noah's Ark after the Arkell's Brewery logo, and more recently renamed the Flag & Whistle.

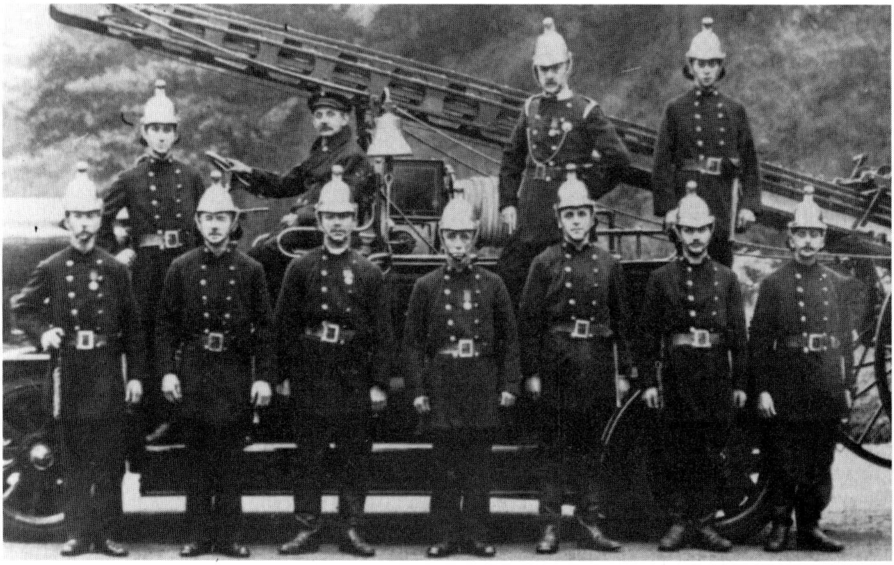

Swindon Fire Brigade, *c.* 1920. Formed in November 1879 under the command of Captain W.E. Morris, son of William Morris (see p. 13). The first headquarters was in Newport Street, but the fire brigade had moved to Cromwell Street by the turn of the century. It remained there until the new station was built in Drove Road in 1959.

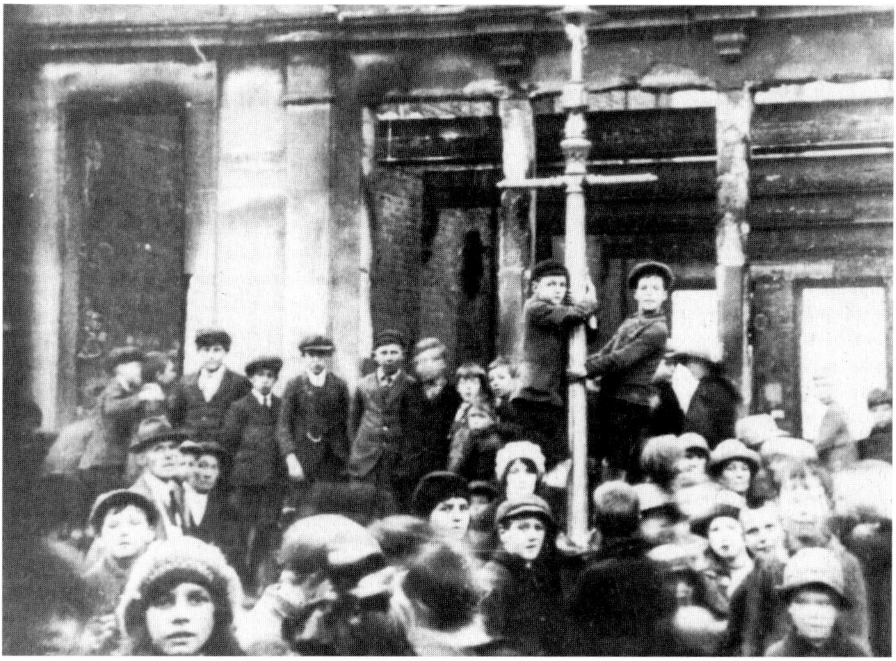

Young boys and other local people outside West Swindon Club, Radnor Street, after the serious fire in October 1923. See also *Swindon in Old Photographs (3)*, p. 127.

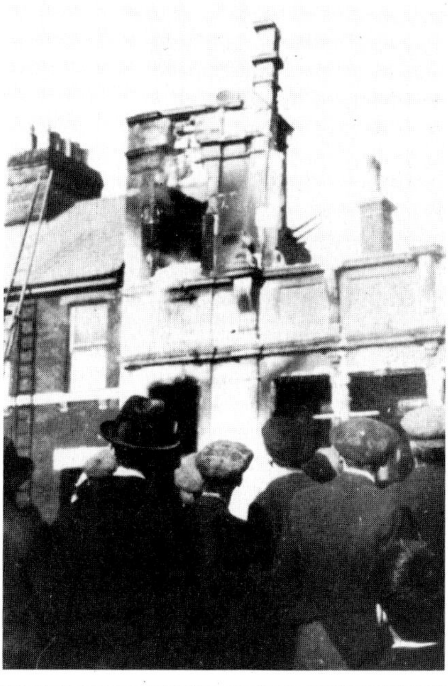

Fire damaged West Swindon Club, Radnor Street, after the conflagration of 4 October 1923.

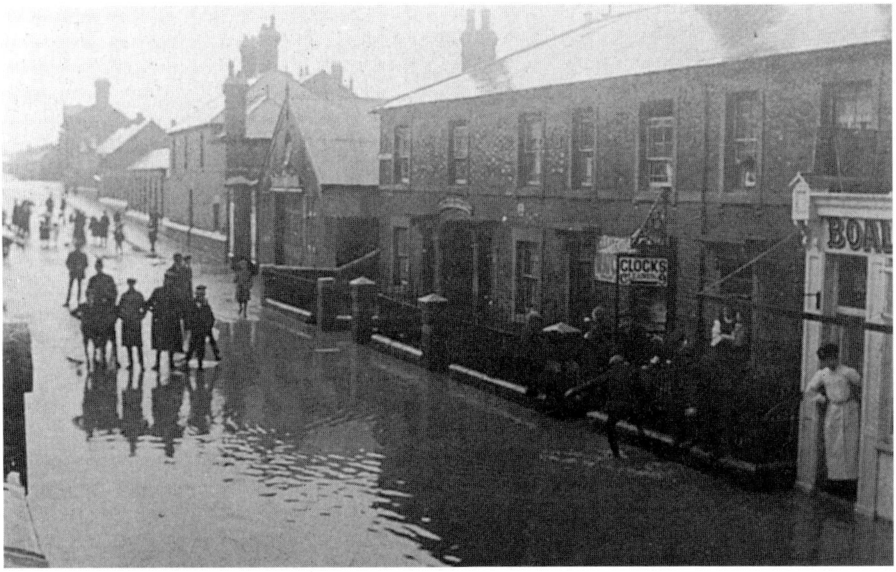

Floods in Cromwell Street, 25 July 1909. William Hooper took this view of the floods from his studio window. The water was just beginning to threaten the premises of T.A. Boalch, family butcher.

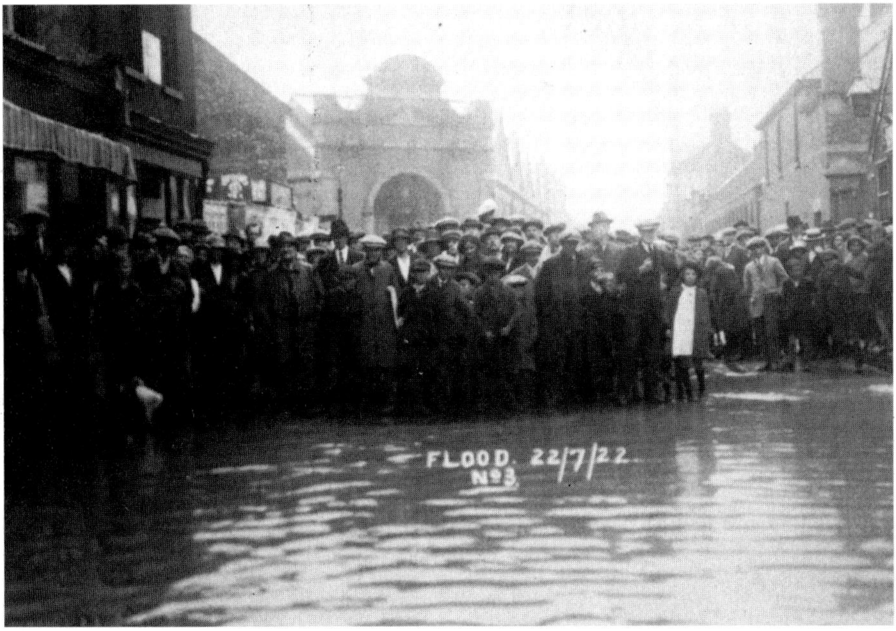

Floods in Cromwell Street, 22 July 1922, looking towards the market. The photograph was taken by Fred Palmer who had just taken over William Hooper's studio in Cromwell Street.

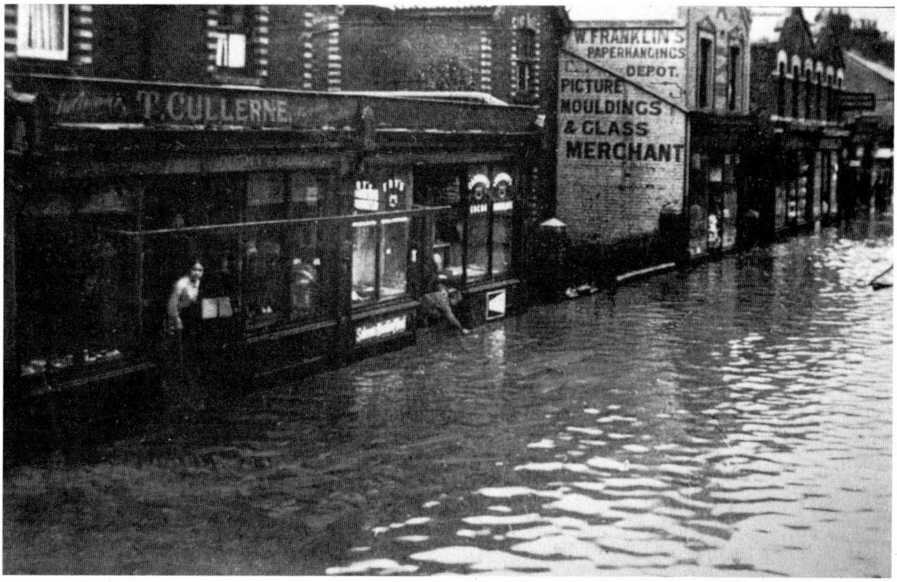

Cromwell Street under flood in July 1922. An assistant at the furniture dealers, T. Cullerne, looks out apprehensively at the scene. Note the decorators' supplies and glass merchants, W. Franklin, who remained trading in Cromwell Street until the area was redeveloped in the 1970s.

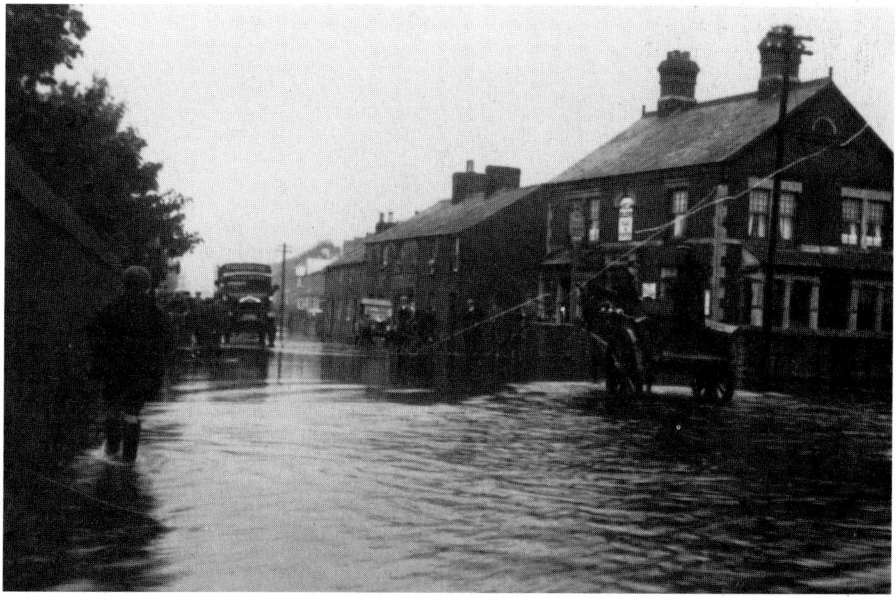

Wootton Bassett Road in flood in September 1927. In the background can be seen the Running Horse public house. The adjoining Ladd's Mill cottages were demolished in recent years to provide car parking space.

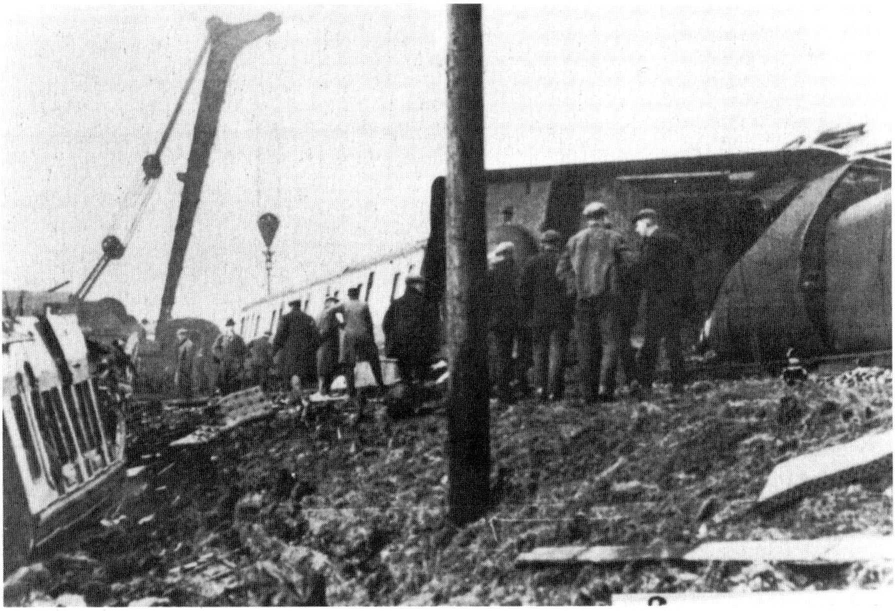

A train accident near Swindon, 15 January 1936. At 5 a.m. the Penzance–Paddington night sleeper train, drawn by 'King' class locomotive No. 6007 *King William III*, collided with some runaway wagons from a freight train. Two people were killed. The locomotive, after repair, was put back into service and not withdrawn until 1962.

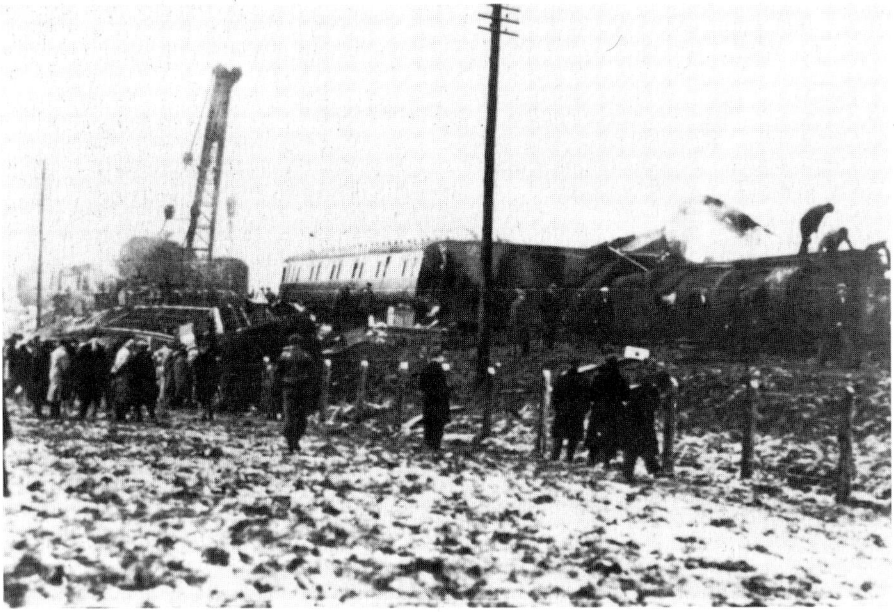

Another view of the accident in January 1936.

SECTION EIGHT

High Days, Holidays, Leisure & Sport

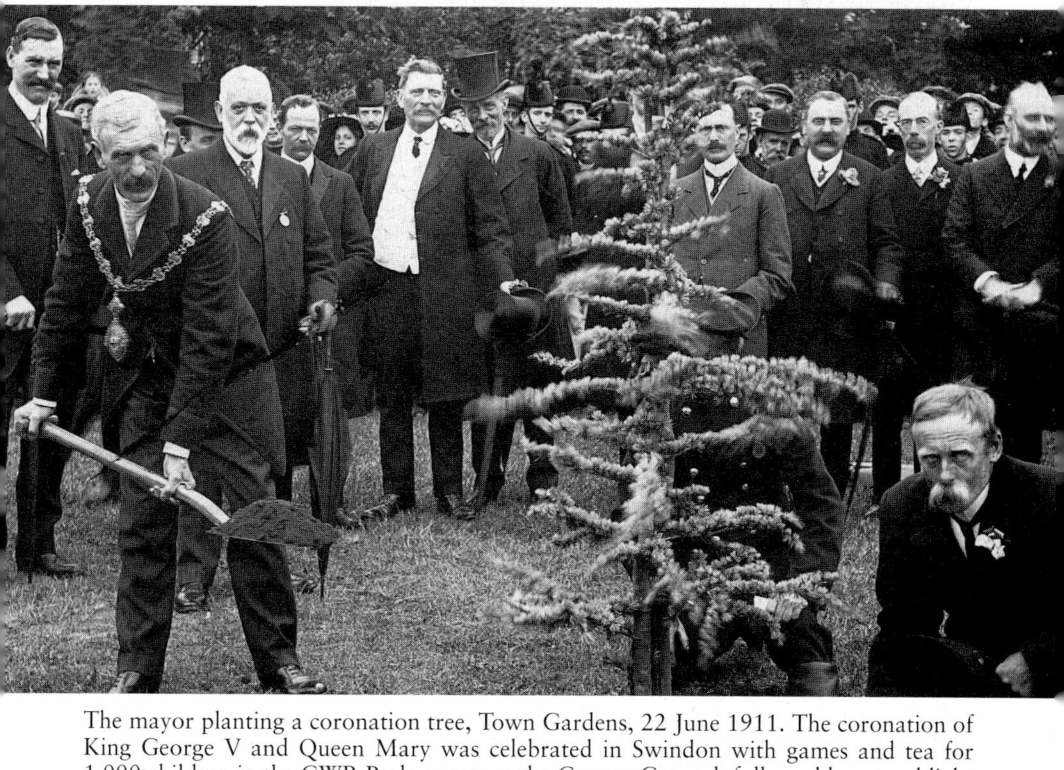

The mayor planting a coronation tree, Town Gardens, 22 June 1911. The coronation of King George V and Queen Mary was celebrated in Swindon with games and tea for 1,000 children in the GWR Park, sports at the County Ground, followed by a torchlight tattoo carried out by local Territorial Army units. Earlier in the day a thanksgiving service was held in Christ Church, after which a procession made its way via Wood Street and Bath Road to the Town Gardens. Here the mayor, Alderman Tom Butler, planted a blue cedar tree (*Cedrus Atlantica Glauca*) to commemorate the coronation. The tree, now fully mature, can still be seen today in the grass close to Quarry Road Lodge in the Town Gardens.

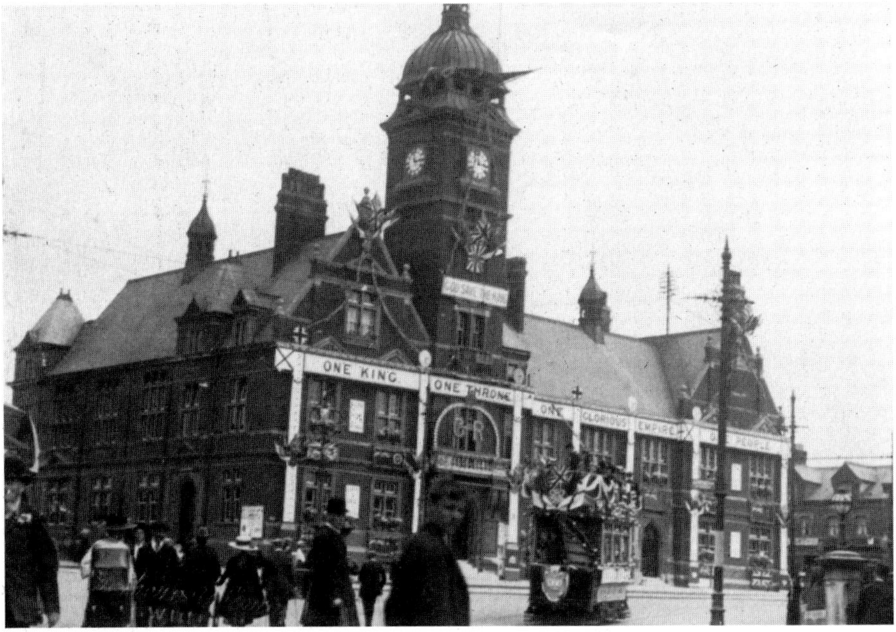

The decorated Town Hall and tramcar during celebrations for the coronation of King George V and Queen Mary in June 1911. The tramcar carried 200 coloured lights. See *Swindon in Old Photographs (1)*, p. 119, and *(3)*, p. 88.

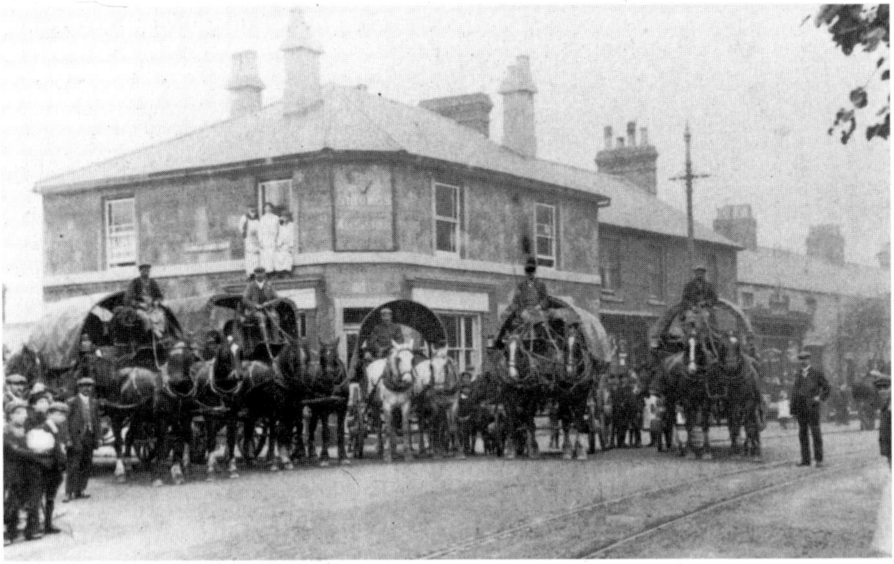

Covered wagons outside The Grapes public house in Faringdon Road, *c*. 1910. The occasion is not known.

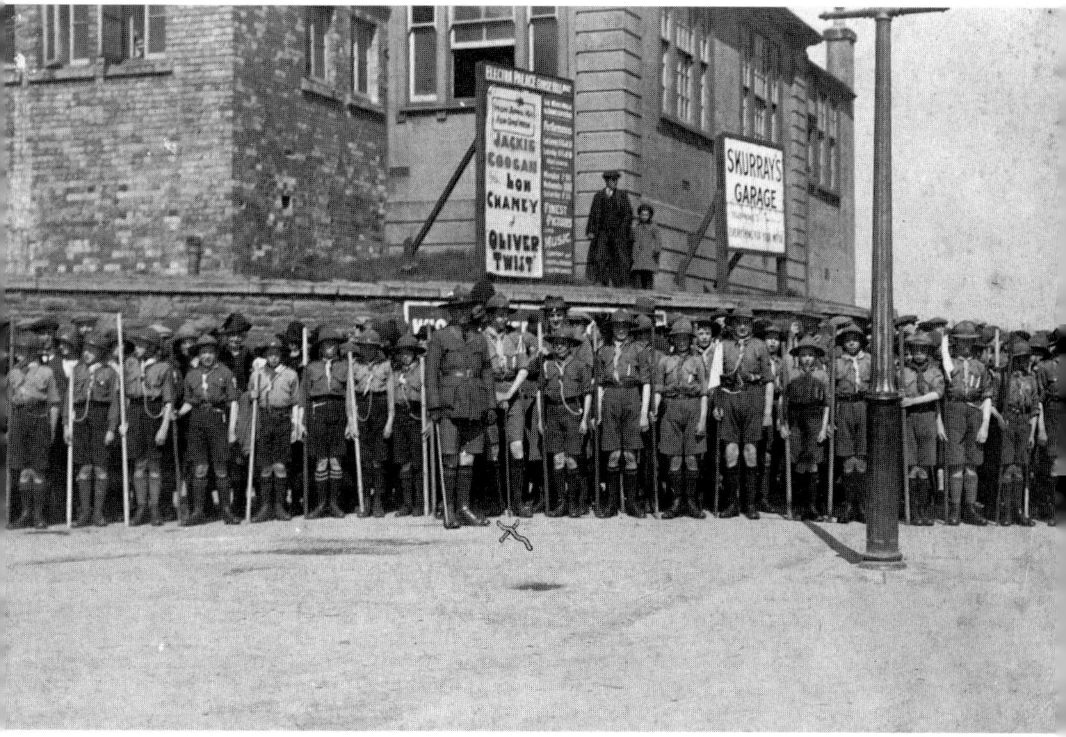

Boy scouts outside the entrance to the GWR junction station, waiting to greet HRH Princess Helena Victoria (granddaughter of Queen Victoria) on her visit to Swindon on Saturday 21 April 1923. The princess, who was president of the YMCA Women's Auxilliary, came to the town to open the YMCA Red Triangle Boys' Club in Fleet Street. She was met at the station by the mayor, A.E. Harding, Major F.P. Goddard, Major General T.C.P. Calley, and other local dignitaries. Luncheon was later held at the Queens Royal Hotel (Refreshment Rooms) at the GWR station after which a procession of cars took the princess and guests to the Town Hall for a civic reception. The Swindon YMCA headquarters and Red Triangle Club at 20 Fleet Street (see *Swindon in Old Photographs (2)*, p. 45) later became showrooms and offices for the Southern Electricity Board and is now an amusement arcade. Note the advertisement for the film *Oliver Twist*, starring Jackie Coogan and Lon Chaney, at the Electra Palace cinema in Gorse Hill.

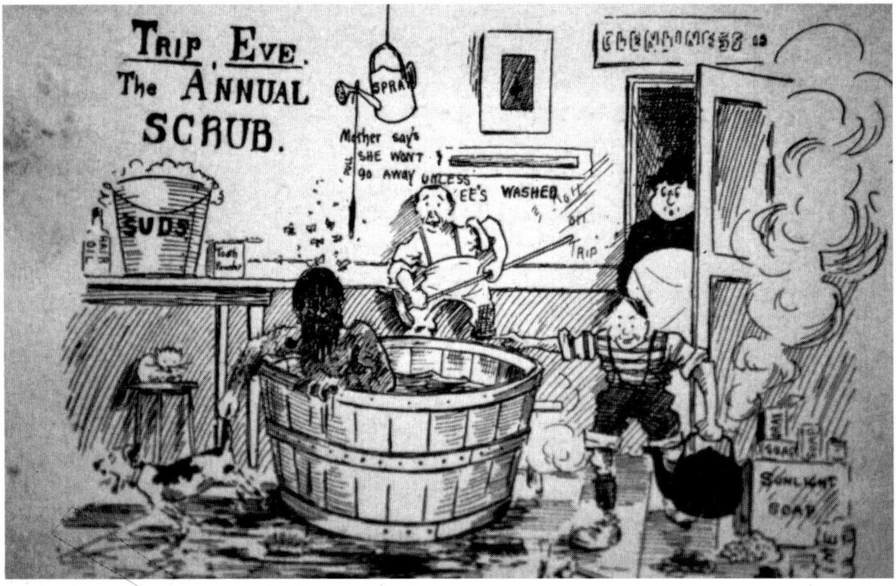

Trip Eve, *c.* 1910, 'The Annual Scrub' for the railwayman. The evening before the great exodus was one of intense excitement, and all the family would dress in their best clothes for the journey. The cartoon shows all the ingredients for the wash – Sunlight soap, tooth powder and hair oil.

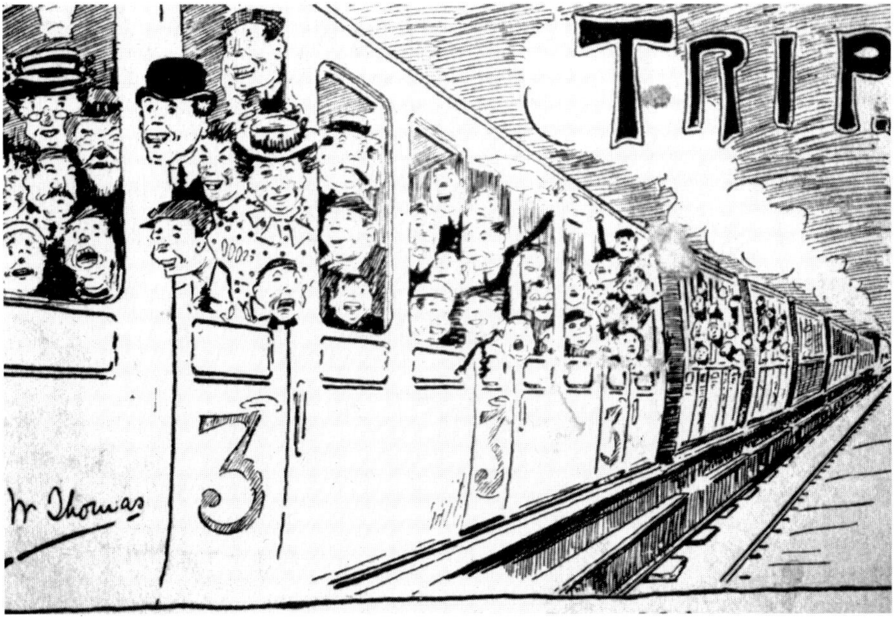

The Departure of the Great Mob, *c.* 1910. Another 'Trip' postcard purchased by the families and sent back to relations who remained at home.

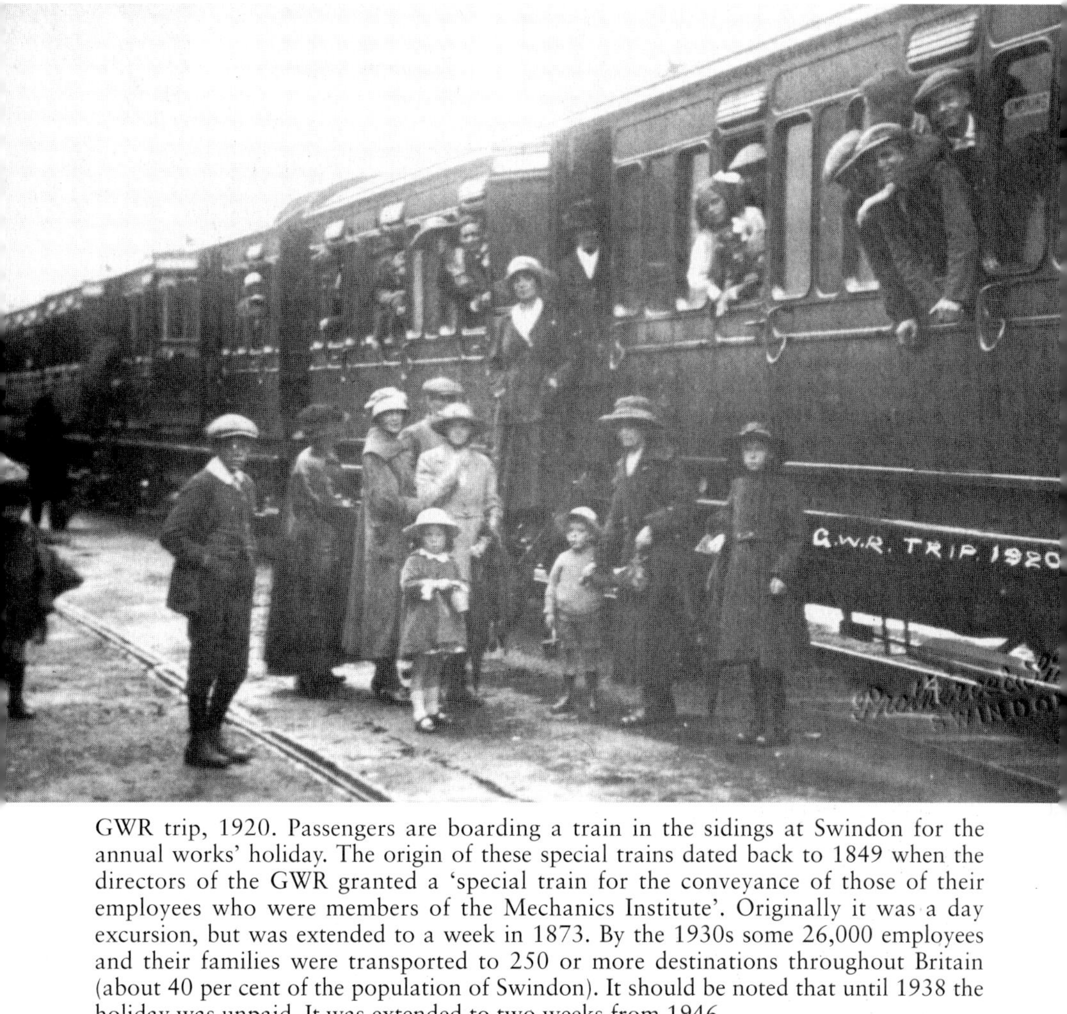

GWR trip, 1920. Passengers are boarding a train in the sidings at Swindon for the annual works' holiday. The origin of these special trains dated back to 1849 when the directors of the GWR granted a 'special train for the conveyance of those of their employees who were members of the Mechanics Institute'. Originally it was a day excursion, but was extended to a week in 1873. By the 1930s some 26,000 employees and their families were transported to 250 or more destinations throughout Britain (about 40 per cent of the population of Swindon). It should be noted that until 1938 the holiday was unpaid. It was extended to two weeks from 1946.

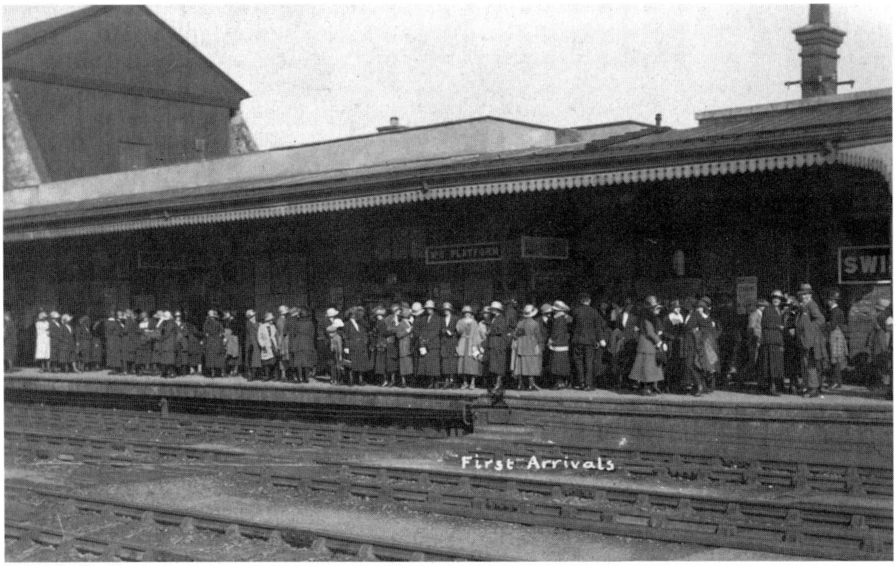

'Trippers' waiting for their trains, GWR junction station, May 1923. This time, however, these were not GWR workers but girls from Wills tobacco factory, off to London on a day excursion.

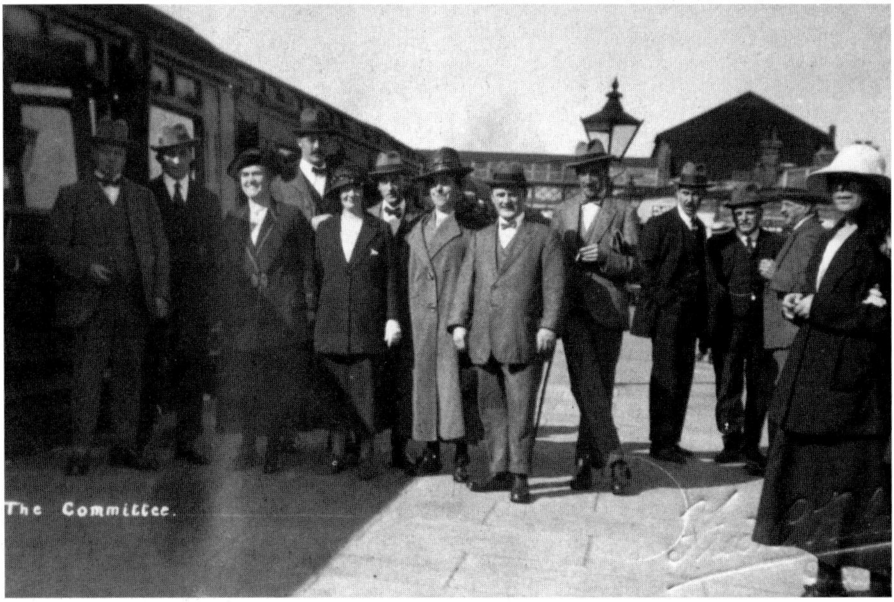

Wills factory outing to London, 26 May 1923. This photograph shows the factory excursion committee posing on the platform at the GWR junction station before boarding their special train to Paddington. Eleven charabancs were hired in London to carry the passengers on a sightseeing trip around the city.

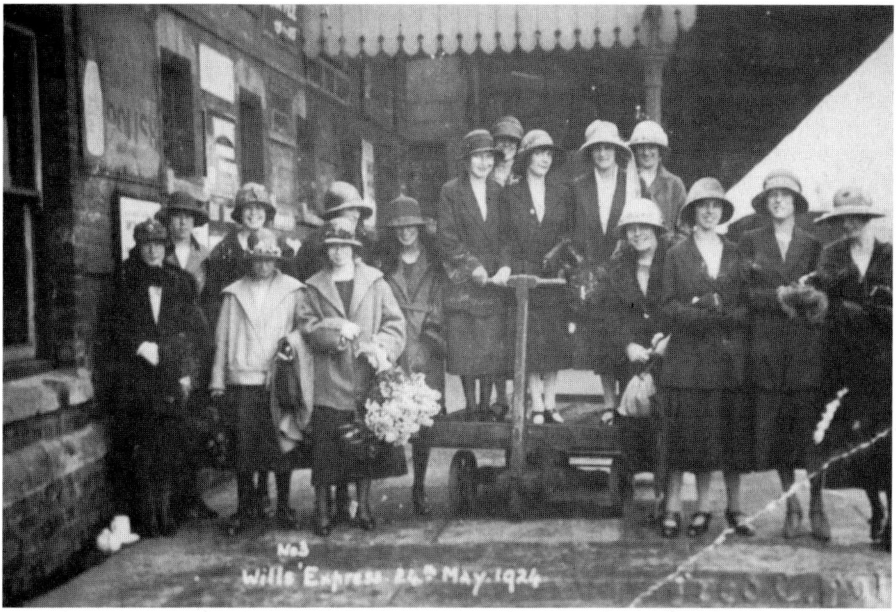

'The Wills' Express.' Wills factory outing from the GWR station, 24 May 1924.

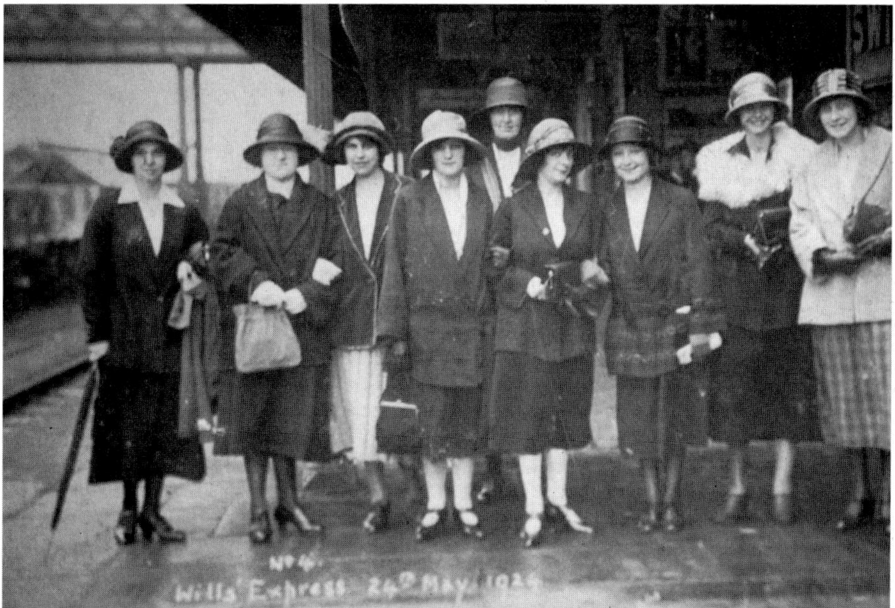

Another view of Wills factory girls, waiting for their train in May 1924. The *Wills Magazine* commented ' . . . a special train has been chartered to visit the British Empire Exhibition at Wembley. Over 400 have signified their intention of going.'

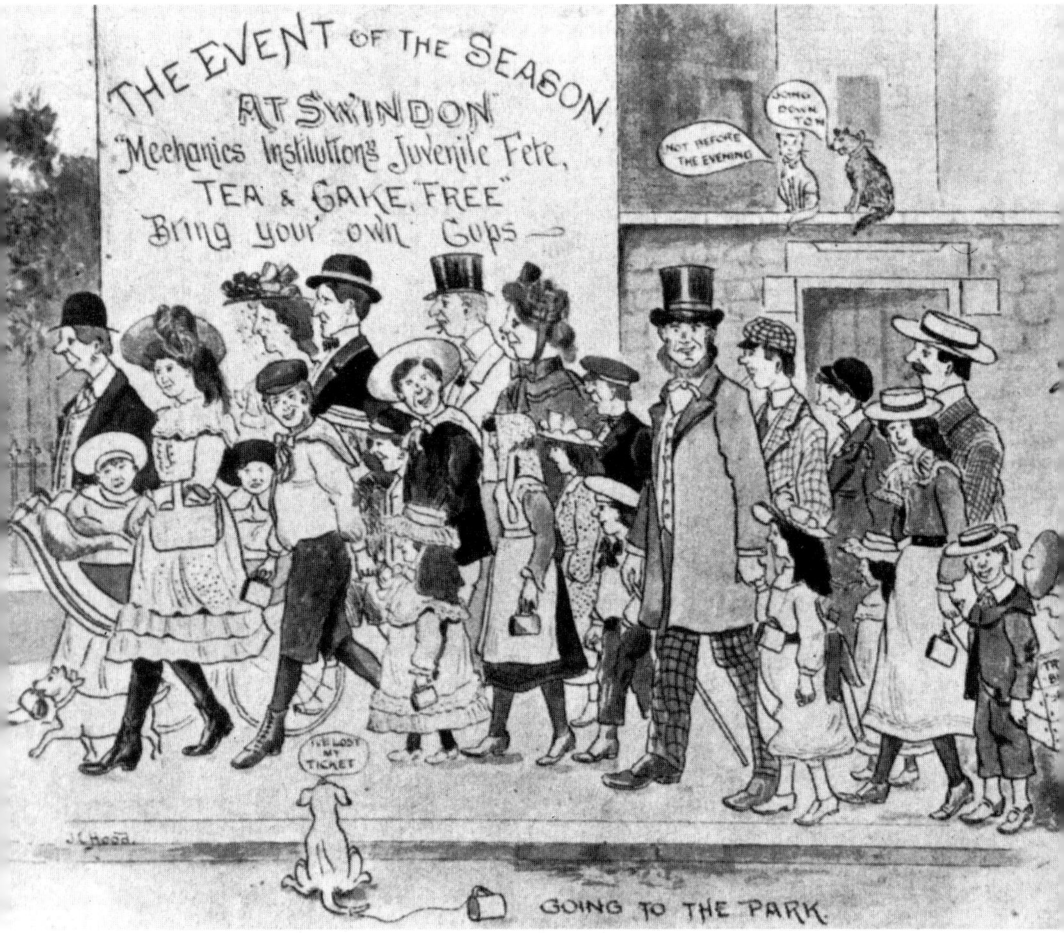

Comic postcard, 1906, depicting crowds *en route* to the Children's Fête in the GWR Park. 'Tea & Cake Free', 'Bring your own Cups'. Note the dog in the foreground with his cup. The Children's Fête was the most important family social event of the year in railway Swindon. Usually held on the second Saturday in August at the GWR Park in Faringdon Road, it was a tradition for each child to receive, on entry, a packet containing a $\frac{1}{2}$ lb slab of fruit cake and a free roundabout ride ticket. Until the 1920s the cake was supplied in 5 lb slabs then cut into $\frac{1}{2}$ lb slices and packed. This task, carried out by volunteers, became increasingly more time consuming over the years and eventually a special cake-cutting machine was designed and built for the purpose by Mr Harvie, manager of the Trimming Shop (see p. 125). In 1904 the attendance at the Fête was 38,000 and some 4 tons of cake were distributed (see p. 91).

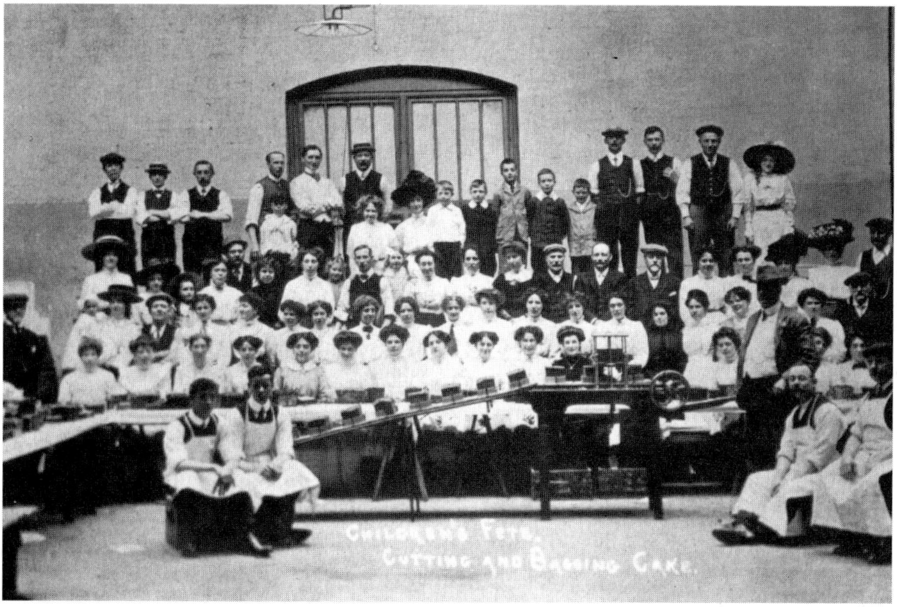

Cake cutting and packing in the Drill Hall, Mechanics Institute Children's Fête, *c*. 1910.

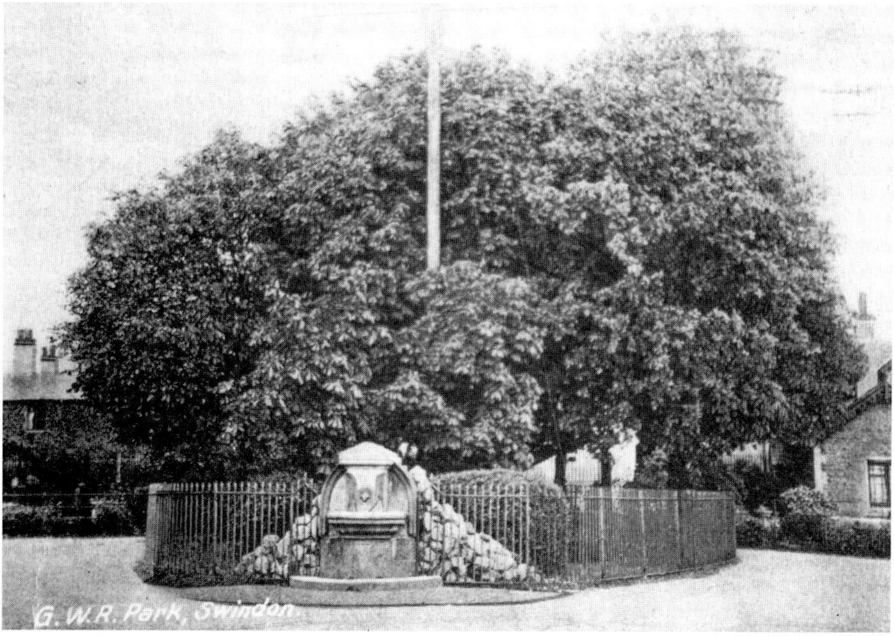

Ornamental drinking fountain, GWR Park, Faringdon Road, *c*. 1910. The metal drinking cups were attached to chains. They were removed during the Second World War.

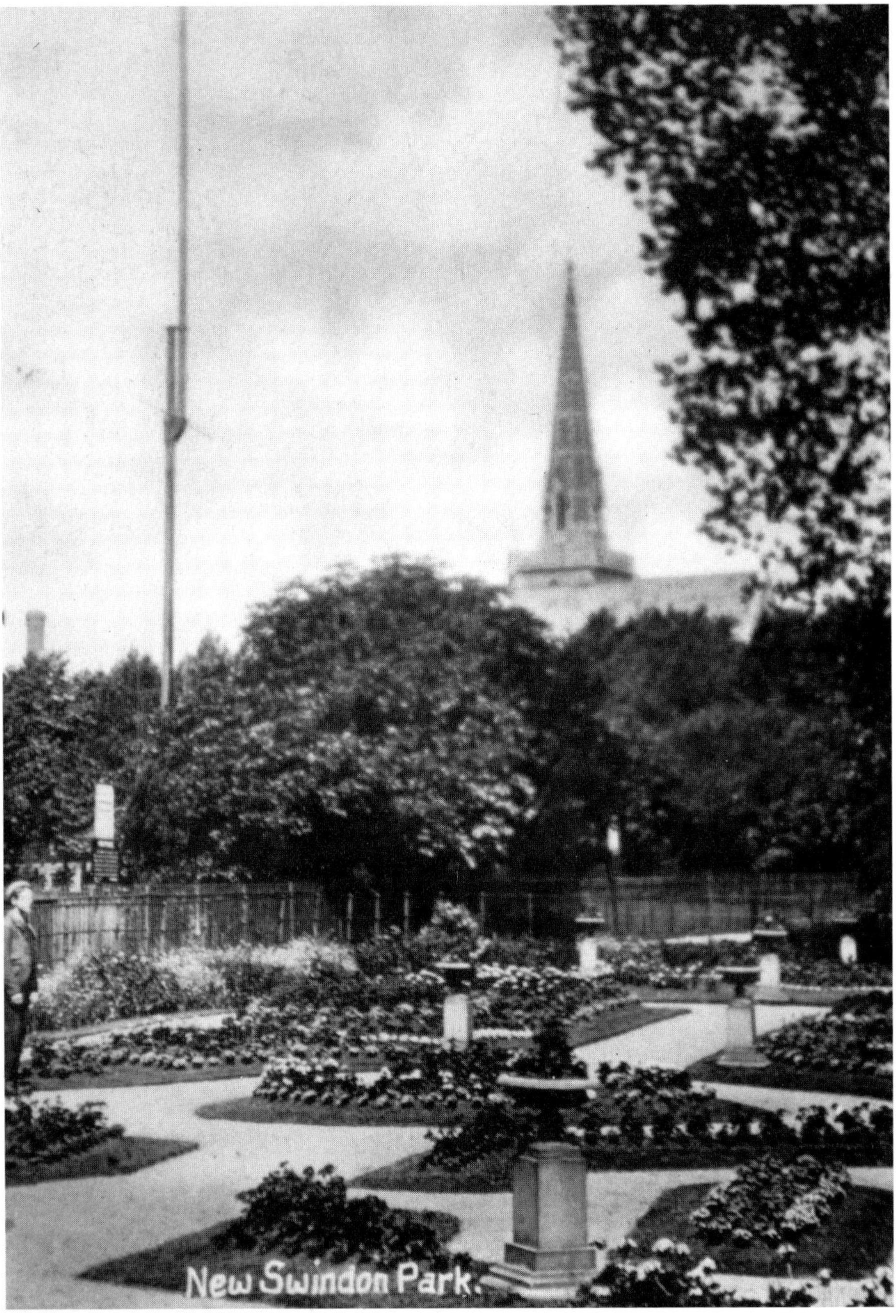

Formal gardens in the GWR Park, *c.* 1910. In the background is the spire of St Mark's church. The church was designed by the young Gilbert (later Sir Gilbert) Scott and consecrated in April 1845.

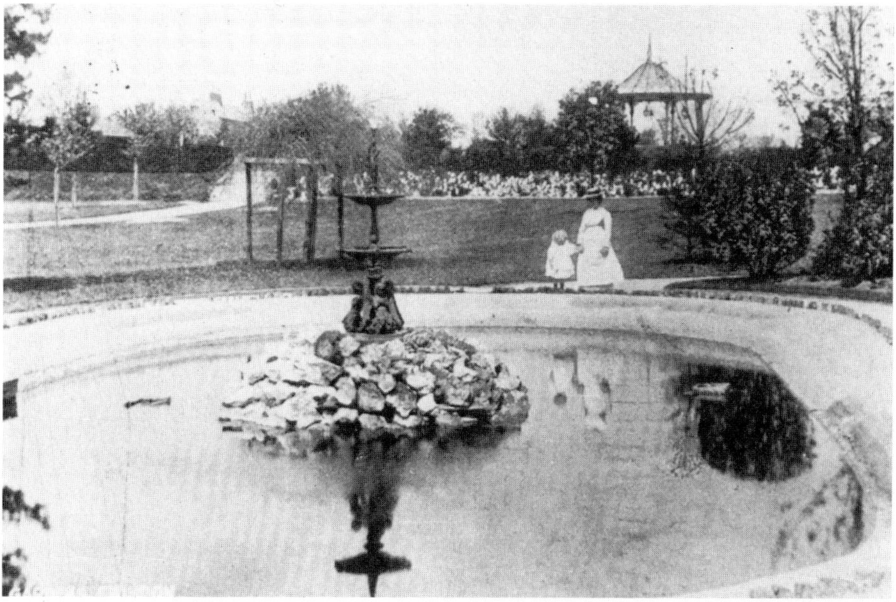

Town Gardens, *c.* 1905, with an Edwardian mother and child admiring the ornamental pond and fountain. Built in 1893/4 on a seven-acre plot of land near the old Okus quarries, the gardens have brought pleasure to Swindonians for a century.

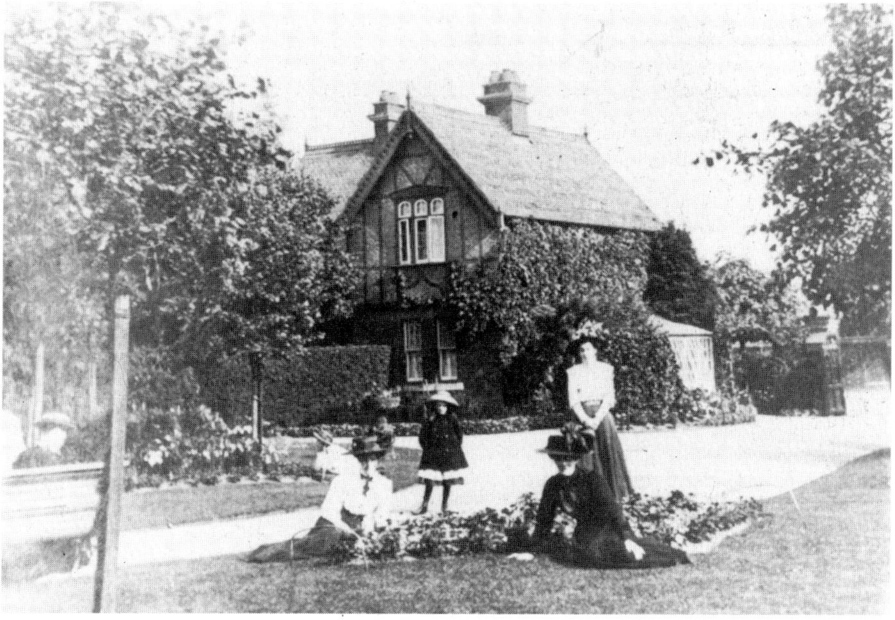

Park-keeper's lodge and Edwardian family, Town Gardens, *c.* 1910. A view little changed today.

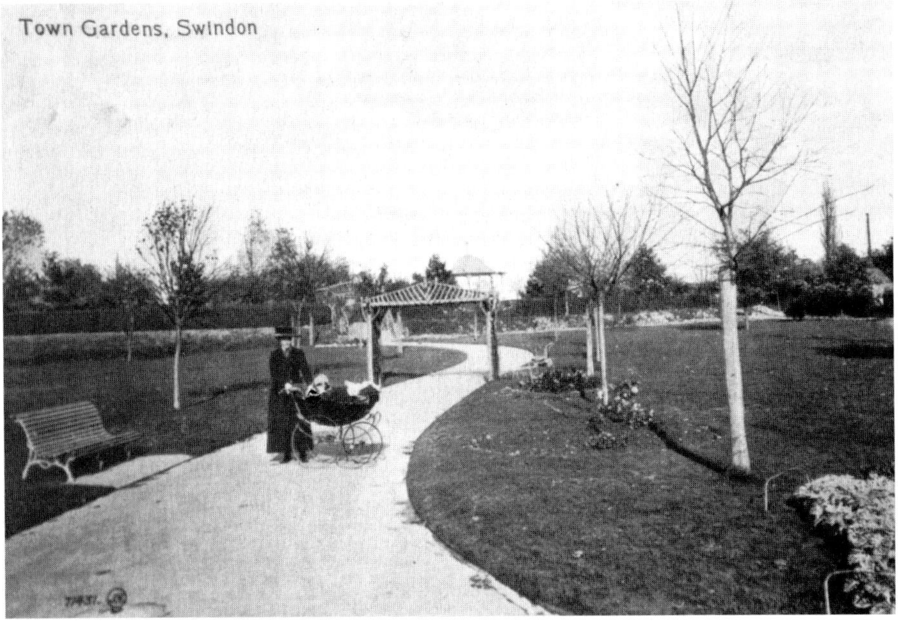

Town Gardens, *c.* 1905. Newly laid out, these saplings are now large mature trees.

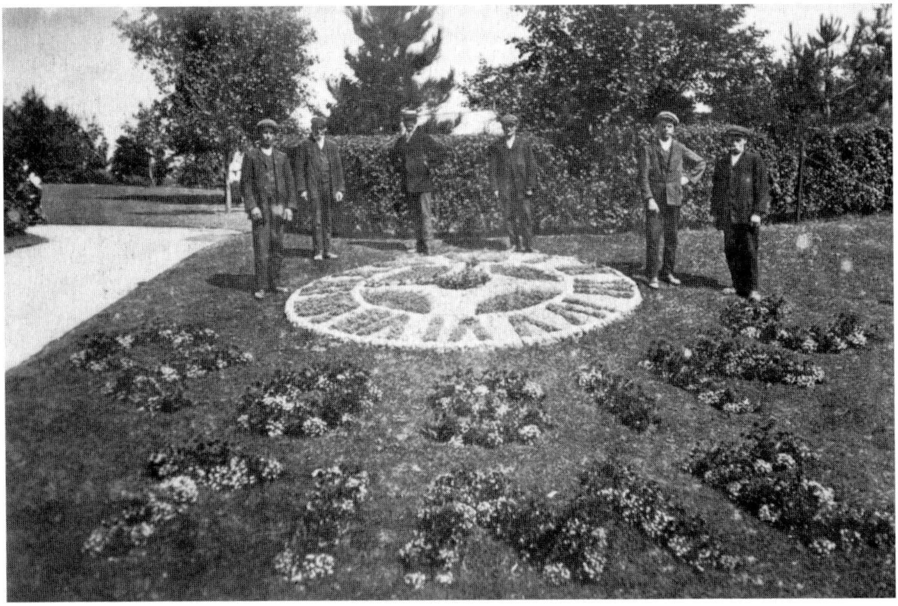

Floral clock, Town Gardens, *c.* 1910. A large workforce enabled elaborate displays to be made.

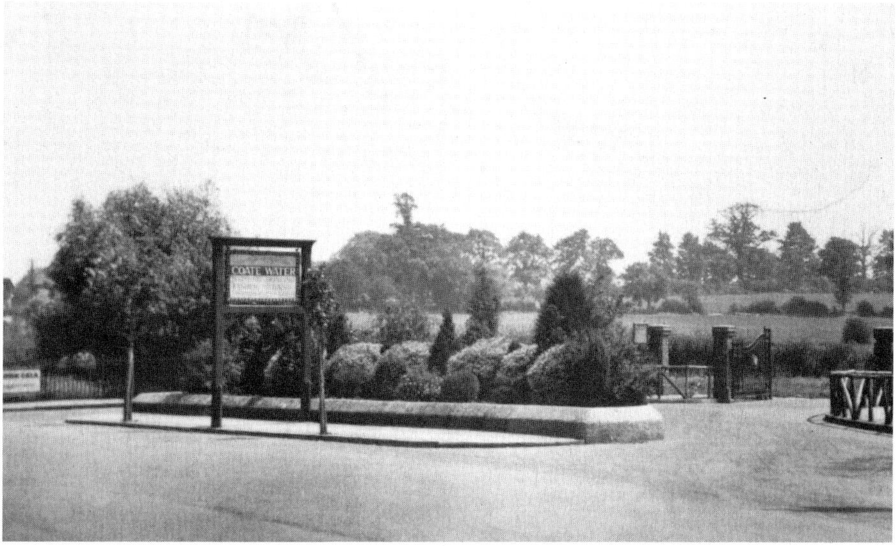

Main entrance to Coate Reservoir and bus lay-by, Marlborough Road, *c.* 1930. Swindon Corporation began its first motor bus service on 15 April 1927, using Leyland Lion single-decker buses to Coate Reservoir. Over 3,400 passengers were carried that day and by the middle of the following week receipts had topped £200 (the single fare being only 3d.).

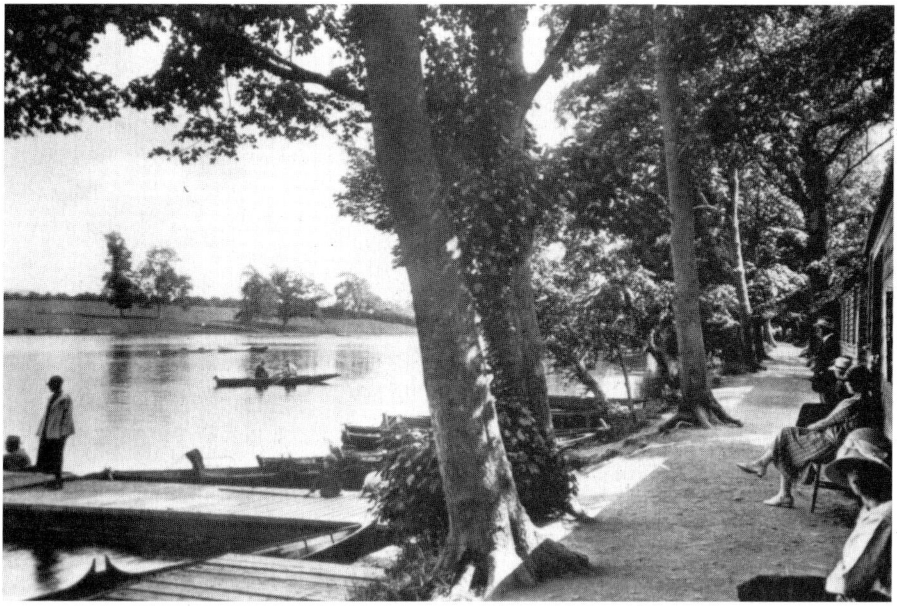

Coate Reservoir, showing the boats and landing stages on the west shore, *c.* 1920. Sunbathing was not fashionable, so ladies wore hats and sat in the shade.

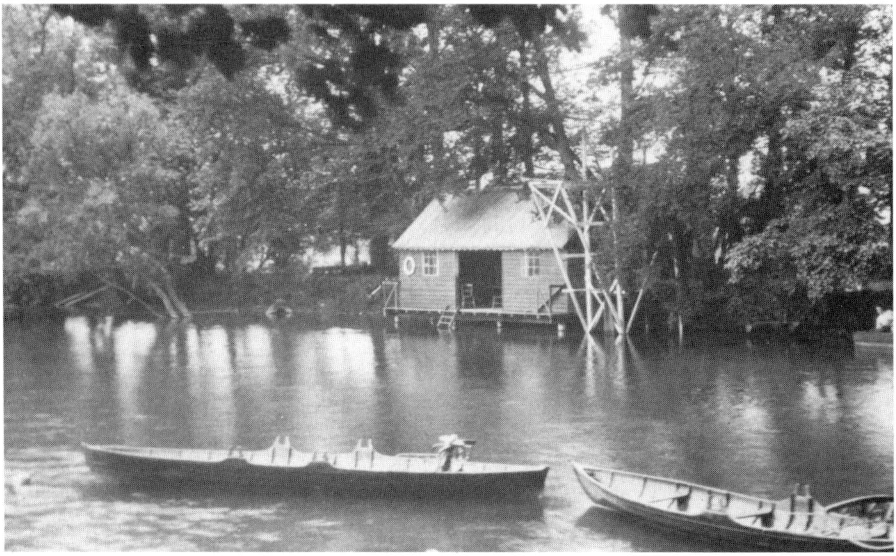

Original boat-house and diving board, Coate Reservoir, *c.* 1905. The reservoir was constructed in 1822 as a feeder for the Wilts. & Berks. Canal. For many generations of Swindonians it has been a place for leisure activities and relaxation.

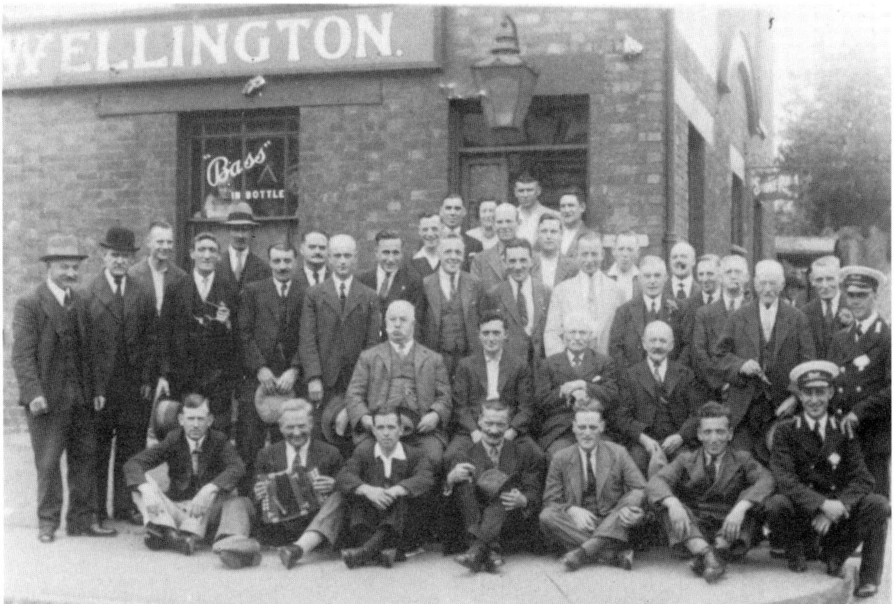

Duke of Wellington, Eastcott Hill, *c.* 1935. A group of visitors on a summer outing to Swindon poses outside this public house with the Bristol Bus Company driver and conductor.

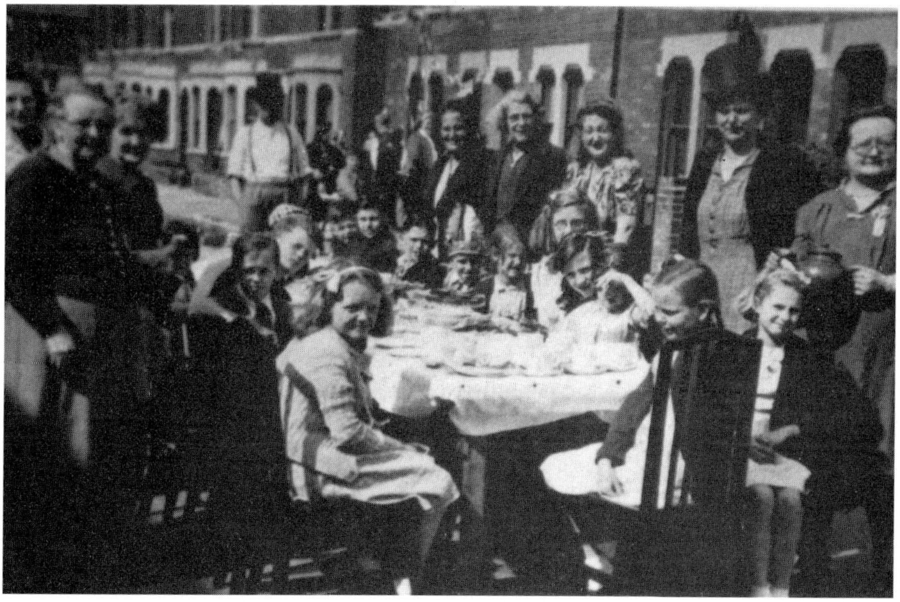

Rosebery Street, VE Day party, May 1945.

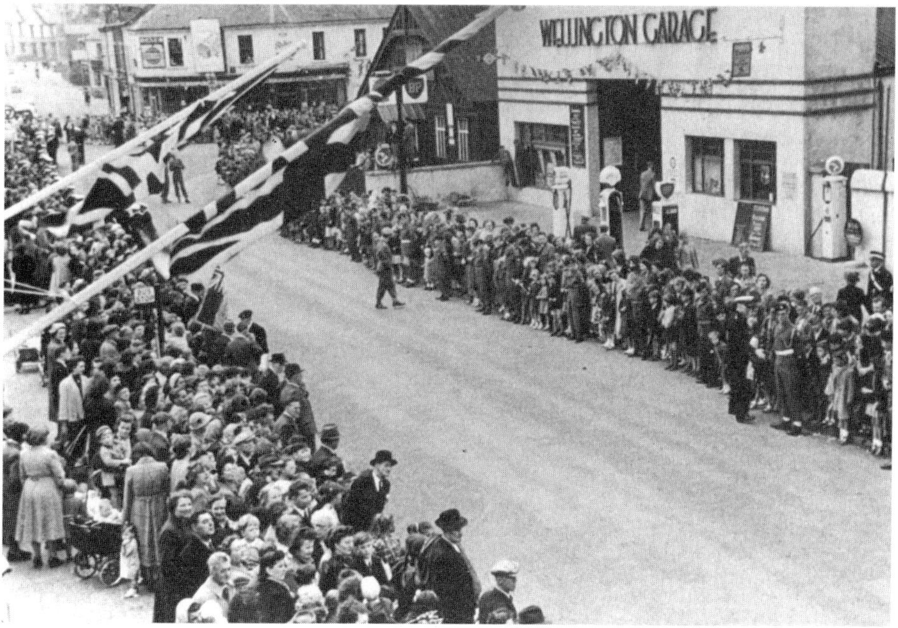

Wellington Street, viewed from a window in the Great Western Hotel, with crowds gathered for the visit of HRH Princess Elizabeth on 15 November 1950. All the buildings seen in this photograph have now been demolished and replaced by modern office blocks.

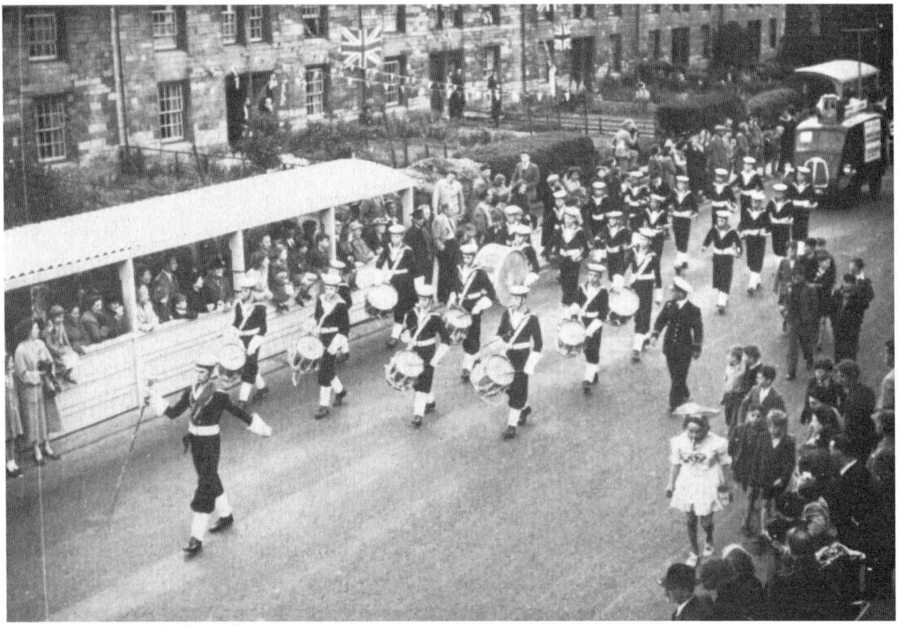

Parade of sea cadets, Faringdon Road, during celebrations for the coronation of Queen Elizabeth II, June 1953. In the background are houses in the Railway Village.

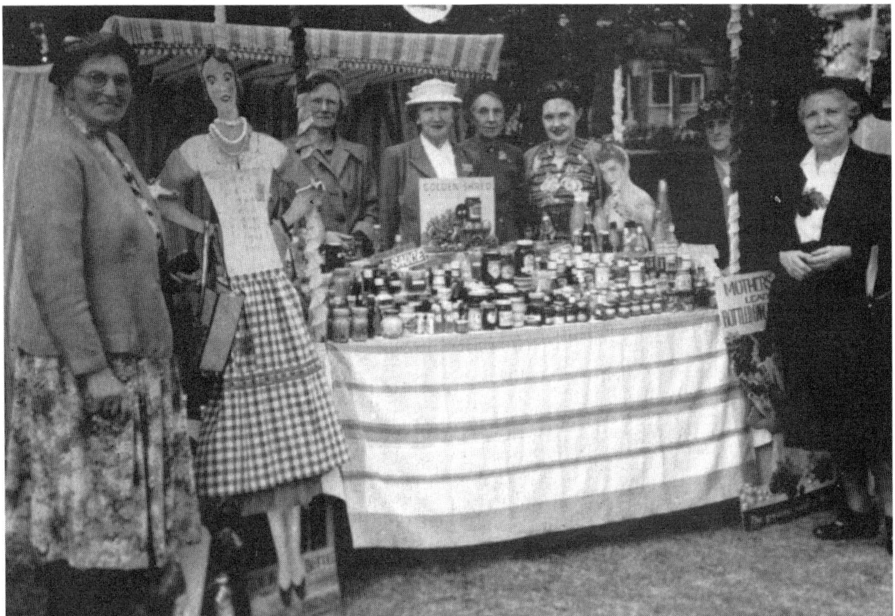

Coronation Fête, 1953.

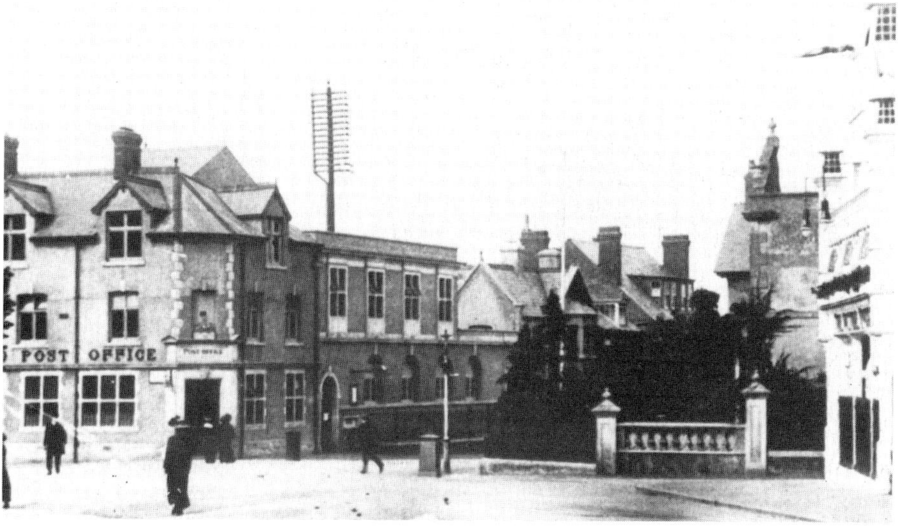

Head Post Office, Regent Circus, 1913. To the right is The Picture House, one of Swindon's first cinemas.

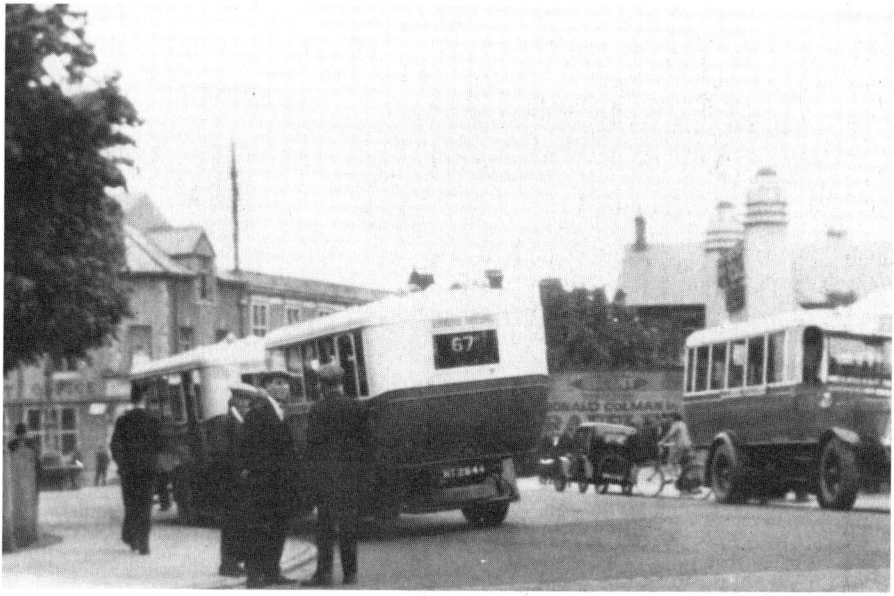

Regent Circus, *c.* 1931. Early 4-ton Bristol buses wait for passengers at their Town Hall terminus. The bus (No. 67) on the left is bound for Fairford, the one on the right for Chippenham. Ronald Coleman is appearing in the film *Raffles* at the Regent Cinema, which opened in 1929.

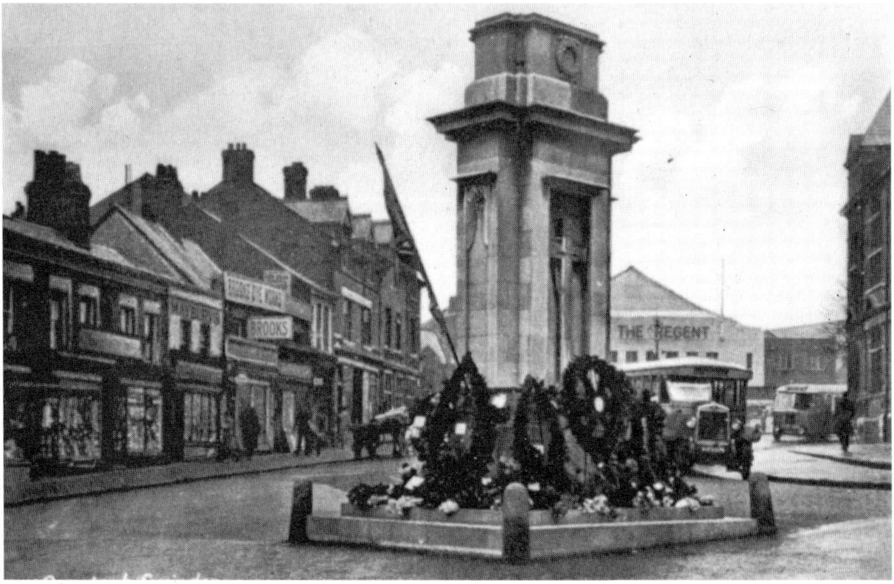

Cenotaph, Regent Circus, *c.* 1936. In the background the restyled and enlarged Regent Cinema and Bristol B-type buses. The cenotaph was unveiled in October 1920 to replace a temporary wooden one (see *Swindon in Old Photographs (1)*, p. 131).

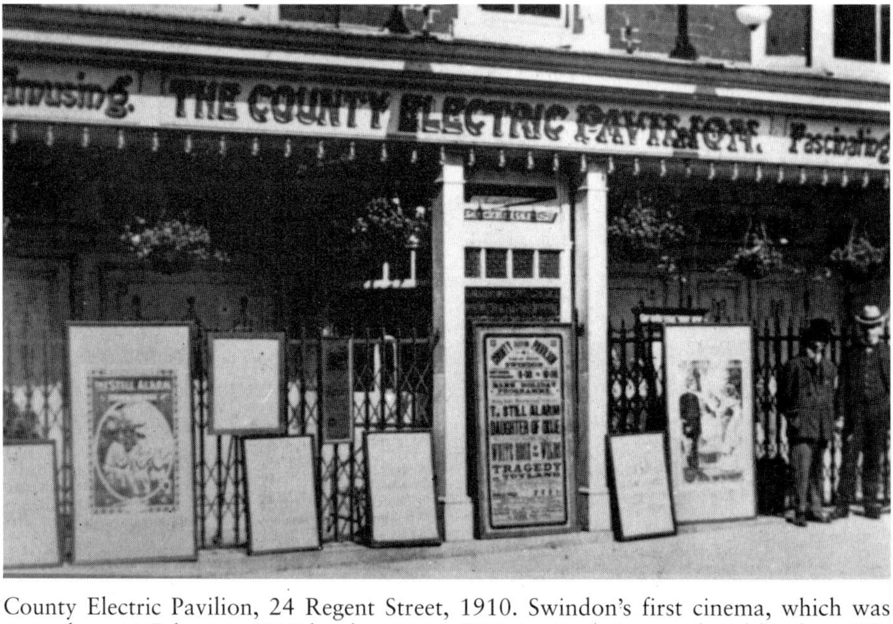

County Electric Pavilion, 24 Regent Street, 1910. Swindon's first cinema, which was opened on 11 February 1910 by the mayor, W.H. Lawson. It was closed by the 1930s when the F.W. Woolworth & Co. Ltd '3d and 6d' stores took over the site.

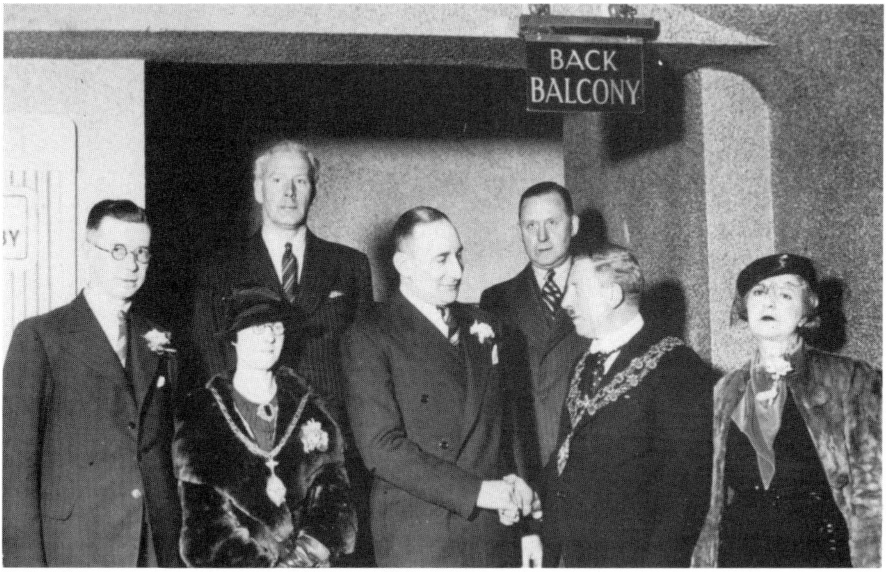

Opening ceremony at the Savoy Cinema, Regent Street, January 1937. Mr A.S. Moss, general manager of ABC Cinemas shakes hands with the mayor, Alderman L.J. Newman. Also in the picture are the mayoress, Trevor Jones (manager), Alex Houre, A.C. Sparie (superintendent) and Mrs Moss. The first film to be shown was *Captain January* starring Shirley Temple. There was seating accommodation for 1,775 people.

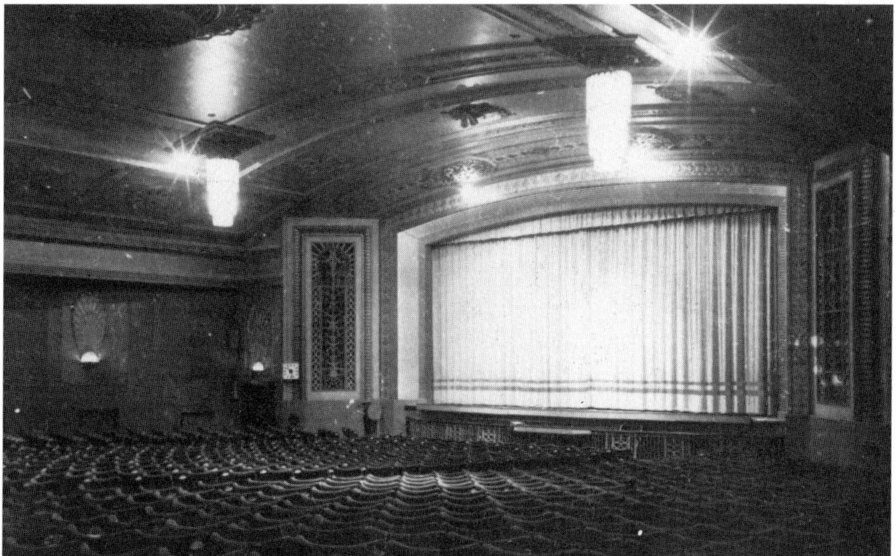

Interior of the Odeon Cinema, Regent Circus, *c*. 1966. Formerly known as the Regent Cinema, it became known as the Gaumont in the 1950s and renamed the Odeon in 1962. Closed as a cinema in the mid-1970s it is now a bingo hall.

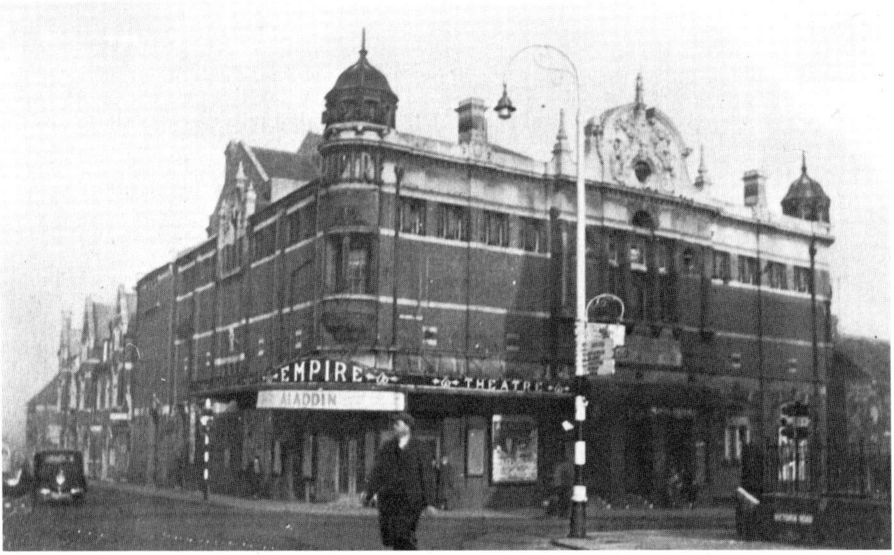

Empire Theatre, at the corner of Groundwell Road and Clarence Street, *c.* 1948. Designed by Drake and Pizey of Bristol, the theatre opened in 1898 as the Queen's Theatre and became the Empire in 1906. Seating over 1,000, it served as a cinema from 1929–47 and closed its doors for the last time on 22 January 1955.

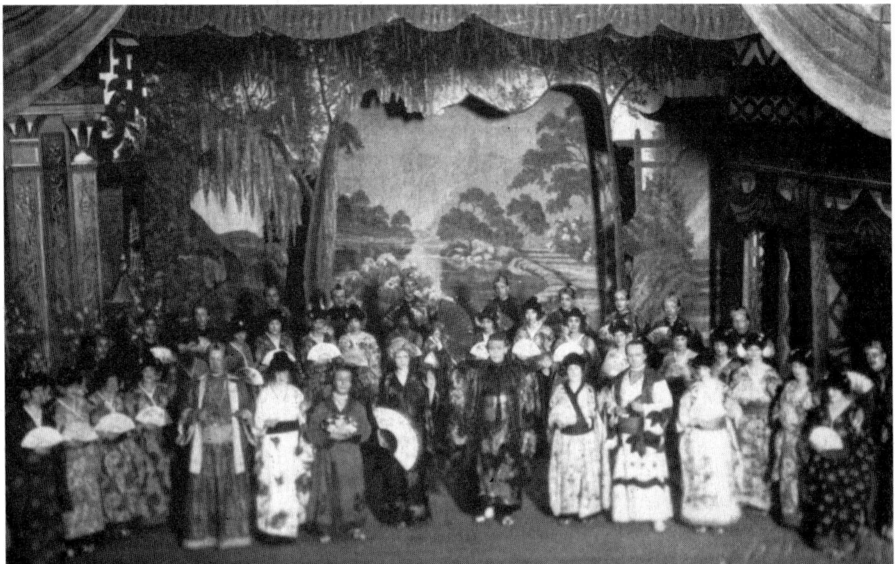

Finale of *The Mikado*, Empire Theatre, 8 October 1915.

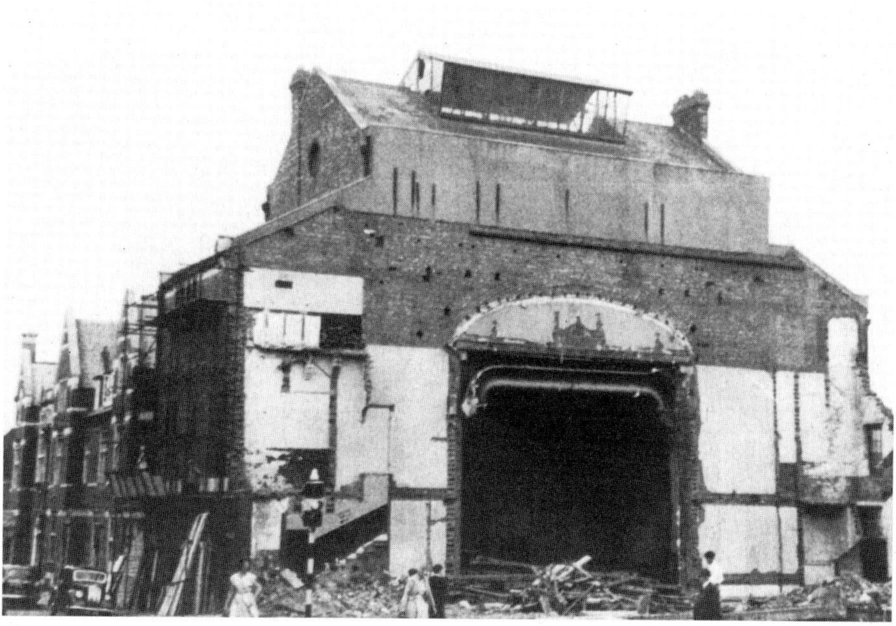

Empire Theatre, while under demolition in 1959. The former stage can be seen clearly in this photograph. Empire House, with shops and offices, now stands on the site.

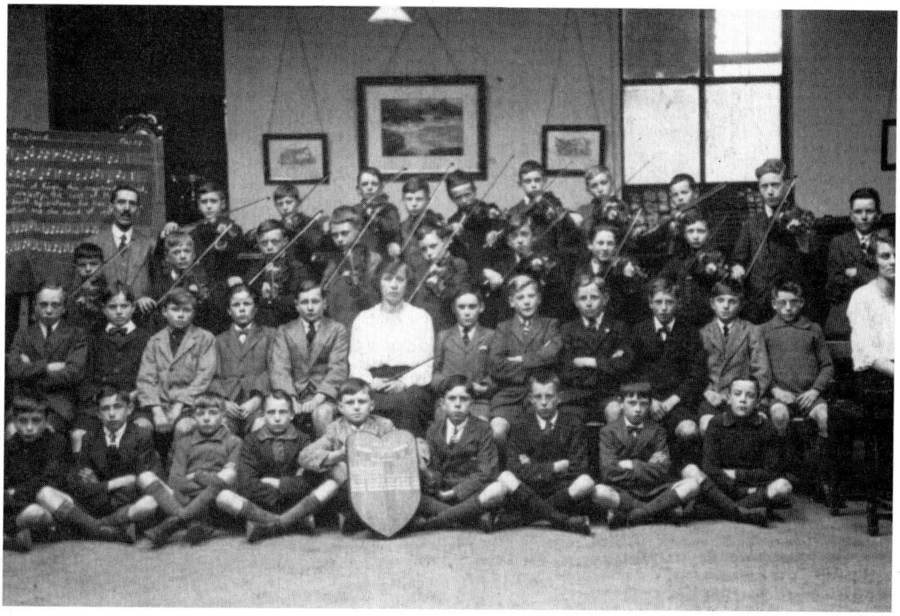

Sanford Street School. The Wilts. Music Festival, 1923. This was the eleventh festival, according to the shield on view, and the music score on the board is *England* by Parry.

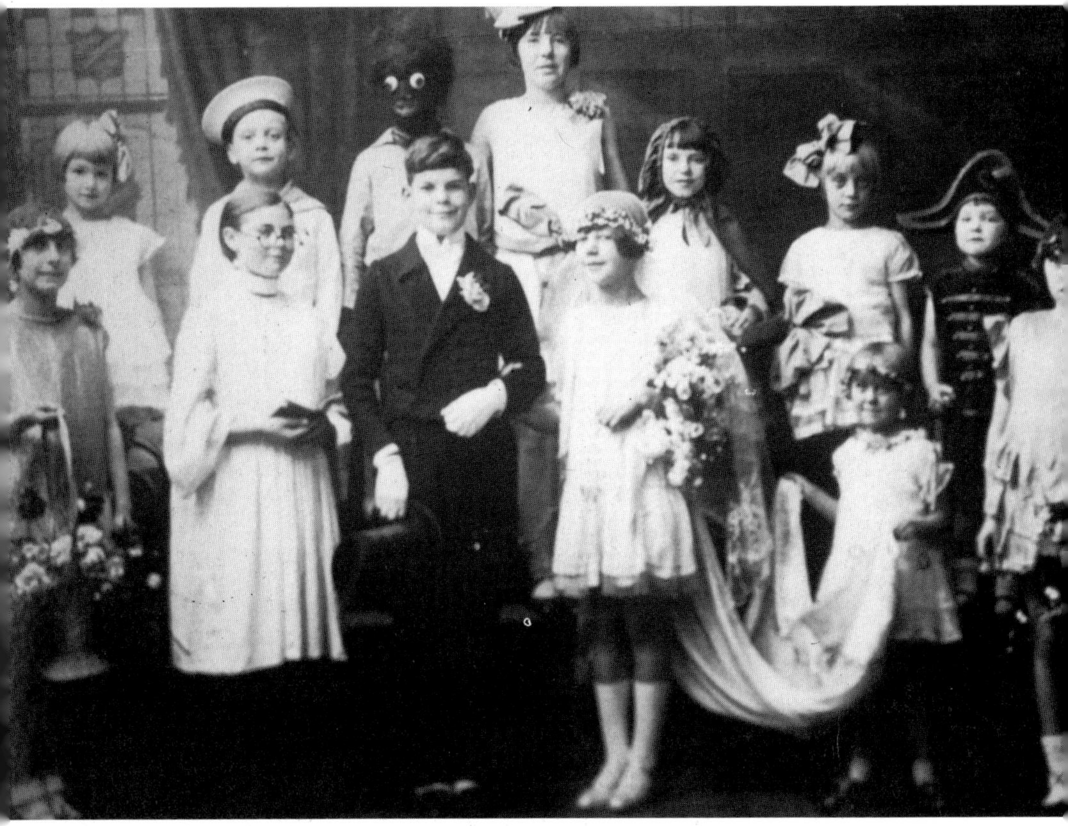

'The Ideal Concert Party'. With no television and only limited radio broadcasting, Swindonians had to make their own entertainment in years gone by. The Concert Party comprised Swindon youngsters who could dance and sing, and entertained audiences in village halls, fêtes and hospitals throughout the county in the 1920s. It was organized by a Mrs Cook, who lived in Plymouth Street, and a Mrs Bailey. The photograph shows the group when they were performing *The Wedding of the Painted Doll* at All Saint's Church Hall in Southbrook Street. Identified are, back row: (sailor boy) Leslie Sealey, (tall girl) Barbara White. Front row: (bridegroom) Peter Bailey, (bride) Madge Burchell. When the Government brought in legislation to restrict child entertainment the Concert Party closed down.

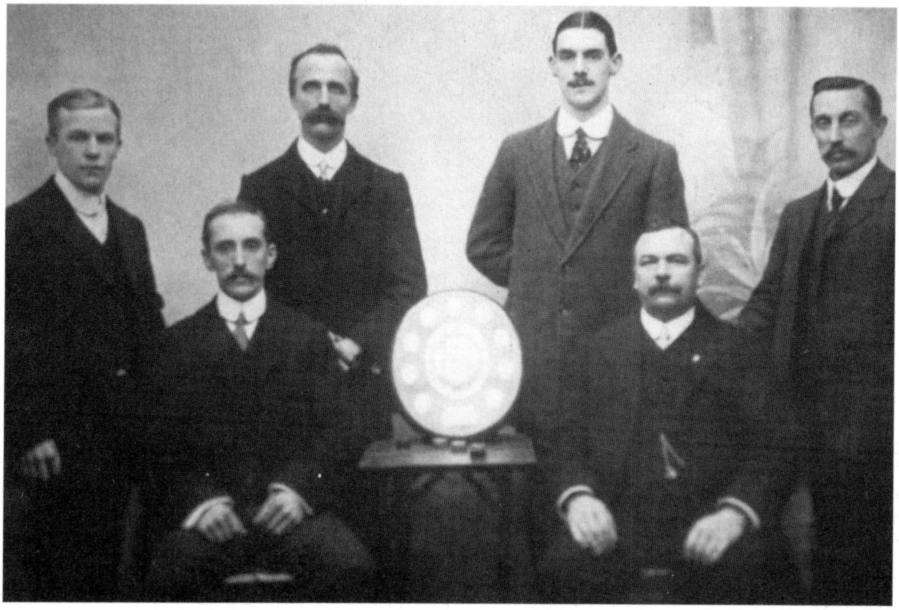

Mechanics Institute draughts team, 1911/12. This particular team were winners of the Wiltshire and Gloucester league that year.

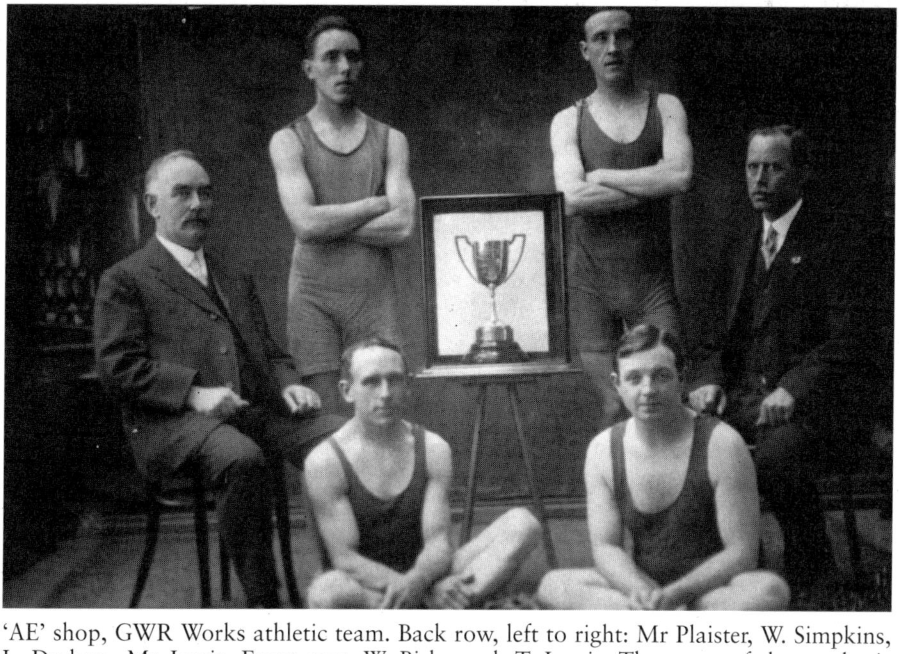

'AE' shop, GWR Works athletic team. Back row, left to right: Mr Plaister, W. Simpkins, L. Dodson, Mr Jarvis. Front row: W. Birkwood, T. Lewis. The name of the trophy is unknown.

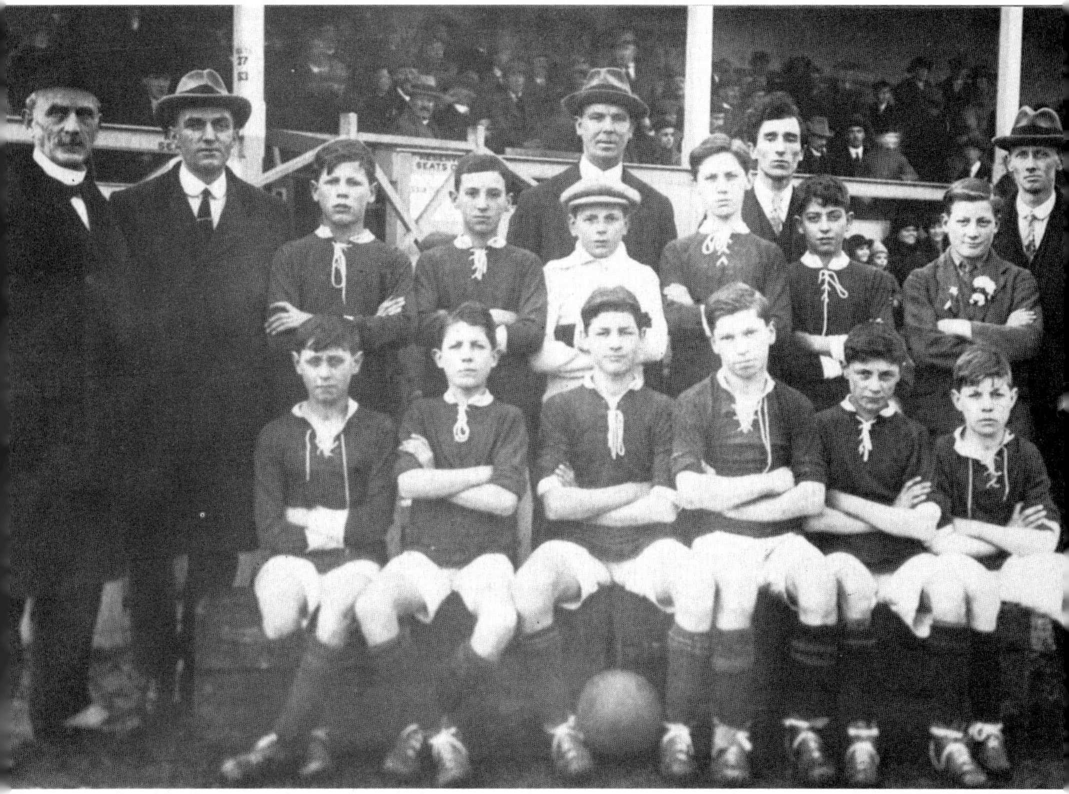

Swindon Boys football team and officials, English Schools Football Shield, 1920/1. During this season the Swindon Boys team were very successful and reached the 1st round proper of the English Schools Football Shield by winning their qualifying section, beating Oxford, Bournemouth and Brighton Boys on the way. Finally they were defeated, after a replay at the County Ground, by Ebbw Vale Boys from South Wales in March 1921. The team were: (goalkeeper) Sheppard, (full backs) Pane, Maslin, (half-backs) Seely, Alley, Cole, (forwards) Hatherall, Boots, Webb, Darnell, Blackford. After the final match both teams were entertained for tea at Sanford Street School.

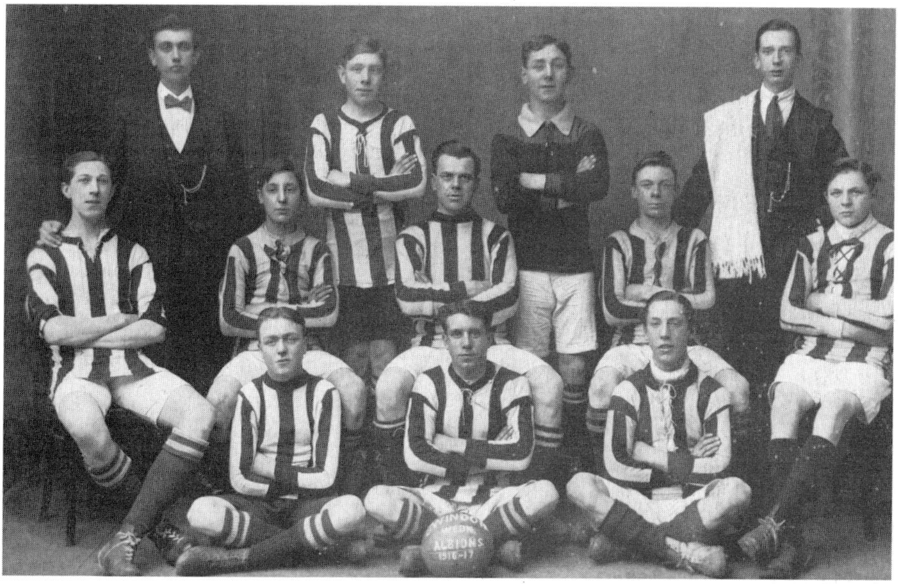

Swindon Wednesday Albions football team, 1916/17. Back row, left to right: E. Hunt, E.M. Woodward, A.C. Bennett, L. Archer. Second row: H. Price, W. Smith, G.H. Craven, T. Newman, M. Willis. Front row: C.G. Ackers, W. Ockwell, N. Clack.

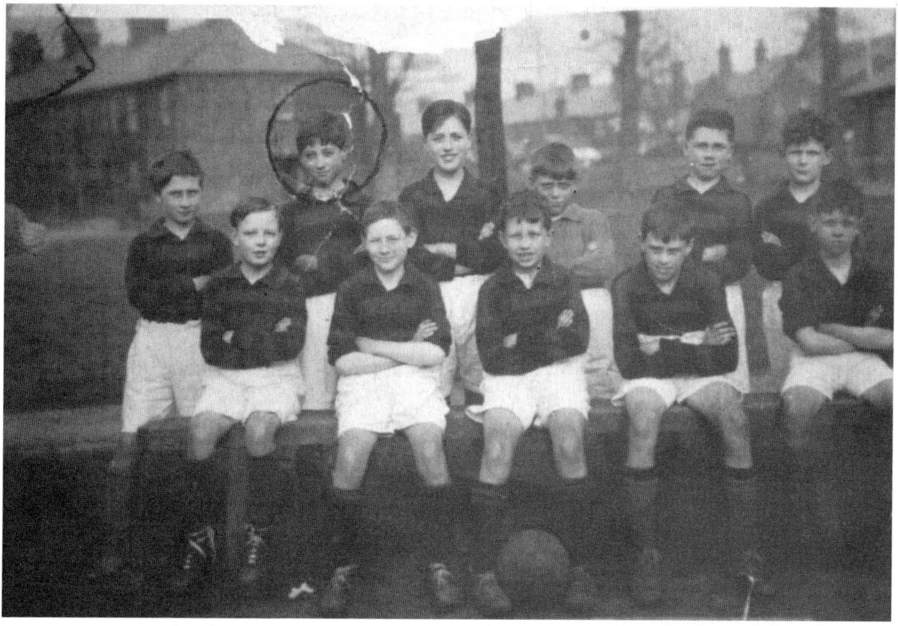

Westcott Junior football team, 1929/30. Back row, left to right: Tim Osman, Jim Bright (circled), George Morrot, Ronnie Adams, Syd Millard, Norman Moulden. Front row: ? Ashman, Bert Wilson, Bert Sawyer, Doug Lane, 'Maggie' Major.

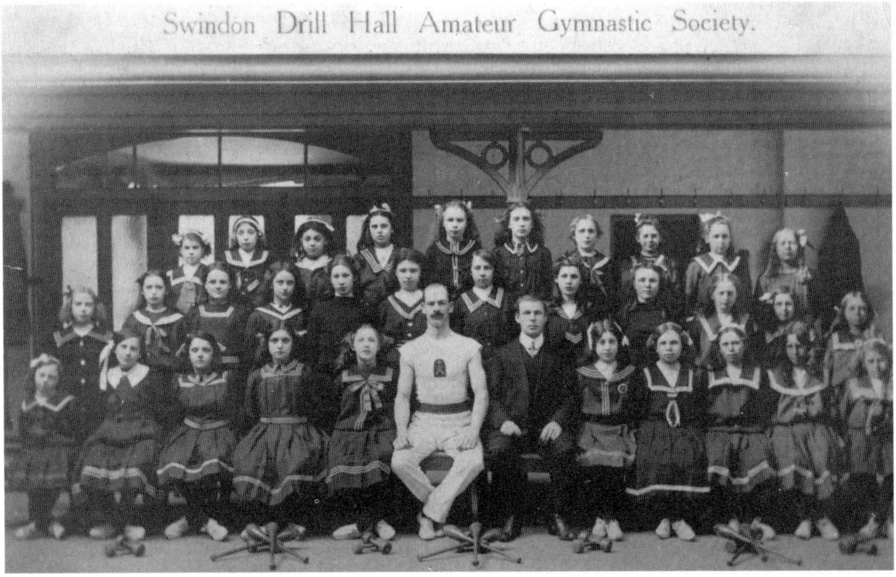

Swindon Drill Hall Amateur Gymnastic Society, *c.* 1912.

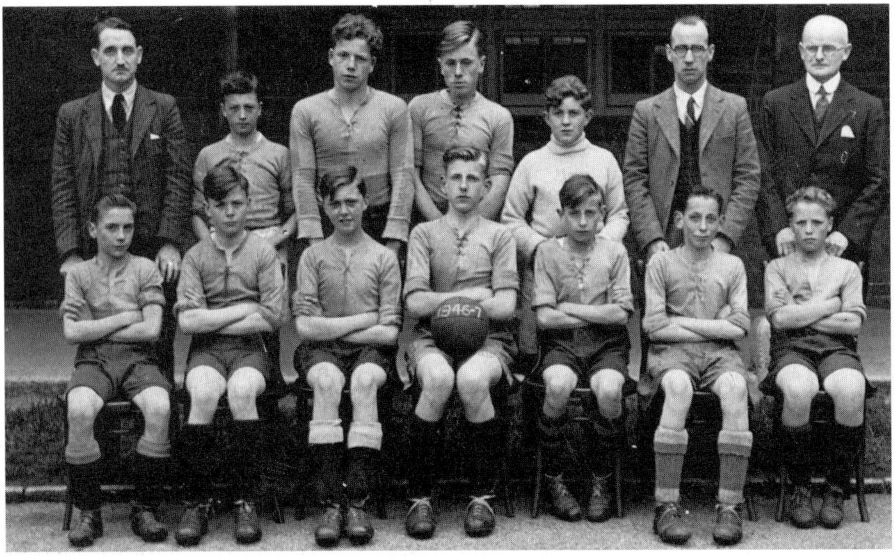

Commonweal School, under-fourteen football team, 1946–7. Back row, left to right: Mr Davies (teacher), Roy Sampson, Merv Gilbert, Peter James, John Pickering, Frank Armitage (teacher), Dr Jones (headmaster). Front row: Frances Twining, Brian Evans (?) Neil Chinn, Graham Haines, Peter Holmes, John Hiscock, Tony Mills. Of some of the team in later years, goalkeeper John Pickering, who also excelled at cricket, played for Swindon CC and Wiltshire, while Roy Sampson made sixty-three appearances for Swindon Town FC between 1953 and 1955. Graham Haines today is vice-president of the Swindon Amateur Light Operatic Society (SALOS).

SECTION NINE

Twenty-five Years Ago: Swindon in 1968 (Photographs by Denis Bird)

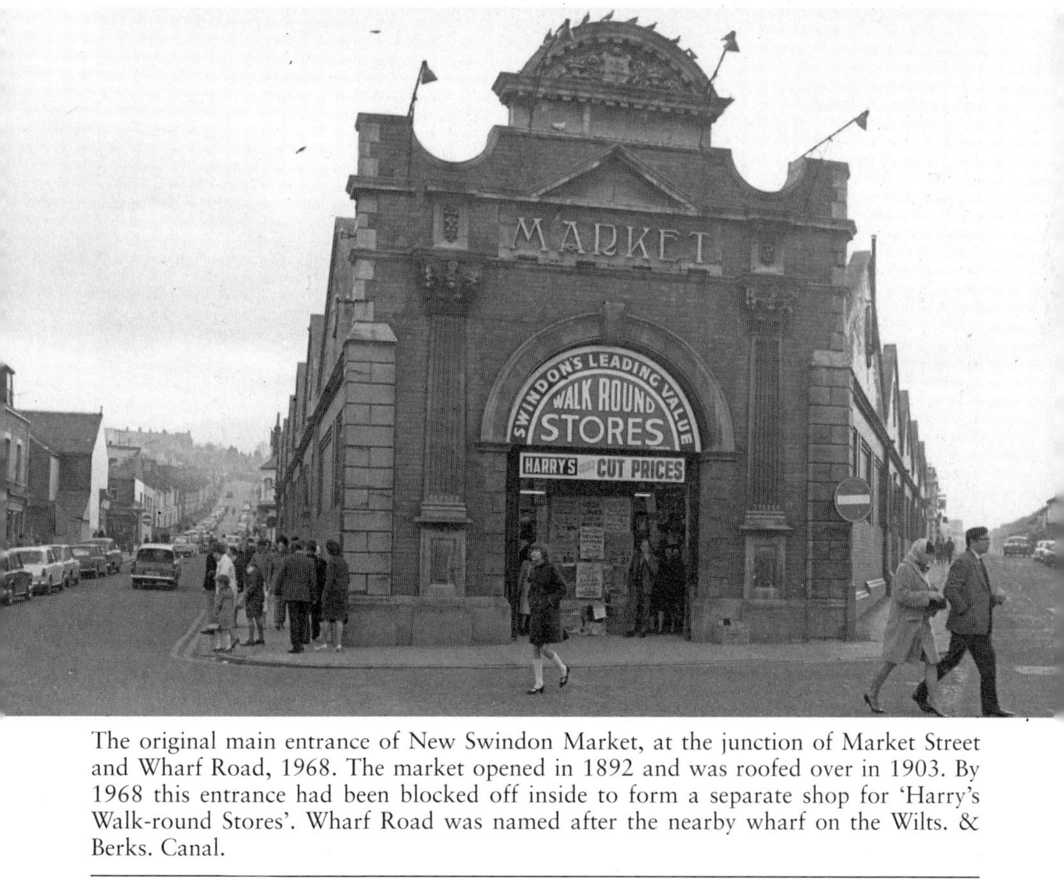

The original main entrance of New Swindon Market, at the junction of Market Street and Wharf Road, 1968. The market opened in 1892 and was roofed over in 1903. By 1968 this entrance had been blocked off inside to form a separate shop for 'Harry's Walk-round Stores'. Wharf Road was named after the nearby wharf on the Wilts. & Berks. Canal.

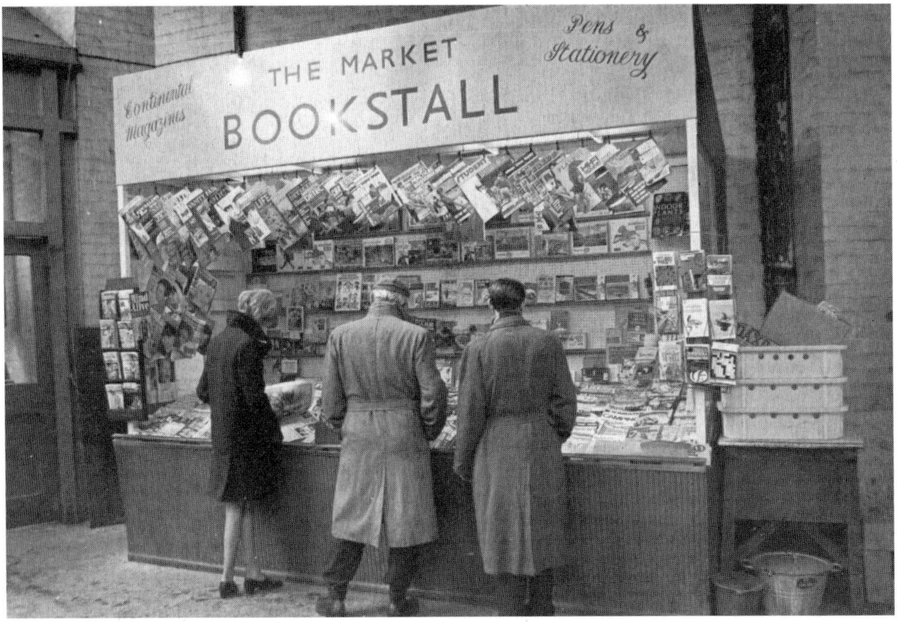

The Market Bookstall, 1968. The doorway on the left led to steps onto Commercial Road; they still exist in the car park today.

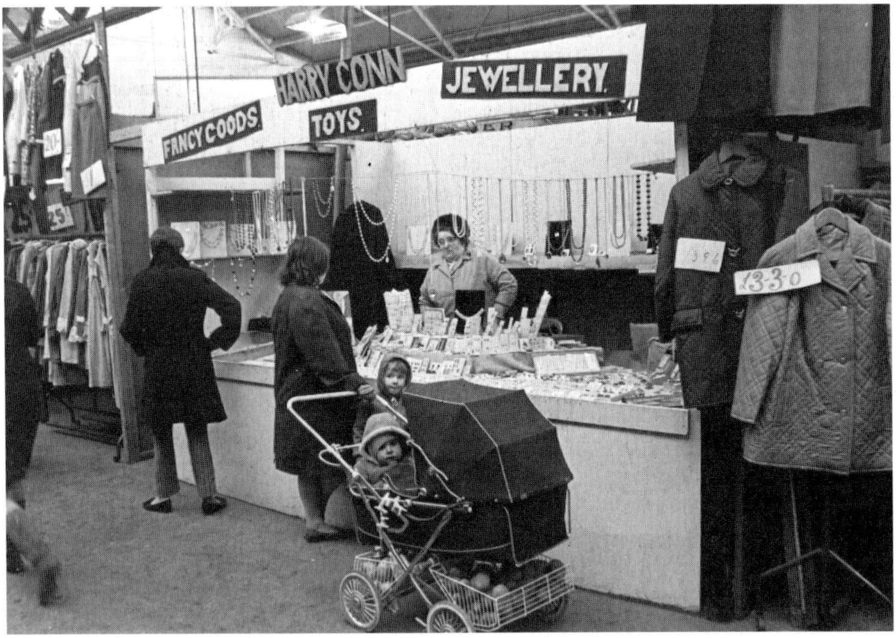

Harry Conn and his fancy goods stall in the market in 1968.

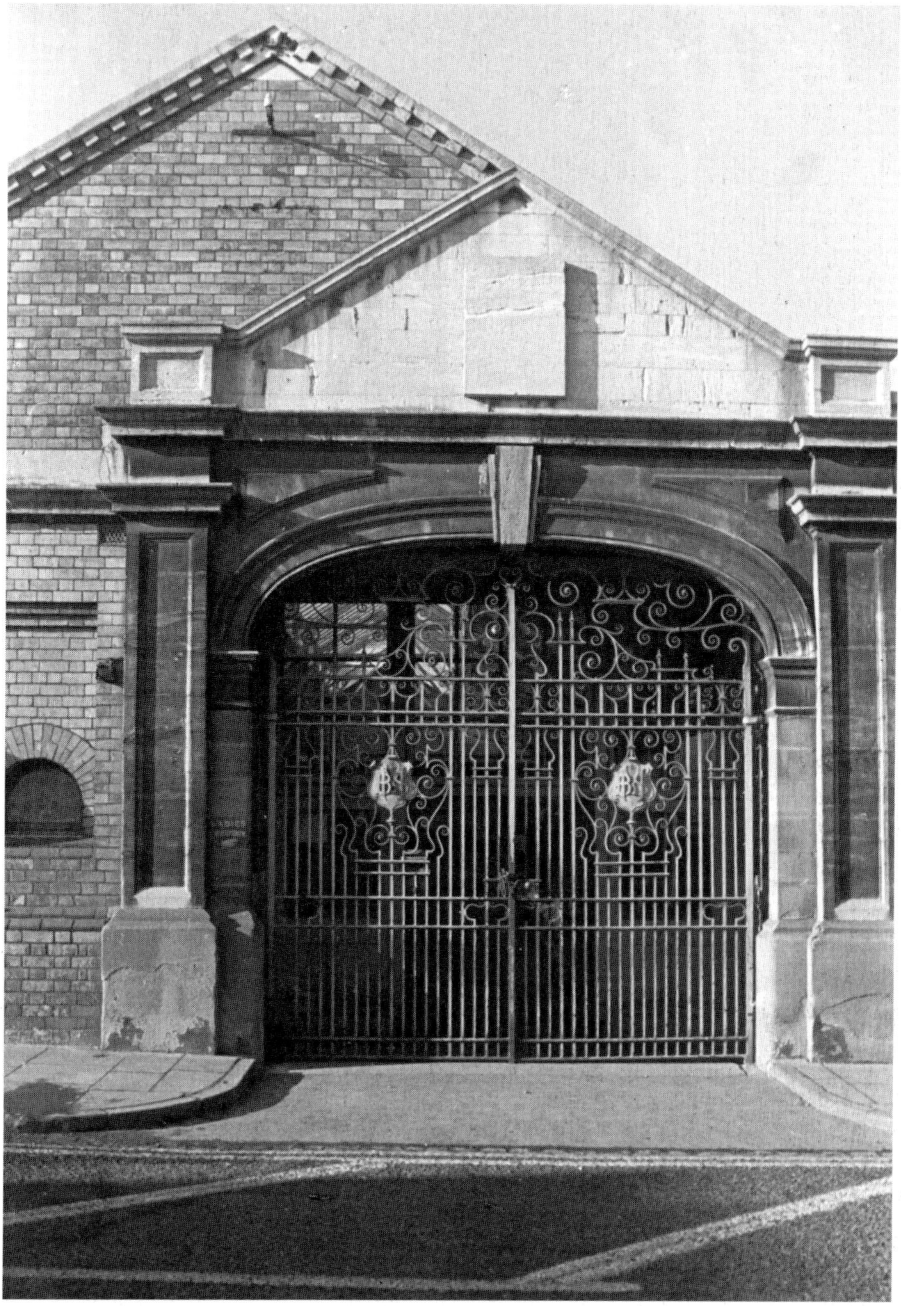

Ornate main gateway to the market, 1968. The market was closed in 1977 and traders were rehoused in the Brunel Centre. The old building was demolished, but a small portion of the exterior walls was retained and the space inside now serves as a car park.

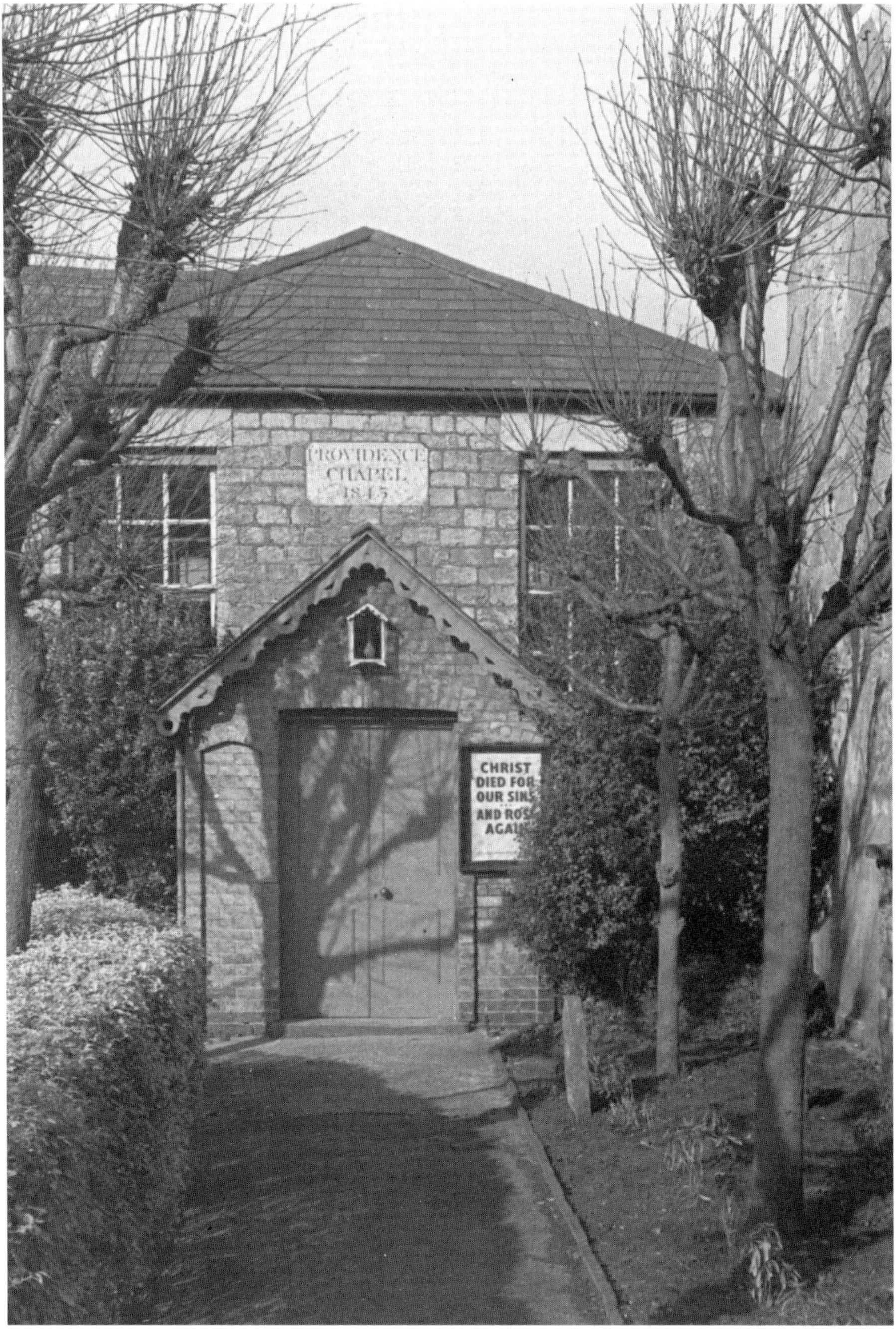

Providence chapel, South Street, 1968. A Particular Baptist chapel, it was built in 1845 with a small burial ground at the front. It is now a private residence.

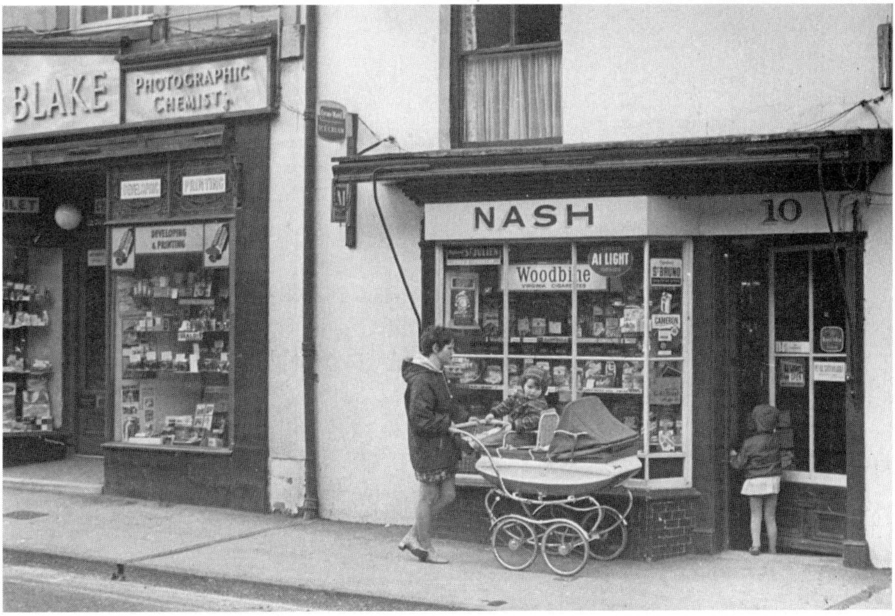

Nash's sweet shop, 10 Wood Street, 1968. The first Nash sweet shop was opened in the 1850s by Mr E. Nash who made his own sweets. Others followed in Rodbourne Road, Bridge Street, and Regent Circus, each run by one of his daughters. In the early days they were renowned for their special bargain packs of sweets known as 'Penny Big Lots' and prize-winning ice-cream. The above premises are now Dandelion.

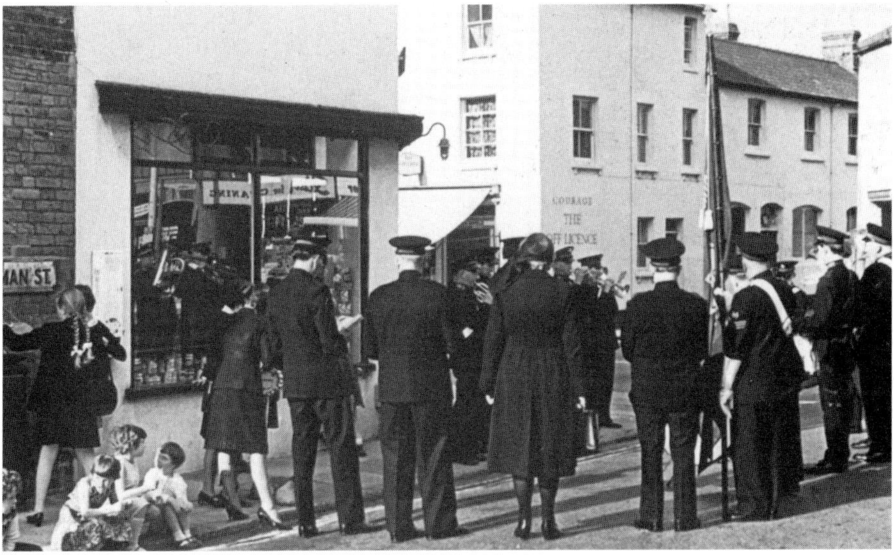

Salvation Army Band playing in Whiteman Street, Gorse Hill, 1968. Note the young children sitting on the pavement while they listen to the music.

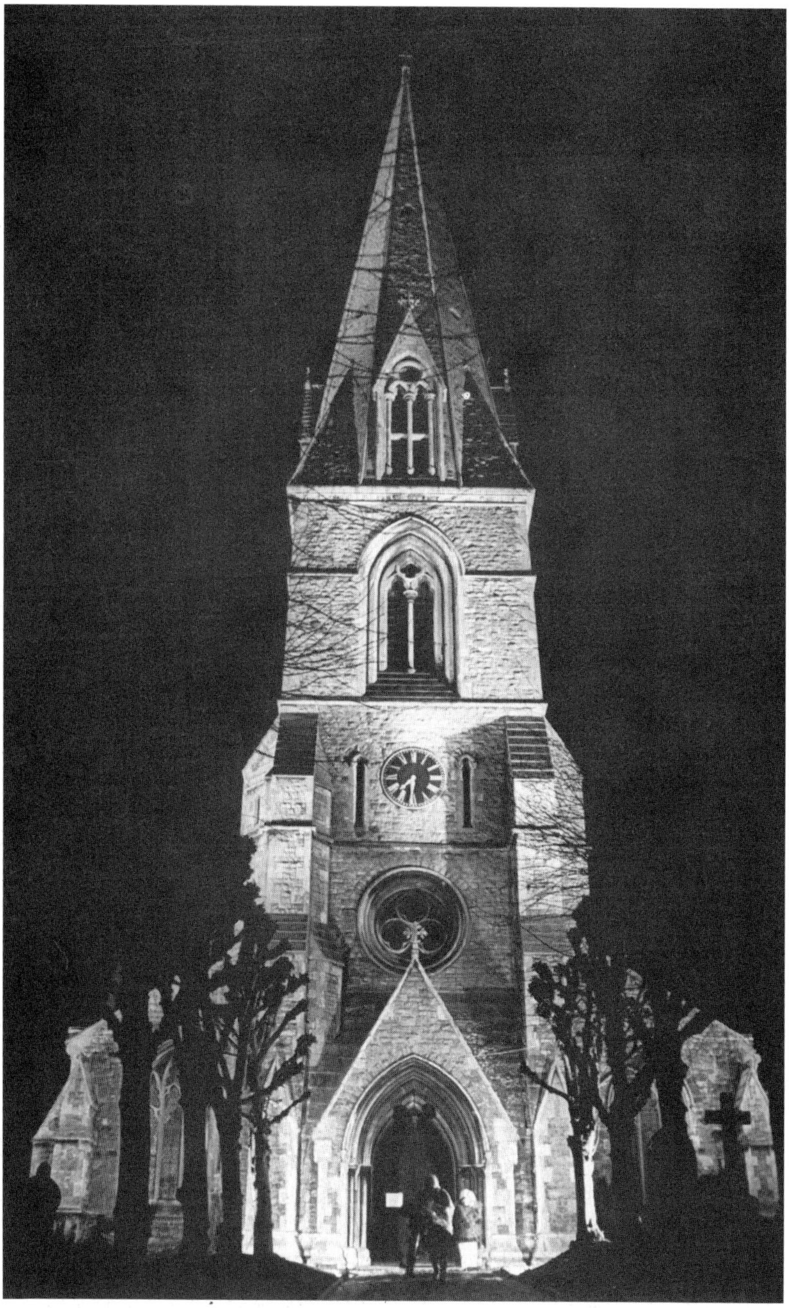

Christ Church floodlit, 1968. The floodlighting of the parish church, installed in 1939, ceased in the early 1970s. Plans are now in hand to install new lighting, and it is hoped that this impressive night-time view may again be seen in the near future.

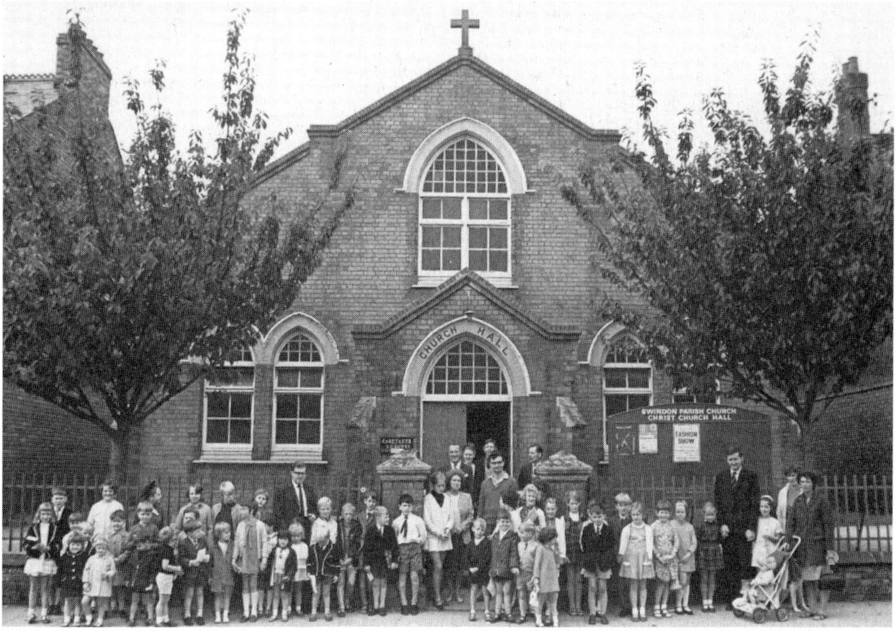

Christ Church Hall, Devizes Road, 1968. Sunday schools pose to have their photograph taken. Opened in 1913, Christ Church Hall was, at one time, used for an overflow service for people who could not get into the parish church!

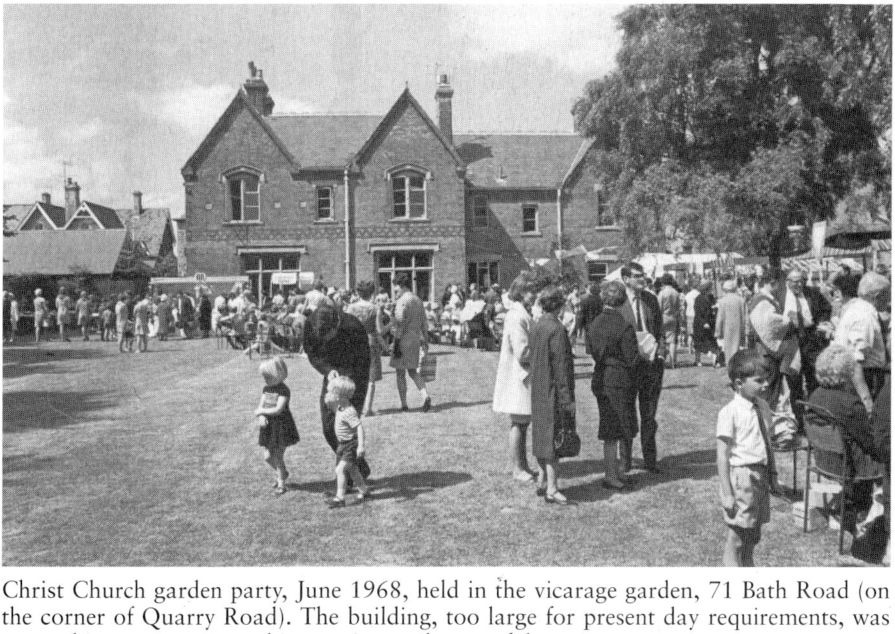

Christ Church garden party, June 1968, held in the vicarage garden, 71 Bath Road (on the corner of Quarry Road). The building, too large for present day requirements, was vacated in recent years and is now in a sad state of decay.

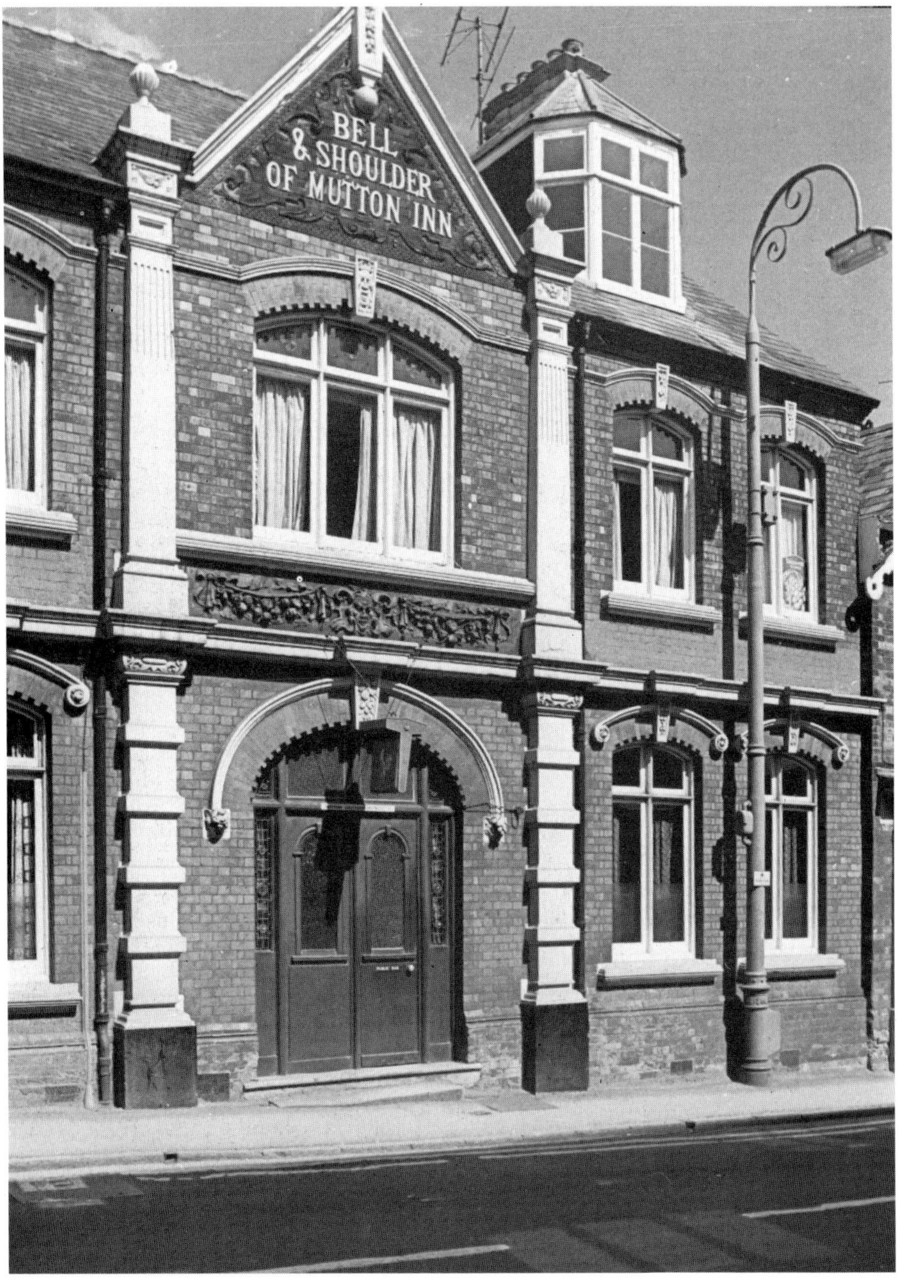

Bell & Shoulder of Mutton, Marlborough Road, 1968. This public house, situated directly to the south of the Masons Arms (see p. 14), was rebuilt in around 1895 to replace the former thatched structure. It closed shortly after this photograph was taken and was demolished the following year.

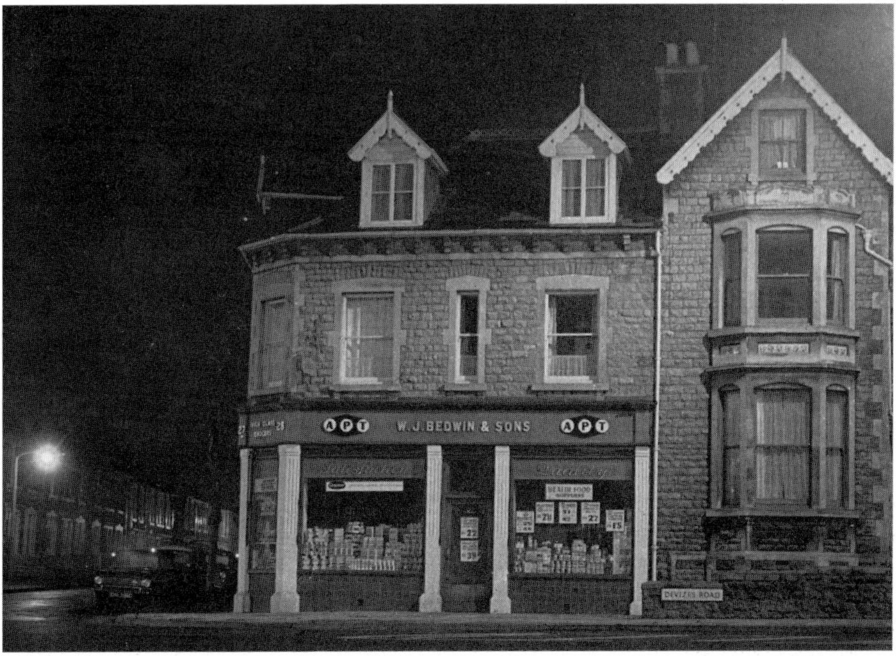

W.J. Bedwin, wholesale and family grocers, 27–8 Devizes Road, 1968.

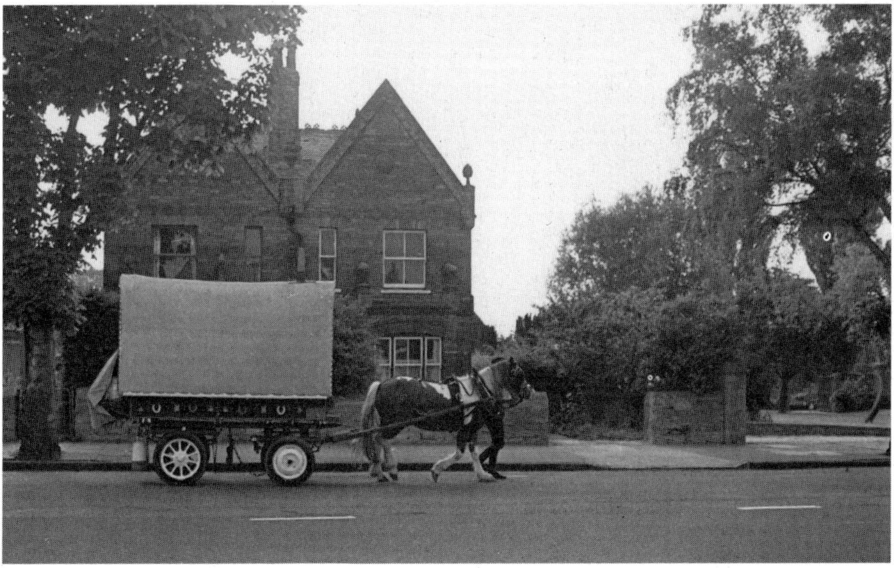

Drove Road and gypsy caravan, 1968. In the background is a pair of Thomas Turner's 'catalogue' houses. This group of houses, fronting his brickyard, was built to show the variety of brick, moulding and terracotta that was available. To the right is the entrance to Queen's Park.

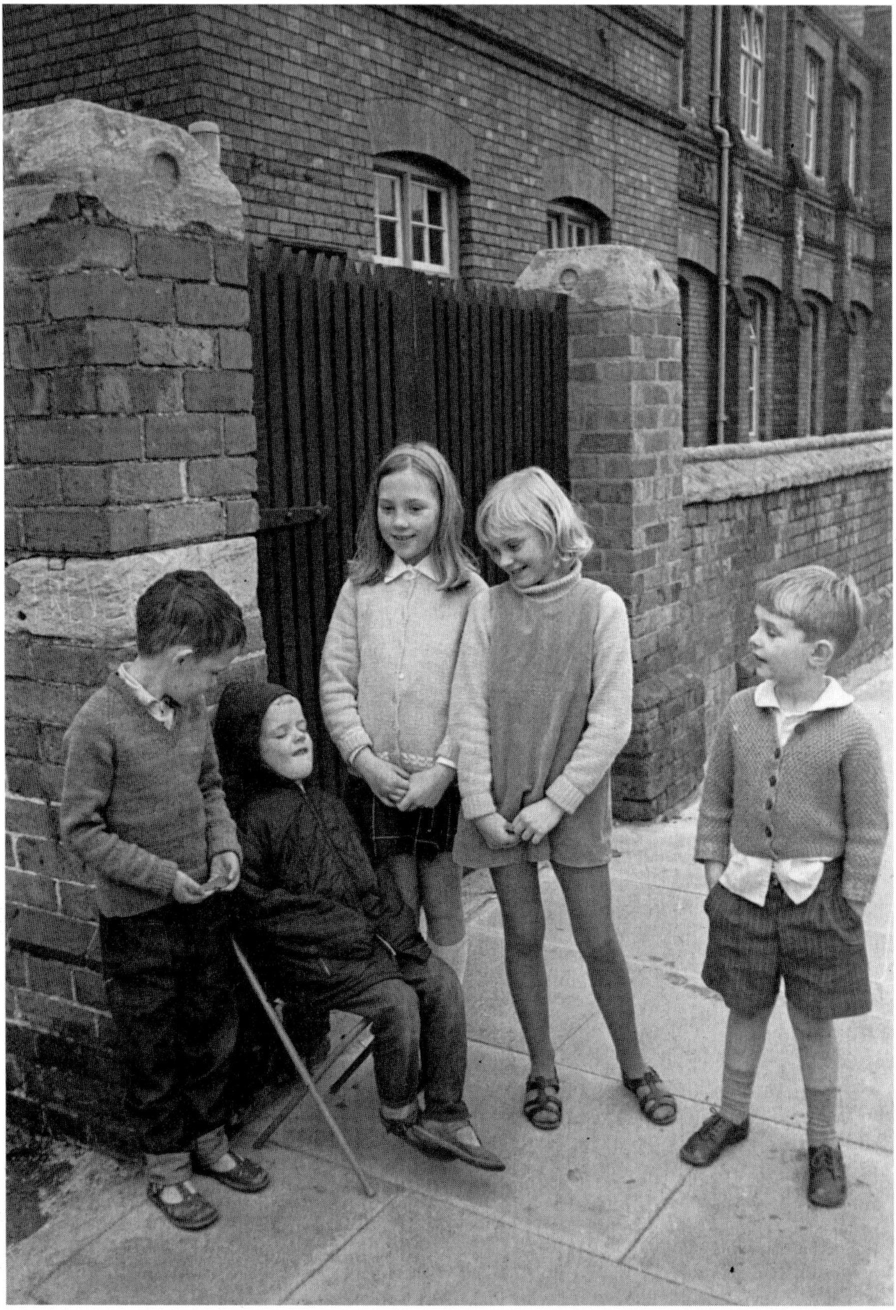

Guy Fawkes Day, 1968. Children outside Gilberts Hill School in Dixon Street try to persuade passers-by to give 'a penny for the guy'. Unfortunately one of them has to stand in for Guy Fawkes!

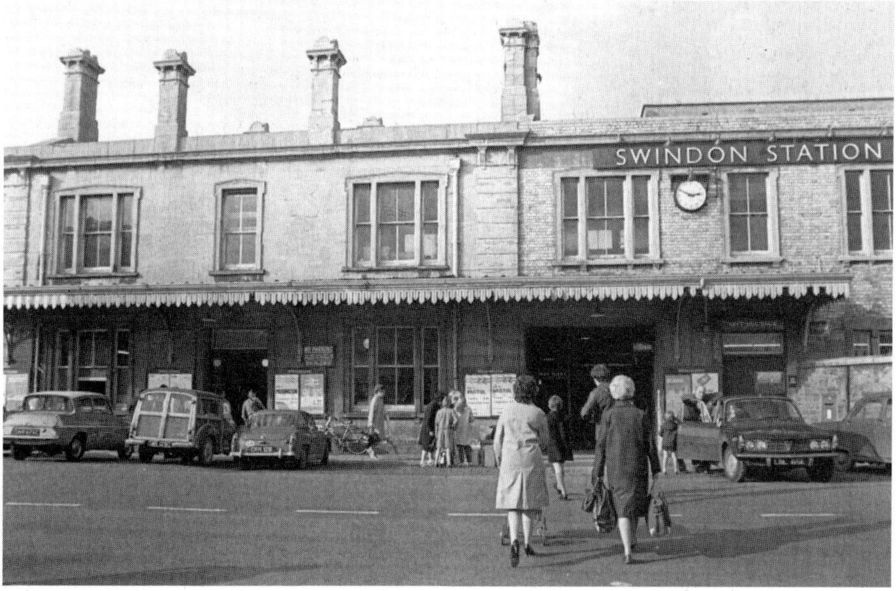

GWR junction station, 1968. The station façade, as remembered by older Swindonians, with a long, dark tunnel to platforms on the right, was completely rebuilt and modernized in 1973.

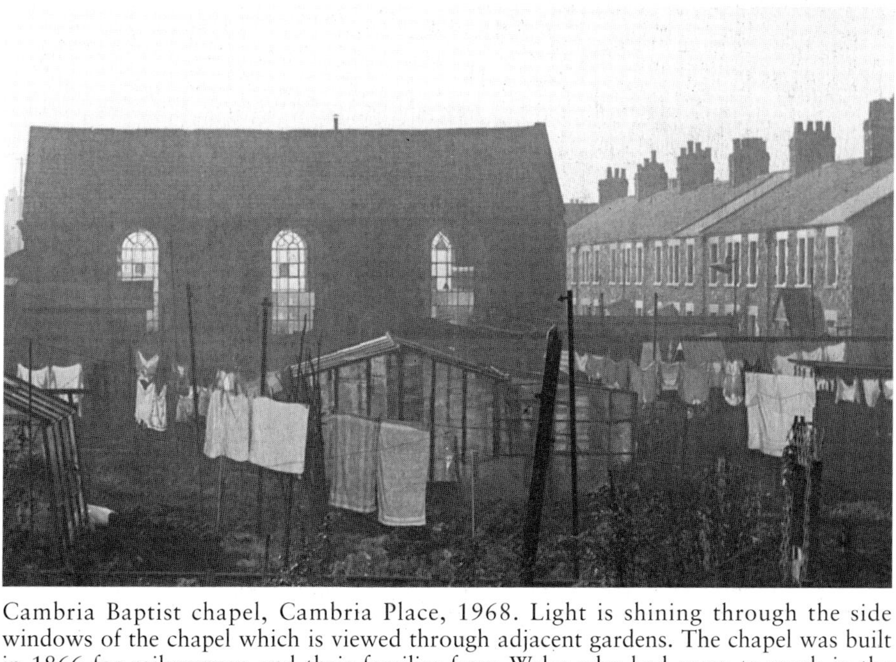

Cambria Baptist chapel, Cambria Place, 1968. Light is shining through the side windows of the chapel which is viewed through adjacent gardens. The chapel was built in 1866 for railwaymen and their families from Wales who had come to work in the GWR Works. It closed in 1986. See also *Swindon in Old Photographs (3)*, pp. 108–10.

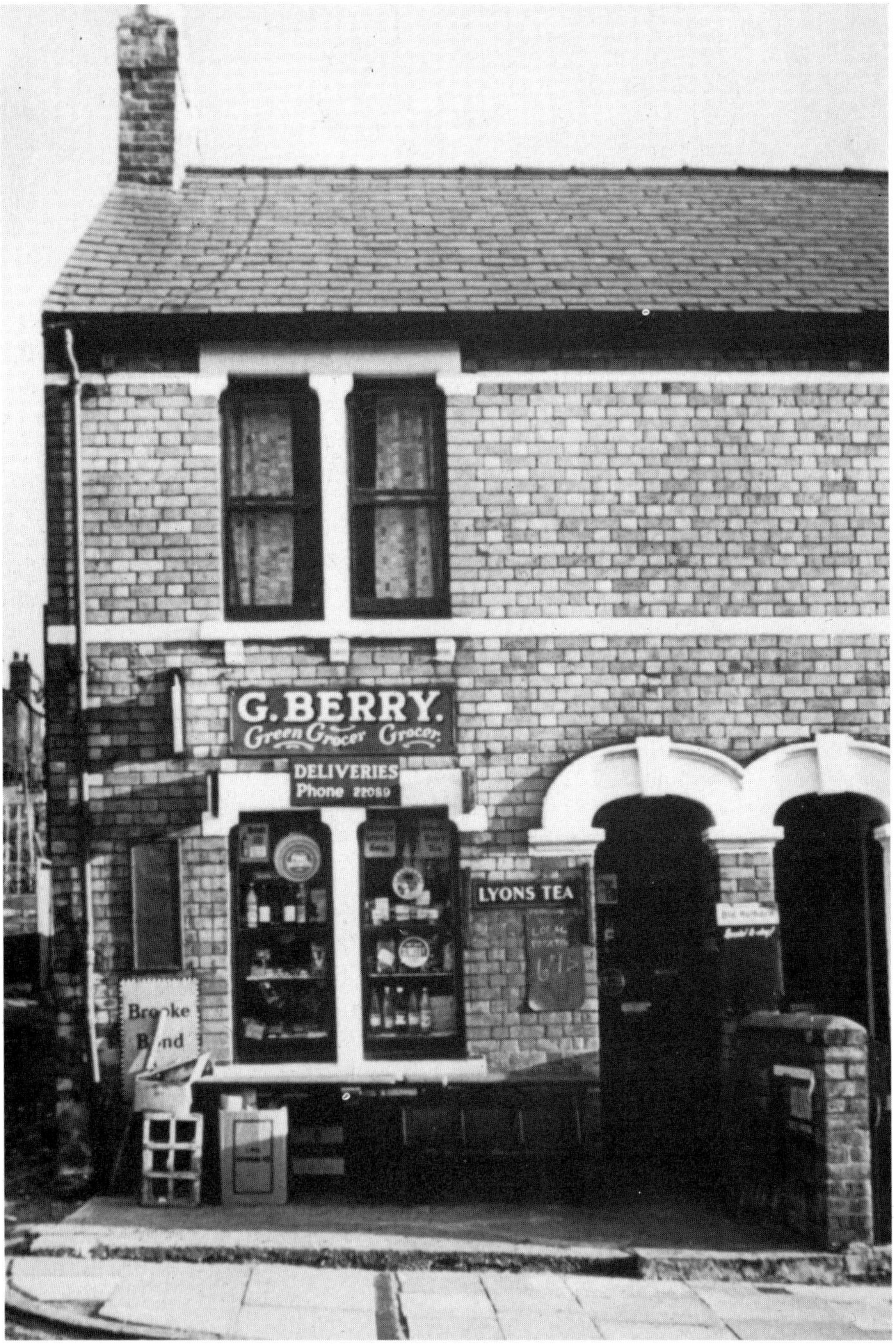

G. Berry, grocer, 33 Dryden Street, 1968. These premises are now a private house again.

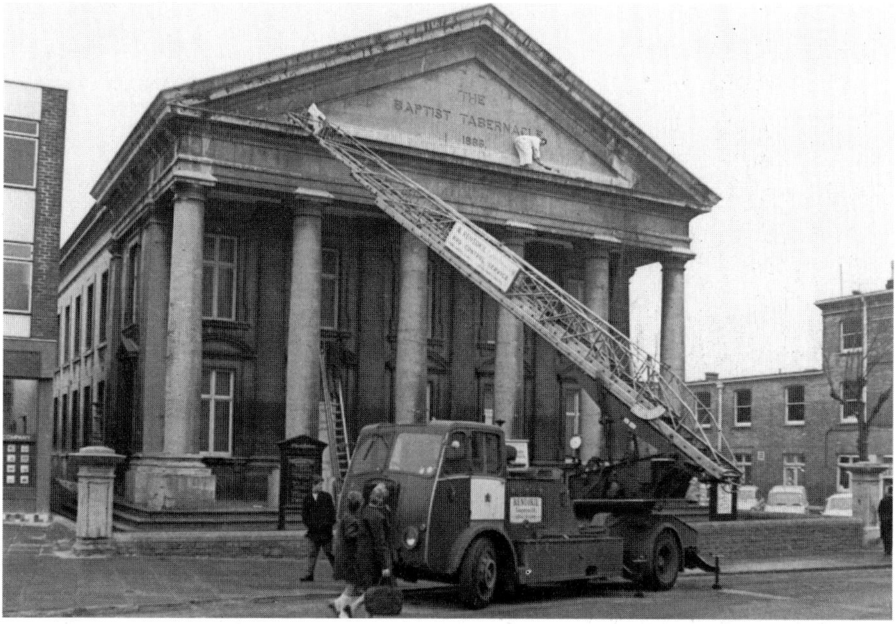

Baptist Tabernacle, 1968. Built in 1885/6 to replace the former church in Fleet Street (see *Swindon in Old Photographs (3)*, p. 100). Here the photographer captured an attempt to prevent pigeons roosting above the portico – a long-standing problem here – but these efforts proved only partially successful. Presumably the pigeons were more used to their precarious perch than the humans trying to remove them!

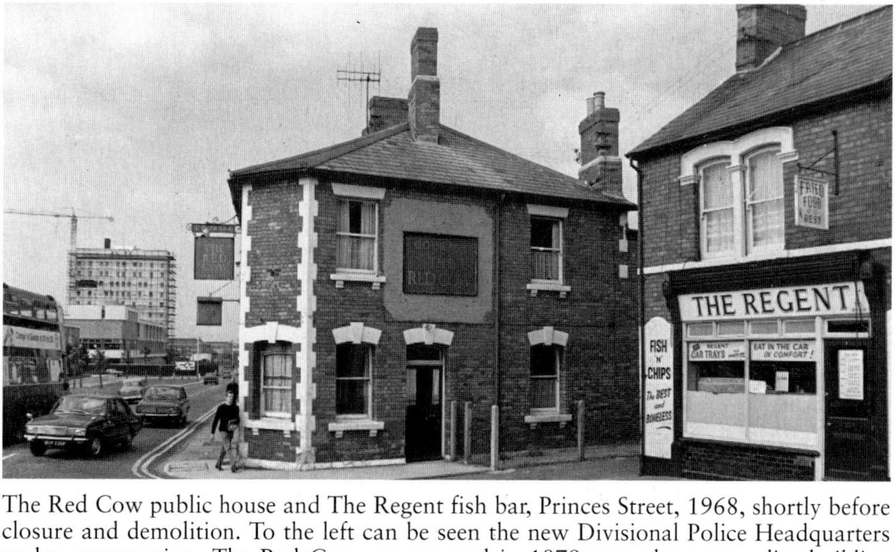

The Red Cow public house and The Regent fish bar, Princes Street, 1968, shortly before closure and demolition. To the left can be seen the new Divisional Police Headquarters under construction. The Red Cow was opened in 1879 to replace an earlier building situated in Cow Lane, one of Swindon's oldest thoroughfares which ran to the west and parallel to Princes Street until the redevelopment of the area in the late 1960s.

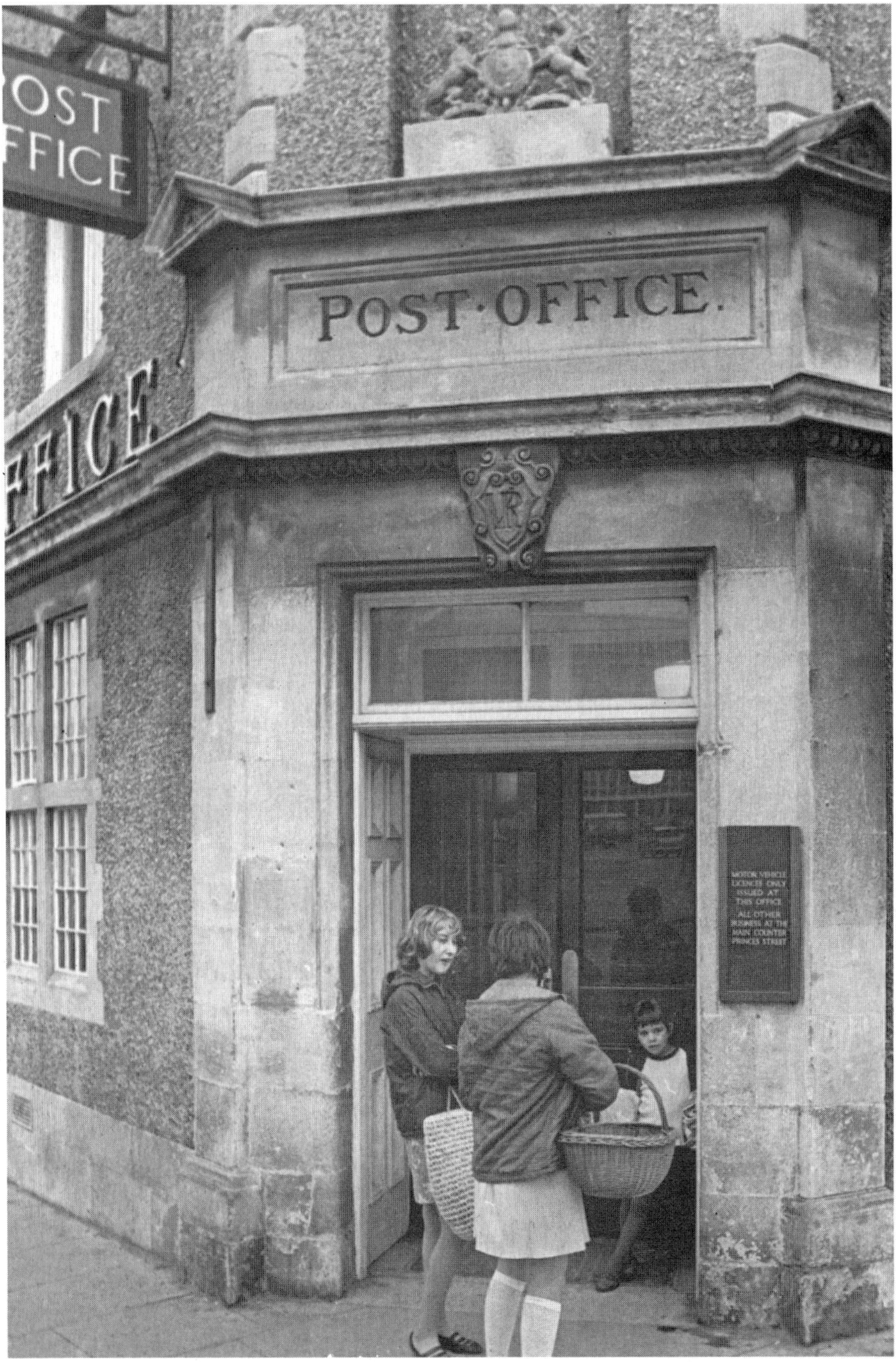

Entrance to the Head Post Office, Regent Circus, 1968.

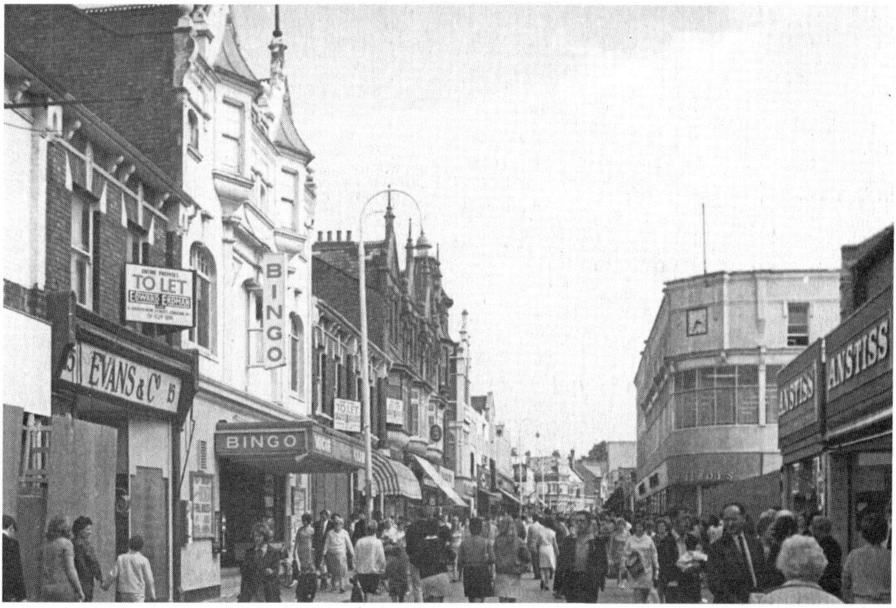

Regent Street, looking south, 1968. On the left is the former Arcadia Cinema, now a bingo hall. To the right the new McIlroy's building and site of Anstiss' store, cleared after a disastrous fire. At this time Anstiss still retained two smaller units adjacent to the site.

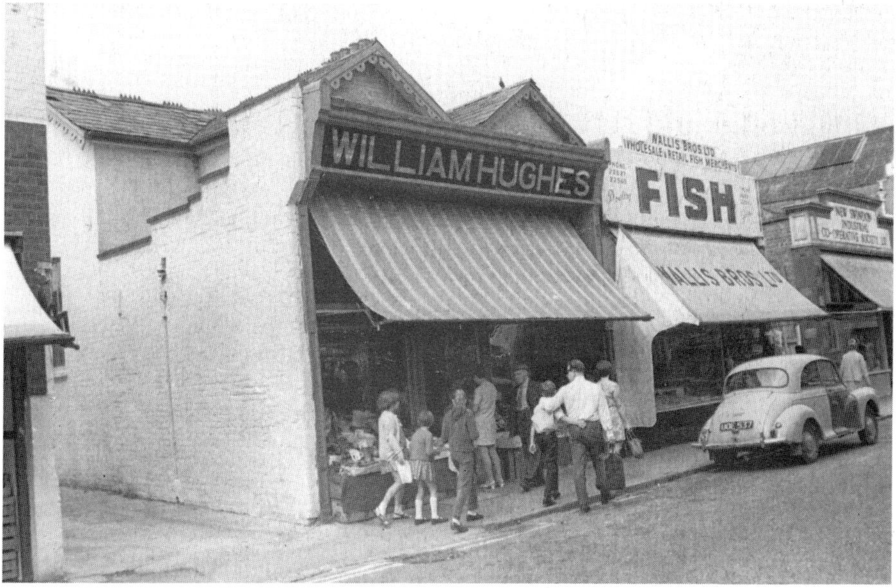

Cromwell Street, 1968. Shops on the north side are, left to right: William Hughes, greengrocer, Wallis Bros., fishmongers and poulterers, New Swindon Industrial Co-op, Franklin's, decorators' supplies (see also p. 59).

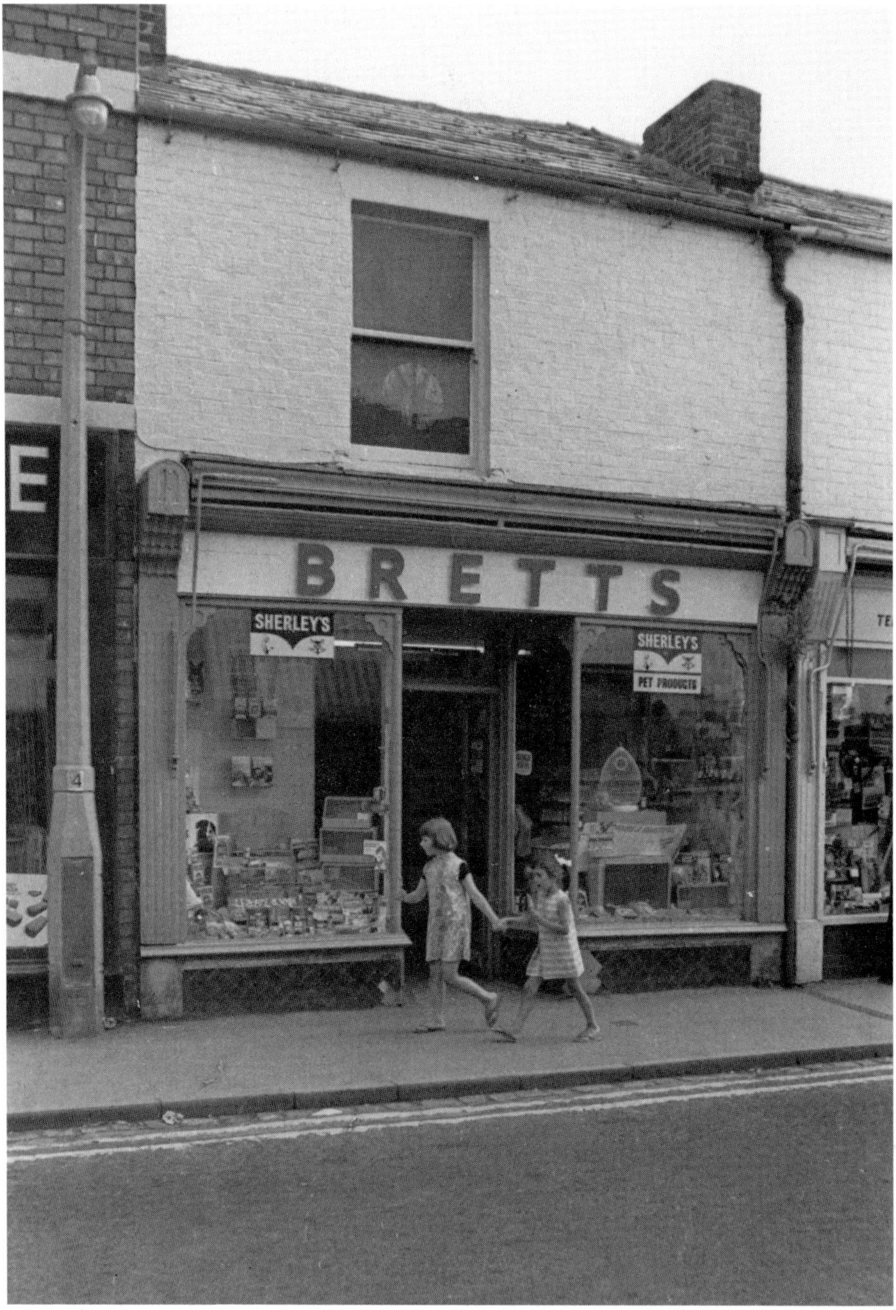

Bretts pet shop, 6 Cromwell Street, 1968, formerly the photographic studio for William Hooper and Fred Palmer. The building was demolished in the 1970s; the Brunel Centre shopping precinct now covers the site.

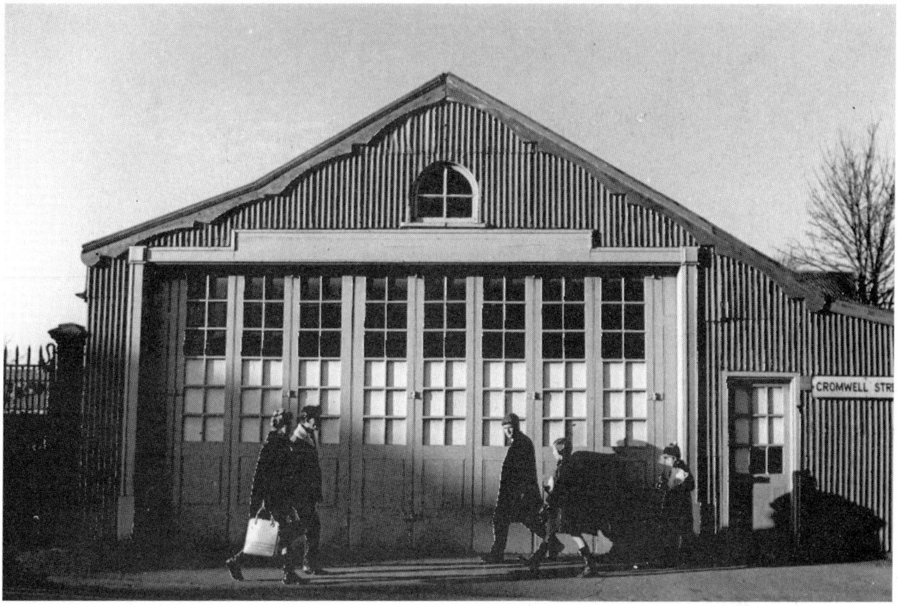

Swindon old fire station, Cromwell Street, 1968. Closed by this time (see p. 112), it was demolished shortly afterwards.

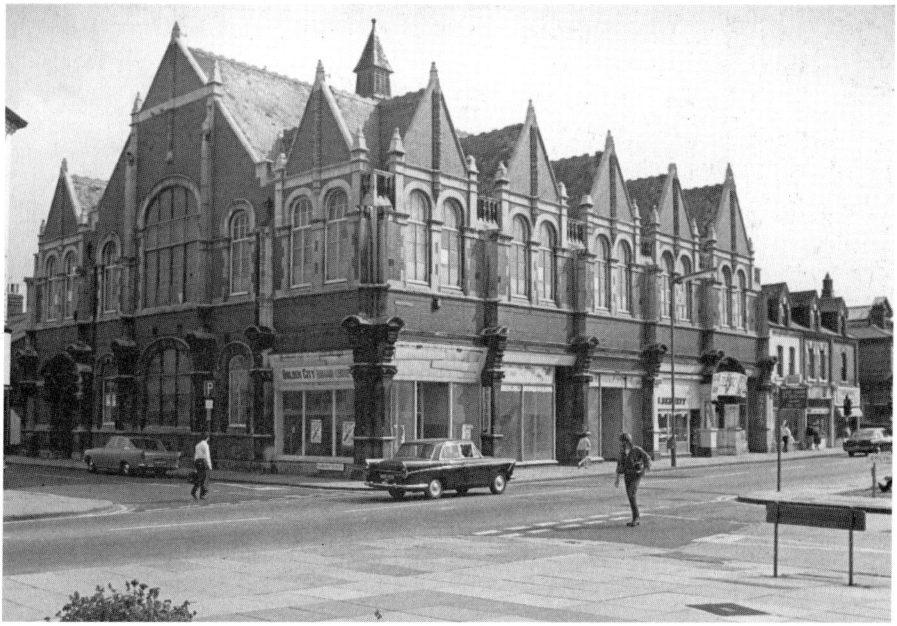

Former Wesleyan Methodist schoolrooms, Faringdon Road, 1968. A modern office block now stands on this site at the corner of Farnsby Street.

Acknowledgements

The Swindon Society would like to thank all those who contributed to the compilation of this book, especially society members Brian Bridgeman and David Bedford, who put the book together and selected the photographs to be used. Thanks also to society members Jean Allen, for all her work towards the production, and Denis Bird, for providing many photographs of his own for the book.

Especial thanks are also due to David Marchant of Ridgeway Studios and Ken Richman for providing many photographs for this volume. Mr Richman also supplied much information on the history of the Co-operative Movement in Swindon.

Our thanks also go to the Borough of Thamesdown Museum Service, and to the staff of Swindon Reference Library (Wiltshire Library and Museum Service) for help and assistance.

For individual contributions the society would like to thank:

Mrs J. Allen • Mr D. Bedford • Mr D. Bird • Mr B. Bridgeman
The Revd T.W. Brighton • Mr J. Bright • Mr R. Burbidge • Mr R. Burnett
Mr R. Clarke • Mrs J. Cole • Mr T.E. Crewe • Mr H.R. Dean • Mr J.R. Dean
Mrs F. Dunford • The Revd F.W.T. Fuller • Mrs P. Gilbert • Mr C. Gwyther
Mr G. Haines • Miss V. Hudd • Mrs B. Hunt • Mr J. Ireland • Mr D. Lacey
Mr C. McLeod • Mr I. Miles • Mrs S. Packer • Mr K. Saunders
Mr M. Smith • Mr F. Watt • Mr G. Weare • Mr G. Wirdnam
Mrs M. Yates

Some doubts exist regarding the original source of some photographs used in this book and the Swindon Society apologizes for any omissions from the acknowledgements shown above. The society would also welcome any comments or additional information regarding the photographs in this book or in the previous three volumes. Please contact Brian Bridgeman, Publicity Officer, Swindon Society, 69 Sandringham Road, Swindon, Wiltshire SN3 1HT.